MOVING WORDS: FORMS OF ENGLISH POETRY

Moving Words: Forms of English Poetry

DEREK ATTRIDGE

OXFORD
UNIVERSITY PRESS

OXFORD

UNIVERSITY PRESS

Great Clarendon Street, Oxford, OX2 6DP,
United Kingdom

Oxford University Press is a department of the University of Oxford.
It furthers the University's objective of excellence in research, scholarship,
and education by publishing worldwide. Oxford is a registered trade mark of
Oxford University Press in the UK and in certain other countries

First published 2013
First published in paperback 2015

Published in the United States of America by Oxford University Press
198 Madison Avenue, New York, NY 10016, United States of America

British Library Cataloguing in Publication Data
Data available

Library of Congress Cataloging in Publication Data
Data available

ISBN 978–0–19–968124–2 (Hbk.)
ISBN 978–0–19–872811–5 (Pbk.)

Contents

Acknowledgements

The debts I have incurred over the forty-five years during which I have been thinking, talking, and writing about the material for the chapters in this book are far too many to enumerate here. If I mention a few by name, this is not to scant my thanks to all those interlocutors who have helped me sharpen my thinking and my analyses, including students, colleagues, audiences at talks, and anonymous reviewers. Early encouragement and advice came from the late John Hollander and Edward Weismiller; more recently I've had fruitful exchanges with, among others, three Toms—Tom Carper, Tom Cable, and Tom Furniss—as well as Martin Duffell, Don Paterson, Natalie Pollard, and Dominic Lash. John Bowen and Robert Douglas-Fairhurst have given me valuable advice, and at Oxford University Press Andrew McNeillie and Jacqueline Baker have been exacting and constructive editors. The three women in my life—Suzanne Hall, Laura Attridge, and Eva Attridge—have continued their tolerant support, for which I am more thankful than I am able to express here.

I am grateful for permission to reprint, in revised form, material first published as follows:

'A Return to Form?', *Textual Practice*, 22.3 (2008), 563–75.

'The Movement of Meaning: Phrasing and Repetition in English Poetry', in Andreas Fischer, ed., *Repetition*, Swiss Papers in English Language and Literature 7 (Tübingen: Gunter Narr Verlag, 1994), 7–29.

'Dryden's Dilemma, or, Racine Refashioned: The Problem of the English Dramatic Couplet', *Yearbook of English Studies* (1979), 55–77.

'Rhythm in English Poetry', *New Literary History*, 21 (1990), 1015–37.

'The Case for the English Dolnik, or, How Not to Introduce Prosody', *Poetics Today*, 33.1 (Spring 2012), 1–26.

'In Defence of the Dolnik: Twentieth-Century British Verse in Free Four-Beat Metre', *Études britanniques contemporaines*, special issue on 'Rhythm in Twentieth-Century British Poetry', ed. Jean-Michel Ganteau (December 2010), 5–18.

'Keats and Beats, or What Can We Say about Rhythm?', in Daniel Thomières, ed., *Le Rythme dans les littératures de langue anglaise* (Reims: Presses Universitaires de Reims, 2005), 99–116.

'Poetry Unbound? Observations on Free Verse' (The 1987 Warton Lecture on Poetry), © The British Academy 1988, first published in *Proceedings of the British Academy LXXIII* (Oxford, 1988), 353–74.

Permission to quote poems has been granted as follows:

'Crazy Weather', by John Ashbery, from HOUSEBOAT DAYS. Copyright © 1975, 1976, 1977, 1999 by John Ashbery. Reprinted by permission of Georges Borchardt, Inc., on behalf of the author.

'Their catch-up is slow and careful', by J. H. Prynne, from *Poems* (2005), 396. Reprinted by permission of the author.

'Stopping by Woods on a Snowy Evening', from the book *The Poetry of Robert Frost* edited by Edward Connery Lathem. Copyright © 1923, 1969, by Henry Holt and Company, copyright © 1951 by Robert Frost.

'September Song' (page 30) from SELECTED POEMS by Geoffrey Hill (Penguin Books, 2006). Copyright © Geoffrey Hill, 2006.

'Poem', by William Carlos Williams, from THE COLLECTED POEMS: VOLUME I, 1909–1939, copyright © 1938 by New Directions Publishing Corporation. Reprinted by permission of New Directions Publishing Corp.

'Correctives' by Don Paterson, from *Rain*. Copyright © Don Paterson 2009. Reproduced by permission of the author c/o Rogers, Coleridge & White Ltd., 20 Powis Mews, London W11 1JN.

'Wells-next-the-Sea', by Sophie Hannah, from *Selected Poems* (2006), 133. Reprinted by permission of Carcanet Press Limited.

'Crossing the Water', by Sylvia Plath, from *Collected Poems*, ed. Ted Hughes. Copyright © Faber and Faber Ltd (1981).

All lines from 'CROSSING THE WATER' FROM CROSSING THE WATER by SYLVIA PLATH. Copyright © 1962 by Ted Hughes. Reprinted by permission of Harper Collins Publishers.

Introduction

Against Abstraction

I

A moment of intellectual satisfaction I remember with particular vividness from my teenage years occurred when, in high school, I was introduced to the principles of Latin scansion and found that what looked and sounded like a random arrangement of words into lines could, after mastering a few rules, be shown to be anything but random. A dactylic hexameter could be relied upon to have six feet made up of long and short syllables, according to strict rules governing their disposition across the line. There were no exceptions, and no uncertainties: whether a syllable was short or long was a known quantity (a phrase apparently from mathematics, but one which could equally well be from classical prosody), there were reliable rules for elision, and with the help of a dictionary one could turn the apparently arbitrary run of words into a lucid and pleasing pattern. That this pattern did not coincide with anything in the sound of the lines (except in the final feet, where accent and quantity were in sync) was not a problem: the pleasure was an intellectual one, not an aural one. In our English poetry lessons we also learned to scan lines of verse, but the process, although involving some of the same technical terms, was a very different matter: all sorts of uncertainties about stressed and unstressed syllables emerged, there seemed to be no clear rules about what kind of foot could occur where, elision was a mystery, and different poets and periods had different understandings of what constituted a metrical line. I found myself wishing there were a way of writing and analysing English verse that, as with Latin, demonstrated the possibility latent within the haphazard forms of the language for precision and order. That English verse *sounded* much more rhythmically regular than Latin verse only exacerbated the problem: I felt that it should be more, not less, susceptible to rigorous analysis.

English studies at university gave me the opportunity to pursue questions of poetic form in more depth, although the terminology and methods of analysis remained frustratingly inadequate in comparison with Latin. When it came to choosing a topic for a Ph.D. thesis, my enjoyment of the short lyric in English, and my fascination with its flowering in the

Elizabethan period (for which I must acknowledge the remarkable Cambridge lectures of Jeremy Prynne), led to a proposal which involved a comparison of Renaissance poetic theory with poetic practice, starting with a detailed discussion of late sixteenth-century poetic treatises. Those treatises, it turned out, included extensive engagement with the question of English metre, and in particular the project of writing English verse in the metres of classical Latin. Four hundred years ago, I realized, poets and poetic theorists were wrestling with the same problem that had bothered me at high school: if the Latin language could be turned from a random sequence of syllables into a patterned series of longs and shorts with unfailing exactness, why could not the English language be transformed in the same way? If the old rhythms that governed ballads and songs were too crude for these lovers of classical poetry (and we must remember that changes in pronunciation had destroyed the subtleties of medieval versification for Elizabethan ears), perhaps the answer, they reckoned, was to identify long and short syllables in English and deploy them in metrical forms derived from Latin examples.

Nothing of what I read in critical studies of the period seemed to account for either the attraction which so many poets felt towards the naturalization of Latin metres or the doggedness with which some of them pursued the project. The best-known names engaged in the enterprise were Sidney, Spenser, and Campion, but many others were drawn in. What dawned on me as I worked on these efforts was that the enjoyment Latin verse offered to Elizabethan readers was similar to that which I was to feel in the school classroom four centuries later: an intellectual satisfaction in the subjection of the unruly matter of language to exact, predictable, calculable forms, which had little to do with the sound of the lines as one read them aloud. (Latin in England—as in all European countries at this time and for centuries to come—was pronounced more or less in the same way as the vernacular.) In examining the numerous treatises on prosody and the many poems written in imitation of classical metres, I found, rather to my surprise, that I had completed a Ph.D. thesis (later published as *Well-Weighed Syllables*).

In answering to my satisfaction one set of problems—essentially problems of intellectual history—I had only increased my awareness of another set. English metre remained a subject where nothing I had read—and there was a great deal to read—offered anything like the precision of classical prosody. Precision in matters of language was the aim of the discipline of linguistics, and it was to linguistics I turned to try to work out for myself how best to account for the varieties of verse to be found in English. The dominant tradition within literary studies—ironically, a descendant of the classical prosody I wished to emulate—seemed at once too powerful, allowing pretty much any sequence of words to be scanned as metrical by means of 'licences' such as 'inversion' and 'substitution', and too weak, failing to account for clear rhythmic differences perceptible by the ear, such as the difference between tetrameter and pentameter verse, or for the specific choices made by poets down the ages. Why was pentameter verse overwhelmingly iambic, for instance, or why was tetrameter verse almost invariably rhymed? (I'm using the traditional terms here; later I will introduce others.) Chomskeian linguistics, in the late 1960s when I started my serious study of metre, offered a compelling model: the aim of a prosodic study would be to deduce the 'metrical competence' which underlies judgements made by English speakers as to the metricality or unmetricality of lines of verse, and, more optimistically, judgements about their smoothness or roughness, weakness or strength, closeness to speech or closeness to song, and so on. Some attempts along these lines had been made, starting with an influential 1966 essay by Morris Halle and Samuel Jay Keyser on Chaucer's prosody,[1] but these were, in my view, too preoccupied with a single verse form—the iambic pentameter—and too insistent on isolating a simple key to metricality.

The result of several years work on this project was my 1982 book *The Rhythms of English Poetry*. My aim was to show what was lacking in prosodic studies to date, and what could usefully be built on in developing a new model of English metre; and then to use this newly minted theory in analyses of poetic examples which would show its potential contribution to critical readings. I wanted to do justice to the variety of English versification, giving the shorter line its due as well as the more frequently studied pentameter. (That I might have achieved the right balance is suggested by two reviews appearing at about the same time, one of which complained that I had privileged the elitist pentameter over more popular forms, the other that I had allowed the shorter metres to determine my account at the expense of the pentameter.) The debt to Chomsky was most evident in a set of English metrical rules I formulated, including formalizations using symbols derived from generative grammar. More important, and I think ultimately more influential, was my emphasis on the physical nature of rhythm, the task of the prosodist (and, indeed, of the poet) being to show how the surface features of the poem's words tap into the familiar rhythmic sequences heard and felt in many places other than language, and learned by children at an early age. These sequences are based on groups of *beats*, those places we are inclined to mark by a physical movement—a gesture of the hand, a nod of the head—or by a mental

---

[1] Halle and Keyser, 'Chaucer and the Study of Prosody'.

registration of this potential bodily act. Beats occur in normal English speech when the series of stressed and unstressed syllables approaches a degree of regularity in its alternation; metrical verse is thus a heightening of a tendency present in the spoken language.[2] I was thus able to account for the differences between the pentameter and the shorter metres based on the ubiquitous rhythmic group of four beats.

The Rhythms of English Poetry turned out to be longer and more complex than I had initially intended, and so in 1995 I followed it up with *Poetic Rhythm: An Introduction*, which was aimed not at the scholar of prosody but the student or writer of poetry. The basic argument was the same, though I used a different set of scansion symbols—more suited to the then new technology of word processing—and set out the types of metre differently; I also included a chapter on phrasal or syntactic rhythm, a subject that remains woefully under-investigated. A third study of metre using the principles of what had come to be called 'beat prosody' was initiated by the poet Thomas Carper, who wrote a more user-friendly introduction entitled *Meter and Meaning*, on which I collaborated and to which I contributed some material. While the subject of poetic rhythm and metre is still for the most part taught—where it is taught at all—in the terms inherited from classical prosody, it is pleasing to note that the alternative approach enshrined in these books is now widely used in the classroom and has proved valuable in a number of critical and theoretical works.[3]

This book is both a continuation of the discussion of rhythm and metre in these earlier volumes, and an exploration of a number of significant issues in poetic form not fully engaged with in them. It combines talks and essays written over the past three decades (in revised versions) with some new thinking about these issues, and uses discussions of particular poems to illustrate the value of close attention to formal detail. The same arguments could, of course, have been made by means of any number of poetic case studies, and a sketch of the earlier texts' origins may help to explain the particular choices within them. In 1979, while writing *The Rhythms of English Poetry*, I attended a performance of Tony Harrison's

---

[2] Here is a recent phonological account: 'In standard varieties of English, speech rhythm is accomplished such that speakers place stressed syllables at roughly regular intervals of time. As listeners we perceive this as creating a rhythmic pattern, with every stressed syllable representing a rhythmic beat' (Reed, *Analysing Conversation*, 139). As Reed goes on to note, conversational speech frequently departs from this pattern, and my use of the term *beat* in this book is restricted to the highly controlled context of regular metre, a context in which stresses and beats don't necessarily coincide.

[3] See, for example, Creaser, ' "Service is Perfect Freedom" '; Duffell, *A New History*: and O'Donnell, *The Passion of Meter*.

version of Racine's *Phèdre*, entitled *Phaedra Britannica*, and found myself wondering why rhyming couplets in English don't work very well on the tragic stage when they work brilliantly in French. The result was an article on the nature of English rhyme in comparison with that of French, an article which, in a revised version that reflects many more recent attempts to Anglicize Racine, comprises Chapter 3 of this book. Invited by the British Academy to deliver the 1987 Warton Lecture on English Poetry, I chose another area to which I felt my book hadn't done full justice: non-metrical or 'free' verse; this lecture has been revised as Chapter 9. The wider question of how stylistic, including metrical, commentary feeds into interpretation continued to interest me, and I attempted an answer, illustrated by an analysis of a sonnet by Spenser, in a 1988 talk which forms the basis of Chapter 6.[4] The focus on the iambic pentameter in this essay allowed me to contribute some thoughts about its particular capabilities as a metrical form. In 1990 Ralph Cohen, Director of the Commonwealth Center for Literary and Cultural Change at the University of Virginia, invited me to contribute to a seminar series on 'Rhythm, Nature and Culture' being convened by Henri Meschonnic; the result was the essay 'Rhythm in English Poetry', which I reprint in an expanded form (Chapter 5) as a way of introducing beat prosody for readers who are unfamiliar with it, and of demonstrating its usefulness in dealing with three different rhythmic styles. Four years later, I was invited to speak at the annual conference of the Swiss Association of University Lecturers in English, and took this as an opportunity to discuss another crucial aspect of poetic form, the movement of meaning. Drawing on the important work on rhythmic phrasing by Richard Cureton, the talk focused on the question of exact verbal repetition and the challenge it poses to a poem's onward motion (and to accounts of such motion). This talk appears in a revised version as Chapter 2. One of the problems with traditional prosody is its inability to deal with one of most long-lasting and popular forms of verse, the four-beat form sometimes referred to as 'dolnik', a term I have adopted. Chapter 7 brings together material from a number of talks I have given on this mode of verse, moving from its early medieval appearance to recent examples. The origin of Chapter 8 was a talk given in 2003 at a University of Frankfurt symposium held in honour of Ulrich Keller, which I seized as an opportunity to analyse a small corner of Keats's

---

[4] A narrower question—how to treat sequences of syllables which appear to have an unwanted stress—became the focus of a 1987 article entitled ' "Damn with Faint Praise": Double Offbeat Demotion', the title of which included an example of the problematic sequence discussed in the article. This is one of the more technical talks and articles I have chosen not to include in this volume.

superb poetic achievement and to demonstrate the usefulness of beat prosody in illuminating the relation between the lexical and rhythmic dimensions of English. Other chapters reflect recent developments in the study of poetic form, including the broad question of a much-discussed return to formal issues (Chapter 1) and new theories of the role of sound in poetry emanating from two of the best known of contemporary poets (Chapter 4).

This book is thus both a demonstration of the potential of a certain way of approaching the formal dimension of poetry and an exploration of a number of topics central to any formal poetics. The first four chapters deal with several issues germane to the discussion of poetic form, including syntax and phrasing, rhyme, and the relation between sound and meaning, and the final five concentrate on various aspects of poetic rhythm, including chapters devoted to the three major traditions of English verse, the four-beat form, the five-beat form, and free verse. Examples discussed range from medieval lyric and Elizabethan sonnet to Dryden's heroic drama, Keats's odes, Tennyson's lyrics, and the contemporary poetry of John Ashbery, J. H. Prynne, and Don Paterson. (This promiscuity is not meant to deny historical change, but it is a reflection of some of the important continuities in poetic practice in English over the past 700 years.) The formal questions discussed here cannot, of course, be separated from questions of what, and how, poems mean, and of the feelings they generate (hence the title of this book); I trust that it will be clear that, whatever emphasis the local argument requires, the larger picture always involves much more than form.

II

Contemporary western culture instils in its citizens a thorough familiarity with the notion of the poem. Though actual poems may be published less often, and less carefully attended to, than ever before, they still seem to be part of the landscape, one of the things to make and do with language. Indeed, they are perhaps more familiar than at any previous time, now that every kindergarten child is encouraged to 'write poems'. As a consequence of the 'free verse' revolution and the doctrine of individual expression, poems are no longer widely associated with 'the craft so long to lerne', with self-discipline and a peculiar intimacy with language. In spite of this—to some extent because of it—we know very little about poems and the reading of poems. There is, of course, no lack of testimony in the history of western culture to their possession of a certain kind of power, well beyond the mild pleasure that might be gained from an amateur effusion in the local press. And there is some evidence of a connection between the writing—and reading—of poetry and the domain of ethics and politics. Even (perhaps especially) historical situations fraught with change have thrown up poetry, often poetry widely recognized as having the highest merit. Men and women have found it worth making sacrifices to write or disseminate poetry in times of crisis. Claims have often been made, explicitly or implicitly, for the moral force of poetry of a certain kind or quality. Yet few would grant poems immediate political or ethical efficacy, except very occasionally—and then in directions that could not have been predicted and that have little to do with what is usually recognized as the power of good poetry. The link between poetry and the ethical remains obscure.

What we mean by 'the power of poetry' is itself far from clear. For a particular reader, caught in the contingencies of space and time, and guided by expectation, training, and ideology, only a few poems, perhaps, will seduce or explode with that full force of which poetry is capable; but those that do so pose a challenge to our accounts of language, of meaning, and of action that we are a long way from meeting. In spite of the immense quantity of commentary that surrounds the poetic tradition, we have little sense of why it is that certain organized arrangements of words can have strong and valued effects (whether for a small or a large number of readers), and hence why writers are drawn to handle language in this way. This is not to say that poems are less well served by their commentators than, for example, prose fiction; it is to highlight the fact that the distinguishing feature of poetry, that which makes it *not* prose fiction, is peculiarly ill served. To assert this might seem to imply a definition of poetry, and I had better state immediately that I have no new definition to add to the already long list of inadequate ones. I'm happy to work with the necessarily vague consensus view that, although there is a gradation rather than a clear borderline between what we might on the one hand call 'poetry' or 'verse' (and I'm not making any principled distinction between these) and what on the other we might call 'prose', the former is characterized by the presence of certain regularities not enshrined in the linguistic system and not immediately decodable in terms of semantics—the minimal instance being, usually, segmentation into units other than those sanctioned by the grammar, signalled on the page by visual means.[5]

---

[5] Here I leave out of account oral poetry, both in the strict sense of poetry that has never been written down, and in the sense of poetry as it is received by listeners to a performance rather than readers who have a page before them. (A poem known by heart constitutes an intermediate case, where the memory may well include a memory of visual cues in addition to temporal unfolding.) In these cases, segmentation is often signalled aurally, either inherently in the poem's metrical or rhyming structure, or performatively, by the reader or reciter responding to the visual cues.

This distinguishing aspect is usually referred to as poetic 'form', and though I shall have to complicate the habitual use of this term, it will serve, with all of its ambiguities, for the moment. Any commentary on a poem that claims to be treating it *as* a poem will necessarily devote some attention to this aspect, and it is here that evaluative criticism is most often disappointing. Turn with a sceptical eye to almost any account of a poem that has a powerful effect on you, and you will find the description of the operation of its formal qualities—if there is one—to be a description that you could imagine being applied to a poem with no evocative qualities whatsoever; read a glowing assessment of the techniques in a poem that has left you cold, and your response is unlikely to change (although, depending on your self-esteem as a reader and the degree of respect you have for the critic, you may be led to feel that it *ought* to change). The enthusiasm of someone you love or admire is likely to be a more effective transformer of your appreciation than any amount of formal analysis, and this is probably how criticism most often works to alter individuals' experiences of particular poems, or of poetry in general.

It's not hard to find the reason for the inadequacy of this kind of commentary; any statement of the type 'in this poem formal property X is valuable because it produces effect Y' seems to imply an algorithm, valid for any poem possessing this property. This implication is usually demonstrably false, for in the next poem in which X is found it will have no such effect; and even if it were true, it would be a mechanical rule of precisely the type all accounts of literature regard as inadequate to explain the special qualities of the 'literary'.[6] On the other hand, if the critic insists that it is only for *this* poem that the statement is valid, we are left wondering what kind of explanatory power it has. We may appreciate formal criticism for its ingenuity and inventiveness, or because it appears to authorize our own enjoyment of a poem, but we're not likely to feel that it has identified the sources of a work's real power. We therefore return to questions of meaning and rhetoric, or biographical source and historical allusion, and the distinct existence of the poem as poem is dissolved (and sometimes the specificity of the work as a *literary* work disappears too).

In a period when the primary focus of critical attention is still for the most part on historical context, on political and ideological issues, on the material, the economic, the psychological, these inadequate accounts of form are rarer than they once were—but only because form is now often simply left out of account. Poetry is talked and written about as though it

---

[6] See Attridge, *Peculiar Language*, and Chapter 6 of this book for further discussion of this issue.

were prose. Although in some cases it may in fact be being *read* as prose, it seems more likely that poems continue to exercise power in the ways that they always did, but that as soon as a reader turns into a writer, the pressures of the institution—and the historical failures of formal analysis—lead to a concentration on content and context, rather than shape, sound, and movement. This is only part of a wider problem of reductive and instrumentalizing readings of literature, but as far as poetry is concerned, it is a crucial one. However, there are signs that the *Zeitgeist* is changing; more and more voices are to be heard arguing for critical approaches that are alert to the distinctiveness of literature as a cultural practice, and regretting the tendency to dissolve literary studies into a minor branch of cultural history.[7] The chapters that follow are an attempt to foreground and sharpen the notion of form, in the hope that criticism can learn to do more justice to poems as poems.

III

When I started reading accounts of the formal properties of poetry in the 1960s, there was, at least among my teachers and fellow-students, something approaching a consensus about English prosody. The dominant critical approach was a blend of American New Criticism and British Leavisism, and the most influential statement of prosodic methodology was probably a 1959 essay by the leading theorists of the former approach, W. K. Wimsatt and Monroe C. Beardsley, entitled 'The Concept of Meter: An Exercise in Abstraction'. Metre was the name for a pattern of 'feet', the verse line being constituted by a certain number of these feet, as in Greek and Latin but with a preference for repeated feet of a particular type. This pattern was said to be 'abstract', which seemed to mean it ticked away mentally with absolute regularity but was not manifested in sound. Playing across this, and hardly ever actually coinciding with it, was the actual rhythm of the line, emerging from the norms of the spoken language. (Just how the spoken language at once produces the metrical grid and moves away from it was never quite explained.) This interplay between regular and varied, abstract and concrete was what was said to give life to the verse. The variations were for the most part understood as 'substitutions': instead of the expected foot, say an iamb, one encountered a different foot, say a trochee. This account of metre is still very common today.

---

[7] See Chapter 1 for a discussion of this 'return to form'.

Let us look at an example. It had better be an iambic pentameter, which for the approach I am delineating usually serves as the paradigmatic metrical line. The following is from Milton's *Lycidas*:

> Batt'ning our flocks with the fresh dews of night
>
> (*Poems*, 447)

These are the five feet a traditional analysis would indicate:

> Batt'ning | our flocks | with the | fresh dews | of night

The second and fifth feet ('our flocks') and ('of night') are clearly weak–strong, and thus regular iambs. The other three feet involve substitutions: the first ('Batt'ning') is a trochee, strong–weak; the third ('with the') is a pyrrhic, weak–weak; and the fourth (fresh dews) is a spondee, strong–strong. (Since we are dealing not with quantity but with degrees of stress, the classical distinction between long and short syllables is replaced by a distinction between stressed and unstressed—or strong and weak—syllables.) As we pronounce these words with these dispositions of strength and weakness, the theory goes, we are aware of the abstract metrical grid behind them; so although we hear the line opening on strong–weak we hear it against an internal, abstract pattern of weak–strong. Here I have to confess my inability to achieve this feat of double hearing; I cannot avoid hearing the first syllable of the line as only strong, with no taint of weakness, and the second as weak, with no suggestion of strength. My experience of Latin verse as a schoolboy, and the similar experience of Elizabethan readers, was of an abstract pattern that matched perfectly the words of the poem as entities on the page; there was no injunction to experience a subtle interplay between spoken line and metrical grid. (Whether there was for the Romans is a question we cannot answer.) And since the metrical pattern was derived from rules that had little to do with the way in which words were pronounced, one didn't face the conundrum of 'hearing' two patterns both built on pronunciation—since there is nothing in the *visual* representation of the language to tell us whether 'Batt'ning' is weak–strong or strong–weak.

Another way of looking at the line, and one that I find more productive, is to say that Milton is using a rhythmic 'figure' earlier poets had used thousands of times, and later poets will keep using: strong–weak–weak–strong. It's frequent at the beginning of the line, but can occur in mid-line as well, often after punctuation.[8] There's no dividing line be-

---

[8] For discussion of rhythmic figures, see Carper and Attridge, *Meter and Meaning*, chapter 5.

tween the two weak syllables, and no need to think in terms of feet—
though one important fact is that the figure contains two stresses we are
made to experience, physically as well as mentally, as rhythmic beats—
places, in other words, where we would tap or nod if trying to feel the
rhythm physically. Others may be able to pronounce 'Batt'ning' with a
normal stress while giving a rhythmic tap on the second syllable; I'm not
able to do so.

The third and fourth feet also involve, in traditional prosody, hearing
one thing and being aware of another, though here a different kind of
argument is often made, or rather two dogmas are enunciated, once the
line has been sliced into feet. It is asserted (a) that all that matters in the
creation of a metrical line is what goes on within the foot, and (b) that
two adjacent syllables of spoken English never receive the same stress. In
our example, 'the' would be said to be ever so slightly stronger than 'with'
and 'dews' slightly stronger than 'fresh'. (Another school of thought within
this approach says that it's the job of the *reader* to give 'the' and 'dews' a
slight push with the voice in order to sustain the metre.) Thus the under-
lying weak–strong–weak–strong will be felt beneath the actual weak–
weak–strong–strong. I have never seen any evidence for either of these
dogmas, and I don't believe a reader unschooled in the doctrine of foot-
prosody would hear (or produce) these variations. The difference in
strength between 'the' and 'fresh' is an overriding phonetic fact, and must
surely play its part in the rhythm. What we have in this part of the line is
actually another very common four-syllable rhythmic figure: weak–weak–
strong–strong. (The third most common figure is its reverse: strong–
strong–weak–weak, as in Keats's line 'And hides the green hill in an April
shower', where the figure in question is constituted by the words 'green
hill in an'.) To read Milton's line expressively as if it were heightened prose
is to give five syllables strong emphasis and, thanks to the inbuilt rhyth-
mic tendencies of the English language, to perceive them as rhythmically
equivalent; there is no need to force the words into a fore-ordained metri-
cal structure. (It's important to give all five stresses full emphasis, because
to weaken 'dews' would be to allow the line to fall into a quite different
metre, one with a triple rhythm and four beats.)

Does the metre, understood as the principle of regular alternation, not
play any part then? Are we simply responding to a series of strong and
weak syllables? Not at all—the underlying metre of any line is an alterna-
tion of rhythmic pulse and rhythmic relaxation, tending always to tempo-
ral equivalence. (The often-used caricature of the iambic pentameter as
di-dum-di-dum-di-dum-di-dum-di-dum is not a matter of an abstract
grid, and wouldn't work if the dums were not pronounced with more
emphasis and at roughly equal intervals.) What we experience, I would

argue, is not two levels, abstract and concrete (a model suggested by Hopkins's unfortunate choice of 'counterpoint' as a metaphor), but a real, physical push towards temporal regularity and an equally real pull towards the more varied rhythms of the specific example of English speech. The five points of rhythmic emphasis in Milton's line from *Lycidas*—'Batt-', 'flocks', 'fresh', 'dews', and 'night'—strive to achieve that ideal temporal pattern, while the other syllables exercise their own rhythmic strength to pull against it; and at the same time the rhetorical emphasis provided by the meaning has its own rhythmic agenda to pursue. To read the line in conformity with the underlying rhythm is to chant it in a way that destroys its subtlety, while to read it simply as if it were prose is to risk losing its hold on the rhythmic norm. (For example, the metre requires that the voice dwell on *dews* and *night* in a way that in prose would be unnatural.) The prosodist's scansion marks may look like abstract grids, but what they represent is something both heard and felt.

IV

As will be evident from my earlier biographical summary, questions of poetic form have continued to fascinate me for over fifty years, whatever other fields of study have tempted me during this period. All the time I have been conscious of this area as something of a byway of literary studies, though I have been exploring it long enough to have experienced both the end of a period in which metre was a significant topic and the possible beginning of a period in which it is returning, if not to centre stage, at least to a respectable role in the chorus. In the field of linguistics, however, the study of metre has remained important throughout this period; it has furnished valuable insights into the phonology of a number of languages, and has encouraged linguistic theorists with an interest in poetry to develop universalizing metrical theories on the model of universal grammar.[9] I have always tried to listen to what the linguists are saying, and have found much of value, especially in countering the woolliness which all too often afflicts literary critics when talking about these subjects. If I have often been critical of the approaches adopted by linguists, it has been because their aims are different from mine, with the result that their analyses don't appear to me to contribute to an appreciation of the singularity of individual poets and poems. In spite of this, I number many linguists among the interlocutors it has been my good fortune to have had in this

---

[9] See, for example, Hanson and Kiparsky, 'A Parametric Theory'; and Fabb and Halle, *Meter in Poetry*.

corner of the literary universe. Sometimes those of us who are fascinated by the minutiae of rhythm and metre forget that our colleagues in literature departments can be less than enthralled by our conversations (whether our jargon is of logaoedic verse and second cretics, or of stress maxima and realization rules); my hope is that in this book I only rarely stray into the realm of technicalities indigestible to all but my fellow prosody geeks.

It remains true that, for the time being at least, what we might think of as technical approaches to the language of literature remain a minority interest in most English departments in the English-speaking world. (Members of English departments in other parts of the world are more likely to have an interest in the workings of the language, as are members of language departments in anglophone countries—and poets.) Better instruction in schools would improve matters, but how many teachers are able to make versification an exciting subject for a lesson? Yet, as I discovered fifty years ago, being able to show how a string of words conforms to patterns that pervade the verse tradition can be an exhilarating discovery. Doing so in a language one speaks fluently, as opposed to the halting Latin which was my portal to prosodic excitement, is all the more stimulating: there can be an interplay between hearing rhythms and noting them on paper, one activity reinforcing the other. And then there is the pleasure of seeing (and hearing) exactly how a poet, while building on an old tradition, has found a way of giving it freshness and new life. What is needed, of course, is a mode of prosodic analysis, and a way of talking about topics such as rhyme, repetition, and sound symbolism, that are not forbidding in their terminology nor confusing in their application.

In revisiting, updating, and in some cases expanding these pieces, I have been struck once more by the amount we still don't understand about the working of poetry as it moves, pleases, and changes us. Although I would like to think that these studies bring us closer to such an understanding, I am not claiming anything like an exhaustive account: part of the reward of investigating formal detail in this way is the enhanced realization of the degree to which poetry resists positivist approaches. Recent developments in 'cognitive poetics', with their aim of providing a neurological basis for the experience of literature, seem to me to demonstrate the same truth. This is not to mystify the realm of the aesthetic (which is already mystified enough), but to point to an essential quality of significant art as a cultural practice, all the more important as the hold of the myth of scientific explanation grows. My goal in this book is to sharpen the questions we ask about poetry, not to solve all the puzzles it poses; and my hope is that doing so will enhance my readers' enjoyment of the poems they read.

PART I

FORMAL QUESTIONS

1

A Return to Form?

To speak of returns is to speak of departures. The crudest thumbnail sketch of literary studies in the English-speaking world would have it that at some point towards the middle of the twentieth century history left town. The 1940s, 1950s, and 1960s, the story goes, were dominated by the formalist modes of New or Practical Criticism (aka Close Reading), the 1970s and early 1980s by the equally formalist modes of Deconstruction and Post-structuralism, and then from about the middle of the 1980s history, in the guise of New Historicism and Cultural Materialism, re-asserted itself, and, although sometimes having to endure the embrace of a less-than-fully-historical Cultural Studies and the dubious attentions of an ever-renewed Psychoanalysis, has been running the show ever since. In recent years, however, more and more voices have been heard proclaiming a return to form as a central issue in literary theory and criticism. Labels such as 'New Formalism' and 'the New Aesthetics' have been bandied about. Is history being edged aside once more as literary form stages a comeback? And if so, in what manner is form best approached, given the changes wrought in our understanding of the literary institution and lit-erary practice over the past forty years?

The coarseness of my sketch (and use of upper case) will have left no doubt that it's misleading in a number of ways, some of which I shall return to in a moment. But in its outlines at least it's widely accepted, and it clearly bears some relation to the actuality of cultural history. It is true, for instance, that much of the most interesting and influential work in literary studies for two decades has involved a close engagement with the historical, cultural, political, social, and economic circumstances within which writing, publishing, reading, and performing have been carried out. Boundaries between what has been traditionally called 'literature' and other kinds of writing have become blurred, and questions of evalu-ation have receded into the dim background. For twenty years or more, the best graduate students in the best English departments—and such students always constitute a valuable litmus test—have by and large opted to undertake historical studies, often of what an older approach would have termed (and perhaps dismissed as) minor authors, and often without fussing about the distinction between the literary and the non-literary. And in all of this, the issue of literary form—so central to many of the critical traditions of the previous half century—has lacked urgency and importance.

What, then, are the signs of a possible return to favour of form, or to use a related word, of an interest in the aesthetic? In particular, has the study of poetry seen a significant revival of interest in what has often been dismissed as the mere mechanics of verse? Let us take the year 2000 as our starting point, acknowledging as we do so that throughout the longer period that I've represented simplistically as under the thumb of historical criticism, publications resisting that dominance were appearing.[1] That year saw the publication of a special issue of *Modern Language Quarterly* edited by Susan J. Wolfson and Marshall Brown, entitled *Reading for Form*, as well as a book that, although more concerned with emotions than form, announced itself as a critique of the prevailing hostility to the aesthetic: Isobel Armstrong's *The Radical Aesthetic*. Taking one book a year to signify this trend in the succeeding years, there was Peter de Bolla's *Art Matters* in 2001, a brave endeavour to articulate the challenge posed by specific works of art, including literary art; Susan Stewart's *Poetry and the Fate of the Senses* in 2002, which the author calls 'a general theory of poetic forms' (ix); and in 2003 a substantial collection of essays, *Aesthetic Subjects*, edited by Pamela R. Matthews and David McWhirter. The year 2004 can be represented by James Longenbach's *The Resistance to Poetry*, which examines the formal features of poetry in order to advance an argument about its strategies of self-resistance, and 2005 by Jonathan Loesberg's *A Return to Aesthetics*, an important study which argues that the avowedly anti-Kantian, anti-aesthetic positions of recent historically in-flected critical theory are in fact deeply indebted to the Kantian heritage. A number of studies of authors or topics which include attention to formal details but lack a polemical edge could be added to this list. How-ever, one would still be left with only a trickle to set beside the unceasing flow of historical and cultural studies from the same period.

Since 2005, the signs of a revitalization of formal study have multi-plied. In 2006, Terry Eagleton's just-published *How to Read a Poem?* was

---

[1] A notable example was *Aesthetics and Ideology*, a 1994 collection edited by George Levine, in which a number of critics addressed the relation between the two terms in the title. In her 1997 book *Formal Charges*, Susan J. Wolfson called for a fuller attention to questions of form in Romantic studies, a field in which historical approaches were dominant.

hailed by Marjorie Perloff in her presidential address to the Modern Language Association: the address was entitled 'It Must Change', and called for, and identified signs of, a return to a focus on what is specific to literature.[2] The year 2007 saw the publication of two highly praised volumes, Angela Leighton's *On Form* and Helen Vendler's *Our Secret Discipline: Yeats and Lyric Form*; while *PMLA*'s regular section headed 'The Changing Profession' featured an essay by Marjorie Levinson entitled 'What is New Formalism?'—a sure sign that the North American academic establishment had perceived an aestheticist straw in the historicist wind (even if Levinson's claim is that the best New Historicists have been formalists all along). The year 2008 brought us Tom Paulin's *The Secret Life of Poems* and 2009 Jason Rudy's *Electric Meters*. In 2010, *The Art of the Sonnet* by Stephen Burt and David Mikics was published; in 2011 *Meter Matters: Verse Culture of the Long Nineteenth Century*, edited by Jason Hall; and, in 2012, continuing the spate of work on Victorian formal issues, Meredith Martin's *The Rise and Fall of Meter: Poetry and National Culture, 1860–1930* and Joseph Phelan's *The Music of Verse: Metrical Experiment in Nineteenth-Century Poetry*.

Two of the books I've mentioned, Eagleton's and Paulin's, are explicitly designed as introductions to poetry and formal analysis (Paulin's is subtitled 'A Poetry Primer'). Because they are by writers well known outside the academic world, these books have received significant attention, but they are in fact members of a flourishing if largely unsung genre. The year 2007 alone saw the publication of David Caplan's *Poetic Form: An Introduction*; Jeremy Tambling's *RE: Verse: Turning towards Poetry*; and the second edition of Tom Furniss and Michael Bath's *Reading Poetry: An Introduction* (to my mind the best of the bunch).[3] Although the *Norton Anthologies* still rely on a dated and over-technical essay on prosody which I discuss in Chapter 7, the publication of Norton's anthology of poetic forms, *The Making of a Poem* (2000), edited by Mark Strand and Eavan Boland, is an encouraging sign. Poets, of course, have never ceased to be interested in form.

Almost all the discussions of the place and purpose of literary study in recent years are marked by curious absences, clearly observable if one

---

[2] Perloff, 'Presidential Address 2006'. Eagleton's book is dated 2007, though it appeared the previous year.

[3] Other recent examples include Ruth Padel's *52 Ways of Looking at a Poem* (2002); James Fenton's *Introduction to English Poetry* (2002); Jeffrey Wainwright's *Poetry: The Basics* (2004; second edition 2011); Stephen Fry's *The Ode Less Travelled* (2005); the second edition of John Lennard's 1996 *Poetry Handbook* (2005); Rhian Williams's *Poetry Toolkit* (2009); and Michael D. Hurley and Michael O'Neill's *Cambridge Introduction to Poetic Form* (2012). I comment briefly on the metrical analysis in some of these books in 'The Case for the English Dolnik'.

conceives of interdisciplinarity as extending beyond a mutual fertilization
between literature and various kinds of history. In particular, the interre-
lation between literary study and linguistic theory, which has continued
to flourish, has been ignored by most commentators on the recent history
of literary criticism and omitted from most surveys and anthologies of
literary theory. For several decades, the discipline of narrative theory has
remained a fertile nursery of literary analysis addressing formal questions,
though overlooked by many critics of fiction.[4] In the study of poetry, the
field of metrics has been equally abundant over this period, with a plenti-
ful supply of books and essays.[5] Both these fields overlap with the wider
discipline of stylistics, the most usual name—if not a very satisfactory
one—for approaches to literature that take advantage of linguistic theory,
and which treat literary form as a major part of their domain. The sus-
tained vigour of these interrelated approaches is indicated by the existence
of several journals dedicated to stylistics and narrative theory,[6] the thriv-
ing Poetics and Linguistics Association in the UK and the Society for the
Study of Narrative Literature in North America (both of which run popu-
lar conferences), the activities of the MLA's division on Linguistic Ap-
proaches to Literature, and the existence of many university and college
courses on the language of literature. Even the area within this discipline
which has been most fertile in recent years, cognitive stylistics, pays due
attention, in spite of its name, to the operations of form. Many of the calls
to return to form that have appeared within the field of literary studies in
recent years would have benefited from fuller acquaintance with stylistic
studies, and from some of the linguistic knowledge that those engaged in
stylistics take for granted.[7]

---

[4] To cite one example only, the series edited by Phelan and Rabinowitz for Ohio State
University Press, *Theory and Interpretation of Narrative*, had, by the end of 2007, produced
27 volumes.

[5] Recent publications include Thomières, ed., *Le Rythme dans les littératures de langue
anglaise*, 2005; Duffell, *A New History of English Metre*, 2008; Aroui and Arleo, eds., *To-
wards a Typology of Poetic Forms*, 2009; Küper, *Current Trends in Metrical Analysis*; and the
special issue of *Études britanniques contemporaines* on 'Rhythm in Twentieth-Century Brit-
ish Poetry', 2010. In a longer version of her *PMLA* article, Levinson acknowledges the
productivity of metrical studies, and provides a somewhat undiscriminating bibliography
(see <www.sitemaker.umich.edu/pmla_article>).

[6] *Style* and *Language and Literature* are devoted to stylistic studies, *Narrative* and the
Journal of Narrative Theory to narrative theory. *Poetics Today* frequently addresses such
issues.

[7] Another discipline which rarely gets mentioned in surveys of literary theory and criti-
cism, and which devotes considerable attention to questions of form, is analytic aesthetics.
The *Journal of Aesthetics and Art Criticism* and the *British Journal of Aesthetics*, for instance,
feature numerous essays dealing with formal questions from an analytic point of view, and
the *Routledge Companion to Aesthetics*, edited by Gaut and Lopes, is, in spite of its comprehen-
sive title, largely committed to analytic aesthetics. Although much writing in this tradition

To depict the past twenty years as barren of studies of literary form is also to ignore the continuing vitality of the continental tradition of aesthetic enquiry, stemming from the significant attention given to aesthetics by both Kant and Hegel. Peter Osborne, in the introduction to his edited collection *From an Aesthetic Point of View*, goes so far as to say that continental philosophy 'views the world from an aesthetic point of view' (5). He continues: 'As such, it tends to attribute an importance to art for philosophy far in excess of anything acceptable to... even the most sympathetic analytic philosopher of art.'[8] The importance of art to Adorno and to Derrida has had lasting effects, and their heritage has by no means been played out, as is revealed by the large number of literary studies that take one or other as a major point of reference. Others continue to mine the writings on art of Heidegger, Gadamer, Lyotard, and Ricœur. Slavoj Žižek and Jacques Rancière both give the aesthetic an important role, and the current continental megastars Giorgio Agamben and Alain Badiou both write on art as a formal practice—Agamben even has volumes entitled (slightly misleadingly) *Stanzas* and *The End of the Poem*. Further places to look during this period for insight into formal properties are the disciplines concerned with other art forms: music and the visual arts. It's true that these disciplines have complex histories in which the notion of aesthetic form has sometimes had a rough ride, but qualities of colour, line, shape, tone, rhythm, harmony, melody, and so on have never been subjected to the dismal fate of the equivalent, and equivalently important, features of literary works. One could also look at the classroom, where the teaching of literature—of poetry, at any rate—has continued to involve at least some attention to form.

Given all this continuing activity on all sides, the picture of literary study as having lost and as now regaining its interest in form betrays a certain obliviousness to the wider domain of humanistic studies. A fuller commitment to interdisciplinarity would have led to a greater appreciation of other approaches to formal issues, and perhaps to a richer interplay between the historical and the aesthetic. Yet within the narrower domain of literary studies the story of the dominance of historical approaches can't be denied. It is perhaps too early to tell whether the current

comes across to those trained in literary studies as somewhat blinkered (and at times disagreeably patronizing), to ignore it altogether is to betray a wilful blindness that is even worse. For a rare example of a discussion across the frontiers of these disciplines, see the 2010 'Symposium' in the *British Journal of Aesthetics*, in which several commentators, including the present author, reflect on Peter Lamarque's *Philosophy of Literature*, and Lamarque responds.

[8] See also the section entitled 'Renewing the Aesthetic', in Elliott and Attridge, eds., *Theory after 'Theory'*.

hints of a revived interest in formal matters are harbingers of a major shift, but it seems a distinct possibility—if only because it is time for the pendulum to swing the other way.

Such a shift, while it would be warmly welcomed by many of those engaged in the business of teaching and commenting on literature (and I include myself), is not without its dangers. One danger is that a return to form would indeed be nothing but a return, a turning back of the clock—what Marjorie Levinson calls 'backlash formalism'. While there are no doubt those who would rather be practising the methods of context-free close reading that were common in the mid-twentieth century, the demonstration of the complicity between those methods and unacceptable ethico-political assumptions has surely been too persuasive to allow a simple revival.[9] Although there is more to learn from the best of the early formalist critics than has generally been allowed in recent decades, they also provide a lesson in the hazards of a formalism that fails to take account of the situatedness of writers and readers, that treats works of literature as self-sufficient, organic wholes, and that allies evaluation with questionable individual and social values. In contrast, there is the danger that increased respectability for formal study might result only in the appropriation of its methods for the continuation of familiar non-literary projects such as the exposure of ideological implications (or the celebration of ideological subversion) and the accumulation of historical knowledge, rather than the revaluation of literary study that a focused attention to form demands. Finally, there is a less obvious danger that arises from the sheer power of the methods of analysis that have been developed over the past century. For the tools we have at our disposal today—enshrined in a thousand guides to reading and teaching literature, analyses of individual works and oeuvres, and decades of classroom practice—*are* extremely powerful; thanks to the brilliant examples of Empson and Richards, Wimsatt and Brooks, Jakobson and Genette, to name only a few, we've inherited techniques of analysis that can be widely taught and put to use, even by those who are left unmoved by the works they are analysing. A great deal that is written or spoken about literary works is governed by an external need—the need to complete a student essay, to give a class, to achieve publication—rather than by an unignorable demand made by a work upon a reader; and we freely detect alliteration or allegory, historical reference or cultural allusion, biographical revelation or ideological deformation, without pausing to ask if this is what the event of the work insists upon when we read it with full

---

[9] Among the numerous critiques of post-war formalist methods to appear in the 1980s were Fekete, *The Critical Twilight*; Lentricchia, *After the New Criticism*; and Eagleton, *Literary Theory: An Introduction*.

attention. I'm not suggesting that we abandon these techniques, just that we make sure they're used to clarify and explain the experience of the work's singularity in an alert and committed reading. Some consideration of recent publications in this area will highlight both the achievements and the dangers that await writers in this field.

II

Eagleton's *How to Read a Poem*, Paulin's *The Secret Life of Poems*, and Vendler's *Our Secret Discipline* have all received a great deal of praise, as I indicated earlier. While the first two are presented as introductions to the art of analysing poems, the third is aimed at an audience of poetry initiates—though it still assumes, no doubt correctly, that in the area of form, even initiates need to have fairly basic matters explained to them. All offer a series of close readings, with plentiful descriptions of formal features; all reveal the weakness of such descriptions when they rely on conventional literary critical language rather than accurate phonetic analysis and when the power of the analytical tools they employ exceeds the needs of scrupulous reflection on the experience of poetry. (It's intriguing that two of these authors found it necessary, or thought it appealing, to refer to the formal aspect of poetry as a 'secret'—a hermetic art, presumably, that has been lost in this age of political imperatives and historical contextualizations.)

A comparison between Terry Eagleton's book and the well-known chapter entitled 'Ideology and Literary Form' in his 1976 study *Criticism and Ideology* suggests that Britain's most visible Marxist critic is less interested in what he then called 'the internal relations between ideology and literary form', preferring now to foster 'verbal sensitivity' as a somewhat unlikely counter to 'advanced capitalism' (17). Eagleton's evaluative comments are revealing, since they demonstrate the danger of using formal analysis to replicate a view of literary value that has been thoroughly criticized over the past few decades.[10] For example, in offering a contrast to that familiar whipping boy of a poem, Rupert Brooke's 'The Soldier', Eagleton says of Heaney's 'Digging', 'it is as though the words absorb into their own bodies the bitter soil and mould of which they speak' (60); the

---

[10] Eagleton's grasp on phonetic detail is not the strongest. Just to give two examples: Tennyson's 'Lotus Eaters' is said to avoid 'sharp consonants' (120), whatever they might be; and in Hardy's 'Darkling Thrush' we are informed of 'the semi-assonance of the last syllable of "Winter's" and the "*re*" sound of "dregs"' (121)—which, even allowing for a Dorset accent, is pretty far-fetched.

idiom of F. R. Leavis, dominant in literary criticism when Eagleton was a student at Cambridge, is unmistakable here. In true Leavisian vein, Swinburne is chastised for the 'narcotic music' of his poetry (46); Tennyson's 'Mariana' is found to be contrived, self-conscious, and lacking in spontaneity (112); and the feelings in Sandburg's 'Chicago' are 'bogus' (113). Eagleton's confidence that 'poems are moral statements' (29) owes something to Leavis as well. (An alternative view that is at least as plausible is that poems are neither moral nor statements.)

Eagleton does, in a short final section, make some gestures towards a reading of form that allies it with ideological rather than Leavisian criticism, though this is of a fairly banal sort—the heroic couplet reflects the world-view of the landowning class, the iambic pentameter rebuffs the voice of the collective, and so on—but it is Tom Paulin's book that exhibits truly impressive leaps from sound patterns to revolutionary movements, uninhibited by anything like Eagleton's common sense. Paulin's approach is not without its Leavisian prejudices either. Thus Auden's 'Musée de Beaux Arts' (one of forty-seven poems or extracts analysed) has, we are told, abandoned the 'Anglo-Saxon alliterative rhythms' of the poet's earlier verse, and the language is 'abstract and artificial', with 'twee adjectives' and 'superficial adverbs' (172–3). (Paulin overlooks the fact that the poem is a reflection on a certain genre of painting, a point which Eagleton, who uses this poem for his opening demonstration, is much clearer about.) By contrast, John Oldham, celebrated by Dryden, is linked 'to all that is robust, bold and liberty-loving in the English language and character', which sounds like a parody of Leavis; and in Ted Hughes we hear 'the English language speaking, the vernacular, with its local dialect energies fighting back against the standard language' (203).

In examining the operation of language in poetry, Paulin goes furthest of these three writers into linguistic detail, and exposes the dangers of an understanding of technique that combines a limited knowledge of phonetics with an over-powerful theory of how sounds work in poetry. He finds it difficult to differentiate between sounds and letters (*dazzling* contains a guttural (41), while *of* contains an *f* sound (163)); he can mistake stress patterns (*midnight* and *banjo* have two strong stresses (18, 234)); he confuses beats with stresses (Coleridge's 'eave-drops fall' is a 'three-beat figure' (64)); and he has a fondness for Ancient Greek feet, even when they produce a four-footed pentameter (165). Paulin is highly inventive in detecting patterns of sound; he has in fact improved on traditional practical criticism, as he repeatedly advances the highly dubious assumption that a repeated sound (or letter) has the effect of making the later examples more emphatic. Thus, for instance, the innocuous word 'home' in a line of Wordsworth's *Prelude* 'is strengthened by the earlier *o* sounds, so that it stands out and slows the movement of the line' (74). He also likes to look for words inside other words, a technique of enormous power, opening the way to almost endless possibilities of (usually misguided) analysis. So Keats's 'winnowing wind' contains two *wins*, part of the evidence, according to Paulin, that the poem is about the revolutionary struggle. Again, this is often a matter of letters rather than sounds: he finds *dead* in 'builded' (206), *ash* in 'asphodels' (215), and *love* in 'shovelled' (228).

Helen Vendler has, of course, been a standard-bearer for formal poetic analysis for a considerable period (I remember a riveting lecture on a Keats ode thirty years ago), but only now has she turned to the subject of her Ph.D. dissertation, W. B. Yeats, devoting 400 pages to the forms of his verse. What links this book to the sense of a newly confident formal criticism in the academy at large is that it is organized not by chronology or theme but by metrical and stanzaic form; thus we have chapters on the ballad, the sonnet, trimeter-quatrain poems, tetrameter poems, blank verse, *ottava rima* poems, and more. This unashamedly formal approach pays large dividends, as it helps us approach the question of form as a poet like Yeats does, asking which form is appropriate for a particular theme, what the potential uses of various forms are, how forms can be developed to cope with new circumstances. Vendler's practice of rewriting stanzas in alternative metrical forms is a particularly useful exercise, one which works effectively in the classroom as well as on the page. Her approach reduces the temptation of jumping from formal detail to large ethical or political themes, something both Eagleton and Paulin are prey to; instead, the link between the formal and the thematic is developed by means of the careful working through of the implications of metrical, stanzaic, syntactic, and other choices. Vendler pays most attention to stanza form, sequence, and the effect of different types of line; she announces 'I leave the rhythmic field aside here, in frustration at the absence of adequate notation' (92). She does, however, make use of the terminology of classical prosody, and it gets her into trouble from time to time. Thus the ballad metre of 'The Wild Swans at Coole' is said to demand a trochee at the end of certain lines, when what is at issue is the common duple or 'feminine' ending; and when she turns to Yeats's accomplished adoption of the four-beat line with varied openings and endings (the verse Milton used in 'L'Allegro' and 'Il Penseroso') she feels she has to classify lines as either 'trochaic' (which for her means beginning and ending on a beat) or 'iambic'.[11] No reader, unless fixated on foot-divisions, hears this very natural rhythmic form as veering from one metre to another.

---

[11] For a discussion of this metre, see Chapter 7 section III.

A problem in much formal commentary, recent and not so recent, is that the power of the semantic dimension of language is so strong that it is easy to imagine we are receiving meanings directly from sounds as well as from the words they constitute. Paulin frequently falls into this trap: we are told, in Donne's 'A Nocturnall upon St Lucies Day', that the *d*s in *midnight* and *dayes* 'carry...death and despondency' (18), and then on the next page that 'the dental *d*s give strength' to the opening lines of the second stanza—presumably because they involve the teeth. Eagleton's commentaries are blessedly free from this kind of thing, and Vendler only occasionally succumbs to the trap of fanciful phonetic symbolism. We hear of 'hard "r's"' and 'brutal "d's" and "b's"' (343), for example—the sort of thing that would (or should) earn an undergraduate a corrective comment in the margin. Another example is in Vendler's discussion of 'In Memory of Eva Gore-Booth and Con Markiewicz', where we are told of the 'harshness rendered by hard *c*'s, *d*'s, and *g*'s' (224) and again of 'the harsh sound effects in "*b*" and in the hard "*c*" and "*g*"' (230) in the later lines of the poem, but not of the hardness or harshness of any of the same sounds in the second, third and fourth lines, where they are just as prominent:

> Great windows open to the south,
> Two girls in silk kimonos, both
> Beautiful, one a gazelle.
>
> (*Poems*, 233)

No one, I suspect, has ever found these lines discordant or grating.

The question of the critic's tone in these engagements with form is an important one. Take Vendler's account of the 'argument' of 'Sailing to Byzantium': she is justifying what is, to say the least, a tendentious reading of the relation between Yeats's imagined condition of being gathered 'into the artifice of eternity' and the final stanza's depiction of an artificial bird:

The argument of the poem...must begin with the attempted repudiation of the 'country' of the young and their 'sensual music'; otherwise the defiant flight to the 'holy city' would not take on high relief. And naturally the poem must conclude with the description of the 'right' choice of embodiment; but prefacing it with a temporarily entertained 'wrong' choice makes the 'right' one conclusive. The balanced arrangement of stanzas points up the antitheses on which the poem is constructed. And although critics have recognized the initial antithesis between country and city, they have missed the equally fierce antithesis repudiating sacred song in favor of secular music. (38)

We should note those 'musts' and that 'naturally' (an interesting word to use in a poem that rejects nature!), and particularly the tenor of the final sentence: it appears that all the many critics (and presumably readers) of this poem before Vendler have missed the fact that the third stanza, far from presenting a prayer that is answered in the fourth stanza, is a wrong turning—in spite of the clear signal of continuity with which the fourth stanza begins ('Once out of nature …'). Now this truth has been revealed we can stop being troubled by the ambiguities and uncertainties that have assailed us when we read the poem (and that, perhaps, some of us have found to be part of its richness and riskiness). There's no place in Vendler's commentary for any sense that poetry might at moments elude the powerful grasp of the critic. It would be a pity if formal analysis, which could play a major part in a revaluation of literature as a cultural practice and an individual experience, became just another tool to 'prove' the critic right.

Paulin's tone is very different. He too has a long account of 'Sailing to Byzantium', and comments as follows on the conclusion: 'Yeats now has another attempt at the *come/Byzantium* rhyme, and this time it's as though he has learnt from the way he muffed it at the end of the second stanza' (165). Unlike Vendler, Paulin doesn't hesitate to say when he feels a poet has made a misstep—he's called the earlier *come/Byzantium* rhyme 'almost literally a bum rhyme which stops the line dead in its tracks'. As a reader, I may disagree, but I appreciate the sense of an engaged individual, thrilled when he finds the language working, dismayed when it grates on his ear. In spite of a barrage of over-interpretation, there's a sense of real engagement with the texture of the poems Paulin discusses. Although too often the claims made for linguistic detail seem far-fetched, one does feel the critic is struggling to explain the effect the poem has had on him. His discussion of Yeats's 'In Memory of Eva Gore-Booth and Con Markewicz' is very different from Vendler's; here, for instance, is his comment on the lines: 'Great windows open to the south | Dear shadows, now you know it all':

In the first we have two identical long *o* sounds followed by *ow*, in the second we have *o ow o*, the same sounds in a slightly different order. The effect is to call back the light, the youth, the beauty of the sisters, while simultaneously representing them as ghosts. (For years I could not understand why this line always made me choke when I read the poem aloud—until I discovered this particular sound pattern.) (169)

Paulin's somewhat idiosyncratic phonetic representation (he is referring to the diphthongs [oʊ] and [aʊ]) aside, this comment conveys more of the poem's power than any of Vendler's pronouncements about its consonantal patterns.

As I suggested earlier, there can be no blueprint for successful criticism. Vendler and Paulin are both distinctive, and both have their strengths, though I think it will be clear why I prefer Paulin's extravagant micro-analyses to Vendler's dogmatic pronouncements. Perhaps the fact that Paulin is an accomplished poet is not irrelevant: something of the inventiveness, the openness, the chanciness, that goes into the writing of literature needs to carry over into our teaching, our criticism, and our research—if, that is, we research not, or not only, as historians, linguists, sociologists, or moralists but as scholars whose primary interest is in literature.

III

In discussing the evidence for a possible shift in critical direction, I've tended to prefer the word 'form' to what is often taken to be a near synonym, 'the aesthetic'. I must confess something of an antipathy to the latter word, partly because it has had such a bad press in recent decades that it's hard to encounter it without thinking 'ideological mystification', but mostly because it brings with it associations which skew the discussion from the start. Although originally coined (by Alexander Baumgarten) with references to the senses, the term became, thanks to Kant's adoption of it in his articulation of a philosophy of the judgement of taste, closely associated with a series of interrelated concepts—among them beauty, disinterestedness, and autonomy. Since I take it that these concepts are among those we most need to question if we are to revitalize the notion of literary form, it seems to me wiser to set the rich tradition of the aesthetic to one side, at least until we have made some progress in thinking through the specificity of literary (and perhaps by extension, artistic) form. Kant, of course, was only marginally concerned with works of art: for him, the major source of beauty (and, for that matter, the sublime) was nature, and the discussion of judgements of taste in the Third Critique is concerned almost exclusively with our experience of natural objects. It is true that the word 'aesthetic' is commonly used today to refer only to art, but the Kantian flavour persists. So although Kant remains importantly, and inevitably, in the background of any consideration of the distinctiveness of the work of art, including mine, I believe I am justified in starting with a somewhat different set of terms. The term 'form', of course, is not without its liabilities either, but I find it a more ductile term, perhaps because it has been used in so many ways, and is thus easier to integrate into an account of the operation of the literary work. It's important, though, that it not be taken as a rough synonym for 'beauty' or 'unity', nor as an abbreviation of 'organic form': fractures, fragments, rigidities, collapses are all possible formal elements.

If there is return to form, therefore, I would like to see it involving a revalorization and reconceptualization of the term. Where for Plato a form (or a Form) is outside space and time, and for Aristotle is yoked to the matter it gives shape to, I would like to think of form as an active principle, as an essential element in the literary event. I don't like the terms 'formalism' and 'formalist'—for me they never quite manage to shake off the pejorative connotations that they have in common speech. (In the *OED*'s definitions, negative senses predominate.) I like the phrase 'new formalism' even less—and in any case one should recognize the prior claim to it staked by a movement in American poetry that favours verse in regular metres.[12]

The event of the poem takes place as part of the event of its reading; outside of its readings, it is nothing but a structure of inert signs. And it seems clear that the event of the poem is a *formal* event, involving, among other things, or rather among other happenings, shifts in register, allusions to other discourses (literary and non-literary), rhythmic patterning, linking rhymes, movements of syntax, echoing of sounds: all operating in a temporal medium to surprise, lull, intrigue, satisfy. I would also include—and this might at first sight seem surprising—the meanings of the words and sentences, for once we conceive of the work as an event, meaning becomes an occurrence, not a substance or an abstraction. Meanings unfold, intertwine, fade, echo, clash; we rely not only on our internal lexicon and familiarity with linguistic and literary conventions to handle the semantic dimension of literature, but on memory (both its powers and its limitations), predictive ability, and the capacity to orchestrate several levels of sense at once. What is traditionally called 'form' is one aspect of this moving complex, inseparable from what is traditionally called 'content'. This is not the familiar inseparability of form that matches content, sound that echoes sense; it is a question of a single process that can't be divided into two separate domains. And because meaning—the occurrence of meaning, meaning as a verb—is so integral an element in the event of the literary work, its relation to the many *contexts* that determine it is also an integral element. A responsible reading of the words on the page, therefore, can't avoid attending to the strands that tie them to the world they arose from—nor, for that matter, the associations they evoke in the world of the reader.

Why do people read novels and poems, or see plays and films? For many reasons, doubtless, but not, we can be sure, primarily to understand

[12] Visible signs of the movement include an online magazine, *The New Formalist* (<http://theformalist.org/>), a large annual conference at West Chester, Pennsylvania, and several anthologies.

the ideological forces at work in the past, or to appreciate the writer's resistance to (or compliance with) those forces, or to gain expert knowledge of a historical period. But a return to form, if that is what is happening, need not be a return to formalism, and it need not be an enemy to historical research or ethico-political commitment. It may bring academic criticism closer to the practices and pleasures of reading outside the classroom and the study, however, and perform the valuable service of recalling us, as literary critics, teachers, and students, to the enjoyable demands of the literary.

2

Meaning in Movement

Phrasing and Repetition

I

Milton's defence of rhymeless verse in the note preceding *Paradise Lost* is one of the best-known comments on the movement of poetry in the history of English literary criticism: 'True musical delight...consists onely in apt Numbers, fit quantity of Syllables, and the sense variously drawn out from one Verse into another' (4). The first two of these properties are clearly metrical phenomena, however problematic Milton's own sense and use of 'apt numbers' and 'fit quantity of syllables' might be; but the third refers directly to the experience of movement produced by *meaning*, as it is propelled by syntactic and semantic connections from the end of one line into the next. Milton understood very well that words occurring in sentences form not just a chain of meanings but sequences of expectation and satisfaction that constitute an important part of the material which the poet shapes and controls. Although the line-juncture is the point at which this experience of varied onward movement can be most obviously exploited—and you only have to read a few lines of *Paradise Lost* to realize how much a part of the poem's distinctive and effective texture the varied enjambments are[1]—it is never entirely absent from the reading process, and even though it is little talked about it is a constantly available poetic resource. Any utterance produces a continually shifting sense of semantic weight and directionality, and reading always entails a continuous process of prediction, continuously modified as expectations are met, intensified, or disappointed. Moreover, these sequences of increasing or decreasing semantic tension occur simultaneously over longer and shorter spans, so that, for instance, a local satisfaction may be part of a broader movement of expectation, or an extended phase of culmination may contain within it brief moments of anticipatory

[1] In *Milton's Grand Style*, Christopher Ricks does ample justice to this quality of Milton's writing.

tension. Syntax is clearly a major engine of this process, but expectations can also be set up by, for example, the use of familiar verbal collocations and idioms, by sound effects such as alliteration and rhyme, and by semantic incompletion or prolepsis. Poetry exploits this dimension of language—which I shall call 'phrasal movement' or just 'phrasing'—to the full.

Thus meaning itself functions in poetry rather like pitched sounds in tonal music: organized into patterns and sequences, it provides the onward drive that impels the reader or listener from the beginning of a work to the end. Phrasing produces periods of slackening pace or gathering momentum, moments with differing degrees of initiatory or closural force, and varying kinds of coherence or disjuncture. Milton's inclusion of these largely semantic effects under the heading 'true musical delight', which might at first seem a confusion of content and form, is thus perfectly appropriate. One familiar manifestation of this inseparability of signifier and signified is *repetition*, for the marked recurrence of an item of language in a poem repeats not just a series of sounds but also a meaning or series of meanings. However, repetition also constitutes a difficult area for any theory of verbal movement in poetry, and I shall turn to it in due course to see why this should be so—and how the resistance of repetition to theoretical accounts can illuminate the working of poetic language.[2]

Of course, it has usually been to the other poetic features named by Milton, 'apt numbers' and 'fit quantity of syllables', that commentators have turned in order to account for the experience of movement in poetry. Metrical analysis can show how different sequences of stressed and unstressed syllables (perhaps what Milton meant by 'fit quantity') produce different rhythms with their own qualities of pace, weight, roughness or smoothness, and so on; and it can show how these patterns produce series of beats falling into sequences of varying length and providing onward movement, anticipation, and closure (perhaps what Milton meant by 'apt numbers'). But metrical effects tend to be quite local, often extending no further than one line (though highly rhythmic forms like the ballad stanza can carry metrical expectation over several lines), and for the most part producing rhythmic variations that involve just a few syllables.[3] Dynamic effects of meaning, however, can function across much wider spans. For an example, one doesn't have to go any further than the opening sentence of *Paradise Lost*, which lasts for twenty-six lines, from 'Of Man's first diso-

---

[2] Theories of poetic language are not the only ones to find repetition a problem; linguistic accounts also come up against its recalcitrance. Jean Aitchison's survey of such accounts at the 1993 conference of the Swiss Association of University Teachers of English was qualified by the remark, capitalized on the handout, 'IT IS DIFFICULT TO MAKE GENERALIZATIONS ABOUT REPETITION!' See Aitchison, '"Say, Say It Again Sam"'.

[3] The most common of these variations are treated in Chapter 6.

bedience…' to '…justify the ways of God to men', and maintains syntactic tension (in a complex, layered, sequence of variations) throughout that extraordinary length. Semantic movement is not confined within the sentence, however; a sentence may produce an expectation of semantic climax in a following sentence, or delay arrival at an expected climax until a later sentence, or prolong the effect of the climax reached in a previous sentence. When we talk of phrasing, therefore, we need not limit ourselves to linguistically defined phrases, but include effects of meanings and syntax operating over spans of any length.

The importance of syntax and sense in the experience of rhythm and movement in poetry has frequently been insisted upon, both by poets like Milton and by many commentators on poetry and theorists of poetic form. But extended and systematic analysis has been rare, compared with the immense effort that has gone into the discussion of metre and its rhythmic effects and possibilities. However, a major step forward in this difficult territory was taken with the 1992 publication of Richard Cureton's *Rhythmic Phrasing in English Verse*, a book which sets out a finely detailed theory of the shaping and patterning of poetic language over spans greater than those usually considered in rhythmic analysis.[4] In the discussion that follows, I am indebted to Cureton's work, though I have chosen to use my own somewhat less systematic and exhaustive approach to these aspects of verse. However, a brief (and necessarily crude) summary of Cureton's arguments will set the stage for my discussion of movement and repetition.

Cureton—following the music theorists Lerdahl and Jackendoff—divides rhythm (which he defines in a very broad manner) into three distinct components, which he terms *metre*, *grouping*, and *prolongation*. Metre involves the perception of beats in regular patterns, grouping involves the apprehension of linguistic units organized around a single peak of prominence, and prolongation involves the experiences of anticipating a goal, arriving at that goal, and extending that goal by further elaboration. The major focus of Cureton's book is grouping, but it dwells sufficiently on the other two components to be able to present a coherent theory of rhythm—in this global sense—as the interrelation of events of these three kinds. Although the three components are separate, they all possess what Cureton sees as the crucial organizational feature of any kind of rhythm: strict hierarchical structure. A rhythm consists of a series of local events or units, perceived as more or less prominent elements within longer events or

---

[4] For a fuller discussion of Cureton's book than is possible or relevant here, see Attridge, 'Beyond Metrics'. I present a simplified form of Cureton's account of phrasing in chapter 8 of *Poetic Rhythm*.

units, which are themselves perceived as more or less prominent elements within even longer events or units, and so on to the entire work.

Analysing phrasal movement for Cureton involves examining the inter-related functioning of grouping and prolongation in a hierarchical organization. At the lowest level, words are grouped into 'clitic phrases', each with a strong syllable and up to six weak syllables. At the next level, these clitic phrases are themselves grouped into units, one phrase in each unit experienced as strong and the others as weak. These units are grouped in their turn, and so on up to the highest level, which usually corresponds to the whole poem. Although grouping is influenced by phonological and syntactic considerations (at the lowest level, for instance, the stress pattern is crucial, and at higher levels the boundaries of groups coincide with syntactic boundaries), the most important factor in determining the length of groups and the position of the peak is what Cureton calls 'the informational organization of the text'. Units are units of meaning, peaks are peaks in the poem's unfolding semantic and emotional drama. A grouping scansion is therefore an attempt to map not the poem's patterning of perceived sounds (as in the case of a traditional metrical scansion) but its patterning of meaning—though it is clear that in practice the two categories will constantly interrelate with and influence one another. In order to account for the way the reader groups potentially rhythmic stimuli, Cureton proposes a number of rules, reflecting both the preferences which readers follow in determining groups ('grouping preference rules') and the structural limits placed on groups by the perceptual mechanism ('grouping well-formedness rules').

Functioning in concert with grouping is prolongation, the reader's response to the existence in poetry of structural goals towards which or away from which the sense moves. Thus at any level of the prosodic hierarchy, there can occur sections of *anticipation*, *arrival*, and *extension*. These sections usually correspond to groups. The movement involved in any sequence from anticipation to arrival or from arrival to extension can be of three kinds: *equative*, where the text pauses to repeat itself; *additive*, where the text progresses by means of analogy; and *progressional*, where prolongation occurs by means of a striking new experience. Cureton does not develop his theory of prolongation very far in this book, but it suggests a valuable way of approaching the question of movement in poetry, reflecting more accurately than the rather static notion of grouping the temporality of the poetic experience.[5] In considering poetic repetition, prolongation is the most relevant aspect of phrasal movement.

---

[5] For a valuable earlier discussion of the movement of poetry generated by syntactic structures, see Sinclair, 'Taking a Poem to Pieces'. A pioneer of the study of poetic syntax was Donald Davie; see his *Articulate Energy*.

II

To illustrate in a very simple way the operation of phrasal movement in poetry, let us take Blake's well-known poem 'A Poison Tree', from *Songs of Experience*.

> I was angry with my friend;
> I told my wrath, my wrath did end.
> I was angry with my foe;
> I told it not, my wrath did grow.
>
> And I watered it in fears,
> Night and morning with my tears;
> And I sunned it with smiles,
> And with soft deceitful wiles.
>
> And it grew both day and night
> Till it bore an apple bright—
> And my foe beheld it shine.
> And he knew that it was mine,
>
> And into my garden stole,
> When the night had veiled the pole.
> In the morning glad I see
> My foe outstretched beneath the tree.
>
> (*Complete Poems*, 212–13)

The opening two-line sentence is a self-contained movement: *anticipation* in 'I was angry with my friend', *continuation* of that anticipation in 'I told my wrath', and climactic *closure* in 'my wrath did end'.[6] At the same time we experience, within these clauses, three shorter movements which we might describe as increasing in semantic weight (emphasis on *friend*), decreasing (emphasis on *told*), and increasing again (emphasis on *end*). The second sentence, syntactically very similar to the first, ends with a climax that is also a moment of strong semantic expectation: 'I was angry with my foe; | I told it not, my wrath did grow.' The forward drive is not produced by anything formal or syntactic at this point (except perhaps our awareness that there are several stanzas to come); it derives from the semantic force of the word *grow* (in contrast to the earlier *end*). Within the clauses of this sentence, we experience three consecutive sequences of

---

[6] Blake's punctuation is less an indicator of syntax than of rhetorical pauses; my references to sentences are to the implicit syntactic structure of his lines. Although one could divide up the poem differently—fewer sentences and more clauses or vice versa—the points to be made about phrasing would be unchanged.

increasing weight, since the new information comes at the end of each sequence (emphases on *foe, not, grow*), the rest being repetition. The parallelism of syntax between these two sentences, therefore, is countered by difference in internal movement.

The sentence that follows does little to satisfy the anticipation aroused by the opening stanza; rather, it increases it by expanding on the implications of *grow*:

> And I watered it in fears,
> Night and morning with my tears;
> And I sunned it with smiles,
> And with soft deceitful wiles.

There is no feeling of resolution in this sentence, just a series of postponements as we wait for the outcome of this nurturing process. The internal movement is balanced; there is little sense of increasing or decreasing weight until the two adjectives that provide strong anticipation before our arrival at the key Blakean word, *wiles*. The second half of the stanza parallels, and is to that extent an extension of, the first half, but there is enough of a new turn in the second half—the unexpectedly pleasant demeanour of the speaker towards his enemy—to propel the reader forward.

The next sentence begins with a summary statement that delays arrival at the semantic goal for one more line, then at last reaches the statement that provides fulfilment:

> And it grew both day and night
> Till it bore an apple bright—

(Notice how the semantic progression is signalled by the conjunctions: 'And—And—And—And—Till'.) The appearance of the beautiful fruit has central importance within the poem, which is concerned with the way hatred can take effect through ingratiating behaviour. Still, the culmination in 'apple bright' of the sequence beginning with 'grow' does not dissipate all the tension produced by the initial announcement of anger, and at the same time as we experience climax and closure at this level, we experience further anticipation over a longer span—anticipation signalled, of course, in the punctuation, and formally increased by our position midway through a stanza. The next line provides a climax to this longer span:

> And my foe beheld it shine.

The next clause, it seems to me, unpacks the implications of that climactic event, and so constitutes a continuation of it:

> And into my garden stole,

We sense more anticipation here: the action of stealing into the garden is clearly not the culmination of the sequence. But that culmination does not come immediately. The line that follows—

> When the night had veiled the pole—

elaborates on and intensifies the action, so that although it ends the sentence it settles nothing and keeps the anticipation alive; in fact the introduction of 'night' sets up a slight anticipation of its own.

The two-line sentence that follows is indeed the climax of the poem, though it achieves that climax with surprising economy. The tension established by the mention of night is resolved by the due appearance of morning, in a natural logic that suggests necessary sequentiality, but the point of view switches back to the speaker as we move not to the anticipated action—the eating of the fruit—but to its disturbingly gratifying effect:

> In the morning glad I see
> My foe outstretched beneath the tree.

The placing of 'glad' renders it ambiguous: we might read it as qualifying 'morning' (as in Blake's well-known painting 'Glad Day'), 'I', or even, momentarily, 'foe', though most readers probably settle on 'I'. This uncertainty increases the anticipation already produced by the adverbial phrase, which is then further increased by the verb 'see' occurring in a strong enjambment that drives the reader on to 'foe'. This is not the true climax, however, since it is the enemy's state that provides the culmination of the narrative logic; 'outstretched' therefore takes the full weight of the expectation, and prolongs it to the significant final word 'tree', which names for the first time the symbol of the poet's destructive but disguised anger. (It is interesting to learn that as a notebook draft the poem was entitled 'Christian Forbearance'.) Meaning in the whole poem thus moves in two waves: first a ripple that takes only two lines, then an onward driving sweep, with its own inner rises and falls, that controls and gives life to the remaining fourteen.

It will be evident that what I've called 'metrical movement' and 'phrasal movement' don't operate in isolation from each other. Milton's focus on enjambment illustrates strikingly the importance of their interrelation, since a run-on line in regular verse is a point at which metrical closure (arrival at the last beat of a five-beat sequence, for instance) conflicts with semantic anticipation (since syntactic continuity always

implies some degree of semantic continuity).[7] Enjambment is usually
discussed more in terms of syntactic linkages than semantic ones;[8] this is
perfectly appropriate as far as it goes, but leaves out of account the dif-
ferent kinds and strengths of expectation that may be set up by identical
syntactic structures with different semantic contents. The relation be-
tween an adjective and a noun, for instance, will depend in part on
whether it is a familiar or an unexpected collocation, whether the infor-
mational weight at this point of the poem falls on the adjective or the
noun, whether the adjective–noun sequence comes within a semantic
peak or within a semantic trough, and so on. Semantic relations over
longer spans are important, too: a relatively weak enjambment in terms
of syntax and word-to-word semantic relations may be part of a larger
forcefully forward-moving unit of meaning. An example would be lines
9 and 10 of 'A Poison Tree', where the lack of syntactic and semantic
connection between *night* and *till* produces a break that coincides with
the line-end, while at the overarching level that takes in the whole cou-
plet the impetus to move on is extremely strong. Syntax and semantics
have to be considered together, then, in their relation to the metrical
patterning of the poem, if we are to understand the production of 'true
musical delight'; and if this is the case, an understanding of the poem's
musicality cannot be separated from an understanding of its play of
meanings.

III

Repetition is, of course, a crucial feature of all poetry; as Jakobson real-
ized in devising his famous definition of poetic language, poetic form
depends upon equivalences—that is, implied repetitions—along the
axis of succession. Even free verse relies, in its division into lines, on
some kind of principled equivalence, and stricter forms of verse use
repetition of features such as syntactic structures, phonological pat-
terns, rhythmic phenomena. What is especially valuable about the con-
cept of repetition is that it highlights temporality (as does Jakobson's

---

[7] A third factor shows itself in verse like Milton's, where the enjambments are frequent
and the metrical form—the iambic pentameter—is one without particularly strong closural
properties: the graphic layout of the poem on the page, which strengthens, for the reader,
the break at the line-ending. In most free verse, of course, this visual interruption of the se-
mantic flow is the only kind possible, since metrical closure does not exist; see Chapter 9.

[8] Useful studies include Hollander, ' "Sense Variously Drawn Out": On English Enjamb-
ment' in *Vision and Resonance* (91–116); and Sinclair, 'Taking a Poem to Pieces'. Cushman, in
William Carlos Williams, summarizes some of the attempts to classify enjambment (31–3).

phrase 'the axis of succession'), the *nacheinander* rather than the *nebeneinander*—even if it problematizes that very distinction.[9] An alternative such as 'parallelism' has its uses, but, like Cureton's emphasis on grouping and his employment of visual metaphors and diagrams, risks reducing the experience of the poem to some kind of static, instantaneous or timeless, abstraction. Of course, temporality or seriality in poetry is not a straightforward matter; poems are made for re-reading rather than reading once only, and though there's a sense in which every re-reading begins anew, there's also a sense in which a re-reading presupposes the simultaneous existence of the whole poem within the reader's consciousness. Nevertheless, insofar as a poem is an oral phenomenon (and poems of course vary in this regard) it is dependent on temporality, albeit a 'staged' temporality, rather than one which unfolds in real time.

What I want to focus on, within the context of this staged temporality, is *the immediate exact repetition of verbal material*.[10] I am leaving aside, that is, several types of repetition that occur commonly in poetry: repetition in conjunction with difference as it occurs in various types of equivalence and in chiasmic patterns, repetition of purely syntactic, metrical, phonic, semantic, and other non-verbal material, and all those kinds of non-immediate, or postponed, verbal repetition which poets use constantly, whether structural, like the refrain, or occasional, like Blake's repetition of the word 'wrath' and the sequence 'I was angry with my...'.[11] My argument is that in the experience of the poem as a temporal phenomenon, immediate exact repetition of verbal material has a rather special role to play, and one that, in thwarting many of our attempts at systematic analysis, highlights the specifically *literary* operation of phrasal movement in poetry. The other types of repetition raise many of the same issues, but they do not do so in as striking a way and are more easily assimilated to traditional aesthetic values and approaches. But to say something and then say it again, in exactly the same words, is to transgress the dictates of good style and good sense; the very phenomenon often regarded

---

[9] I am grateful to Adolphe Haberer for helping me to see the importance of this qualification.

[10] Madeline Frédéric, in her comprehensive treatise *La Répétition*, calls this 'répétition en contact immédiat' (46) or 'répétition lexicale immédiate' (156). Gunnar Persson's *Repetition in English* is a study of this phenomenon—which he terms 'immediate and identical repetition of lexical items' (8)—as it occurs in contemporary spoken English.

[11] I take the distinction between 'structural' and 'occasional' repetition—a fundamental one in discussing poetic repetition—from Barbara Herrnstein Smith's invaluable book, *Poetic Closure*. For a discussion of some aspects of the structural sonic repetition of rhyme, see Chapter 3.

as the distinctive feature of poetic discourse becomes, in its purest form, a mark of poetic collapse.[12]

A poem's temporal dimension is a matter of directedness, of a movement from the beginning (in the past) to the end, somewhere ahead. As Cureton's analyses demonstrate in minute detail, the pace of this movement continually varies; at any given moment the language can be driving ahead, coasting in the wake of a dynamic climax, idling slowly forward, or cresting at a point of structural arrival. And as Cureton has also shown, this happens simultaneously over spans of different duration; a small-scale conclusion may be part of a larger-scale anticipation, which in turn may be part of an even larger-scale extension. Within the multi-layered onward movement, repetition of various kinds clearly plays an important role, and one that in its multiple effects is not easily analysable.

We may recall that for Cureton, onward movement is termed 'prolongation', and can occur as anticipation (leading towards an arrival) or as extension (moving away from an arrival by elaborating on it in some way). We may recall further that there are three types of prolongation, all of which may occur as anticipation or extension: equative, additive, and progressional. Within this analysis, repetition is included in the category of equative prolongation, which is described as 'movement which does not significantly move' (147)—the whole problem of repetition being caught in this paradox. 'In poetry', he continues, 'this "pausal" movement is usually articulated by overt repetition or apposition. In moving towards or away from a goal, the text pauses on the path to name and rename some part of the path rather than getting on to the journey's end.' By 'apposition' Cureton appears to mean a semantic repetition that does not actually use the same words, and it is not difficult to see how this can qualify as equative prolongation: the poem is carried forward by its new language even while its meanings repeat what has gone before. This type of equative movement is only partially equative.

'Overt repetition' of the kind I am interested in is a little more problematic, however. It presents equative prolongation in the strictest sense, an unmoving movement that stalls the progress of the poem. Yet this raises the question of how such an event can produce the experiences of arrival and extension (the only two prolongational movements that Cureton identifies). The movement from a linguistic item to its exact repetition

---

[12] In her suggestive essay on 'The Paradoxical Status of Repetition', Shlomith Rimmon-Kenan makes a similar point, with the aid of a citation from Christine Brooke-Rose (153–4). Wordsworth, in his note in *Lyrical Ballads* to 'The Thorn', insists on the value of exact repetition as a marker of passion: 'From a spirit of fondness, exultation, and gratitude, the mind luxuriates in the repetition of words which appear successfully to communicate its feeling' (289). He cites several biblical examples.

can be neither a sequence of anticipation and arrival nor a sequence of arrival and extension (since an extension is a moving away from a goal by developing its implications). We have to conclude that equative arrival and equative extension in fact exclude the purest form of equativity, exact repetition, which remains something of an embarrassment to a theory of prolongational movement. This is not, I should add, a criticism of Cureton's impressive attempt to arrive at a systematic description; it is an indication of the odd status of repetition in poetic movement. If we turn to Cureton's theory of grouping, we find that exact repetition poses a difficulty here too. The peak of a rhythmic group—often also a point of prolongational arrival—is the point of greatest informational prominence (197–9), which would imply that a repetition, whose informational weight is zero, is the very opposite of a peak, a kind of ultimate trough or nadir.[13]

We know, however, that repetition of this exact and overt kind in poetry need not produce a sudden experience of total emptiness or nullity, a black hole in the poem—in fact, a repeated phrase or sentence can be a very positive addition, and we shall be examining some examples shortly. But its effectiveness often depends on the way it is treated by the reader, since—as the bearer of no information whatsoever—it does not contain any indication of how it might best be read. Should it be treated as an additional emphasis that produces a climax? A post-climactic release of tension? Stalling or blockage? Momentary backward movement? Of course, in any given instance, the context of the repetition will limit these options, but the point I want to make is that the repeated item itself— insofar as it is read as repeated—cannot signal what kind of repetition it is. As a result, it will often pose a challenge to the schematic description of the rhythm and movement of verse.

Usually this challenge is experienced only as a momentary refraction in the apprehension of form and content; but occasionally a writer will exploit to the full repetition's resistance to interpretation. No one has done so more exhaustively, not to say exhaustingly, than Gertrude Stein. A short passage will serve as a reminder of the extraordinary effect of her repetitions, working over and over a limited set of words until they seem to be emptied of content, only to inject a fresh set, suddenly radiant in their meaningfulness, until they too lose their power to signify or refer. The following is a paragraph from 'Patriarchal Poetry':

---

[13] One of the difficulties of transferring theories of musical movement to language is evident here: despite some parallels, there is no real equivalent in music of the semantic dimension of language. Repetition in language works against informational progression in a way that cannot be equated with the operation of musical repetition.

Made a mark remarkable made a remarkable interpretation made a remarkable made a remarkable made a remarkable interpretation made a remarkable interpretation now and made a remarkable made a remarkable interpretation made a mark made a remarkable made a remarkable interpretation made a remarkable interpretation now and here here out here out here. The more to change. Hours and hours. The more to change hours and hours the more to change hours and hours. (*The Yale Gertrude Stein*, 136–7)

Such writing defies analysis in terms of directional movement and arrival at goals; unanticipated peaks are provided by the irruption of linguistic difference, but they tend to melt away as the new series of repetitions begins.[14] In what follows I want to focus on less extreme examples, moving from shorter to longer repetitions.

The least problematic form of immediate repetition is the repetition of *single words*. Known in rhetoric as *epizeuxis*,[15] it usually suggests a speaking voice at a moment where repetition would be a natural emotional outlet. King Lear's dying moments include several examples: 'Howl, howl, howl!'; 'Cordelia, Cordelia!'; 'No, no, no life'; and, of course, 'Never, never, never, never, never!' In the decisions which the actor faces as he prepares these lines one begins to see the way in which immediate repetition eludes interpretative rules.[16] Should he treat such a sequence as moving towards a climax on the last repetition, that is, as a prolongational sequence of anticipation and arrival? Should there be an attempt to equalize the repetitions, in order to bring out the deadening despair that produces this mechanically reiterating language? (This would produce either a group with no peak, which is impossible by Cureton's rules, or a series of one-member groups, which, according to those rules, we habitually try to avoid.) Is the first utterance of the word the peak, followed by a series of weaker echoes? Or should the actor try for more varied effects, countering the repetition by giving a different value to

---

[14] Stein herself emphasized the slight differences which she continually introduced into her repetitions (see 'Portraits and Repetition', in *Lectures in America*, 178–9). These variations are obviously important in providing a feeling of slight but continual movement that runs through even the most repetitive passages; but they can be appreciated only against the background of the massive effect of the repetitions.

[15] A different type of immediate verbal repetition is *anadiplosis*, or what Frédéric calls 'répétition lexicale pseudo-immédiate' (157), where a word that ends a syntactic segment is used again to begin the next one; Shakespeare's Sonnet 129 contains an example: 'On purpose laid to make the taker mad; | Mad in pursuit, and in possession so.' I am excluding this type from my discussion, as the repeated term is rendered different by its syntactic and semantic context. Persson makes the same exclusion (9–10).

[16] The difficulties of categorizing different uses of immediate repetition in speech are evident from Persson's study; some of these can be gauged from his list of types alone— repetition is said to be 'intensifying', 'emphatic', 'conjoined', 'mimetic', 'simple', or 'purposive' (15–16). The author admits that these are not 'watertight compartments' (17).

each instance of the word? Of course there is no final answer, and differ-
ent decisions will have different results.[17] It is hard to see how grouping
preference rules would help here—which is not to cast doubt on the
usefulness of such rules, but to demonstrate that the unique effect of
repetition lies precisely in its evasion of rules.

Repetition of single words can also be used mimetically, as in the re-
markable ending of Seamus Heaney's poem 'A Constable Calls' (part of
the sequence entitled 'Singing School'). The deceptively simple poem de-
scribes from a small boy's perspective the visit of a policeman, by bicycle,
to the family farm to check on the crops being cultivated. Here is the last
stanza, suffused, like the whole poem, with a sense of the mundane
become ominously, but indeterminately, meaningful:

> A shadow bobbed in the window.
> He was snapping the carrier spring
> Over the ledger. His boot pushed off
> And the bicycle ticked, ticked, ticked.
>
> (*North*, 67)

Repetition is used here not just to mimic the slow clicks of the cycle's gear
mechanism as the policeman rides away, but as a closural device—or more
accurately, as an anti-closural device that nevertheless has closural force.
Exact repetition is not in itself closural: it does not let the poem progress
towards an end, but it does not bring it to a satisfying halt either.[18] All it
does in itself is mark time, but without any internal information or struc-
turing principle to suggest when it should stop. A word or line that has
been repeated once implies an infinity of possible repetitions. However,
the greater the number of repetitions, the more obvious their anti-closural
effect; a single repetition can be read as an emphatic and final reiteration.
We can rewrite the last line of Heaney's poem to show this:

> *His boot pushed off
> And the slow bicycle ticked, ticked.[19]

---

[17] Carruth observes, 'I can arrange those five repeated nevers in a half-dozen ways that
are easily enunciated and appropriate'—though this surely doesn't mean that the play is not
'feasible in dramatic production', as he asserts ('Lear', 518).

[18] In *Poetic Closure* Smith points out on several occasions that systematic or structural
repetition in poetry is an anti-closural force (42, 48, 57, 157), but she identifies non-sys-
tematic or occasional repetition as an effective closural device (155–66). Although she
confines her examples of closural repetition to formal patterning such as internal rhyme,
alliteration, and assonance, she mentions 'the recurrence of whole words and phrases'
(161). My argument is that the latter operates in part like structural repetition, especially if
the repetition occurs more than once.

[19] I adopt the convention used in linguistics to indicate a constructed counter-example:
an asterisk at the start of the example.

This, to my ear, has more finality than the original. What Heaney actually gives us is more suggestive of a continuous sound going on beyond the end of the poem, as it is of the boy's continuing meditation on the dark significance of the visit. If we rewrite the ending with no repetition at all, however, the singular power of the poem's conclusion is lost altogether:

> *His boot pushed off
> And the slow bicycle quietly ticked.

In this example there's little sense of the interpretative blockage I talked about in relation to Lear's words: the dominance of the mimetic effect requires a repetitive reading, perhaps a diminuendo, like the fade-out of a recorded piece of music. What it does make problematic is a grouping and prolongational analysis; the final repetition produces a peak and an arrival—perhaps the climax of the whole poem—only by virtue of the repetition itself, and not by virtue of its semantic content. (My last rewrite indicated how the significance of *ticked* is reduced when it occurs only once.) An additional grouping preference rule to deal with this phenomenon might help, but—as a preference for linguistic emptiness—it would operate against the rule which states a preference for peaks that are linguistically dense.[20]

Immediate repetition of *short phrases* is rarer than immediate repetition of single words, but when it occurs it usually produces similar effects. A well-known example—this time in a prose speech—is Hamlet's, 'You cannot, sir, take from me anything that I will not more willingly part withal—except my life, except my life, except my life' (II.ii.215–17). No doubt many readers and auditors have agreed with Coleridge's comment that this repetition is 'most admirable' (I.24), but it is hard to say exactly why. (Coleridge didn't attempt it.) Hamlet's richly varied language, full of the rushes and sallies of rhythmically orchestrated phrasing, suddenly starts reiterating itself like a stuck needle as he confronts his own death-wish (which Freud, we may remember, linked closely to the phenomenon of repetition-compulsion). Once again, an actor may choose to speak it as a crescendo or a diminuendo instead of an uninflected repetition, or with three different tonalities; however he does it, it represents a resistant moment in the text, a moment where the mobile forward-moving energy that animates almost every literary work is suddenly thwarted.

---

[20] Grouping preference rules are not necessarily consistent with one another, however; Cureton points out, for instance, that our preference for a grouping peak of unusual linguistic density usually runs against our preference for groups that are informationally and physically 'heavy' (244). It may be that some poems achieve forcefulness by pitting preferences against one another. A version of optimality theory might offer a way forward (see Prince and Smolensky, *Optimality Theory*).

An example of a repeated phrase which functions closurally like Heaney's ticking bicycle, but is expressive rather than mimetic (though the example contains a mimetic single-word repetition of 'talk' as well), is the final line of Sylvia Plath's scathing account of marriage, 'The Applicant', coming as the climax of a series of jaundiced assertions of the needs fulfilled by a wife:

> A living doll, everywhere you look.
> It can sew, it can cook,
> It can talk, talk, talk.
>
> It works, there is nothing wrong with it.
> You have a hole, it's a poultice.
> You have an eye, it's an image.
> My boy, it's your last resort.
> Will you marry it, marry it, marry it.
>
> (*Collected Poems*, 221–2)

Unlike the Heaney example, I find this ending extremely difficult to read. There's no question mark—clearly this is less an offer than a command—and the repetition (itself repeating a phrase already used twice in the poem) seems to produce a kind of sheer linguistic violence, increasing in intensity as the meaning is emptied out. Once again, it is hard to see how a grouping or prolongational analysis would capture what is happening in this most powerful of conclusions.

Another example of 'expressive' closural repetition, but one which is tonally very different, is the ending of D. H. Lawrence's 'Song of a Man Who Has Come Through':

> What is the knocking?
> What is the knocking at the door in the night?
>
> It is somebody wants to do us harm.
> No, no, it is the three strange angels.
> Admit them, admit them.
>
> (*Complete Poems*, 250)

Notice that the first phrasal repetition in the excerpt functions as a kind of anadiplosis, since the repetition is part of a new syntactic and semantic unit and thus shorn of some of its quality of pure repetitiveness; whereas the final repetition is a strict one, allowing a variety of readings but clearly contributing to the reader's experience of closure.[21]

---

[21] Repetition of a phrase that, on its second occurrence, leads on to a new thought is a distinctive device in poetry. Two of the best-known are Tennyson's 'The woods decay, the woods decay and fall' ('Tithonus') and Empson's echo of this phrasing in 'The waste remains, the waste remains and kills' ('Missing Dates').

Immediate repetition of *longer phrases or sentences* is much rarer, and reveals even more clearly the way in which repetition poses an obstacle to our norms of poetic processing.[22] It is almost always occasional, though one fairly familiar type of structural use is in poems that deliberately imitate the form of the blues, like the following opening stanza of Langston Hughes's 'Blues at Dawn':

> I don't dare start thinking in the morning.
> I don't dare start thinking in the morning.
> If I thought thoughts in bed,
>   Them thoughts would bust my head—
> So I don't dare start thinking in the morning.[23]
>
> (*Selected Poems*, 261)

In this example, of course, we hear the strains of a blues melody as we read, and the repetition can be said to work 'musically' to restate the opening theme and at the same time to postpone, and hence increase anticipation of, the climax that comes in the third and fourth lines—which in a more typical blues would be the end of the stanza.[24] Read outside that context, the repetitions seem merely laborious.

One of the most effective exploitations of the peculiarly resistant power of the immediate repetition of a long phrase is the strangely potent ending of Robert Frost's 'Stopping by Woods on a Snowy Evening', which will be our final example. It is worth quoting the whole poem, in spite of its familiarity.

> Whose woods these are I think I know.
> His house is in the village though;
> He will not see me stopping here
> To watch his woods fill up with snow.
>
> My little horse must think it queer
> To stop without a farmhouse near
> Between the woods and frozen lake
> The darkest evening of the year.

---

[22] One of the most striking examples of the repetition of longer units is Alice Oswald's long poem *Memorial*. The poem moves between accounts of the deaths of the heroes of the *Iliad* and translations of Homeric similes from the epic; almost all the latter—up to twelve lines long—are repeated verbatim, giving the poem a distinctive eddying rhythm, especially marked in the poet's own performance.

[23] It is interesting to note that blues singers, and Hughes's imitations of blues songs, usually vary the immediate repetition slightly, if only with an added initial 'Oh,…'.

[24] In music, of course, where semantic directionality is not at issue, repetition can be used much more freely and with much less drastic effects. The employment of the *da capo* symbol is not a sign of flagging creativity.

He gives his harness bells a shake
To ask if there is some mistake.
The only other sound's the sweep
Of easy wind and downy flake.

The woods are lovely, dark and deep,
But I have promises to keep,
And miles to go before I sleep,
And miles to go before I sleep.

(*Complete Poems*, 250)

Throughout its length, the poem progresses without strong prolongational effects; it is, after all, a poem about stopping when one would be expected—by the human community, even by the habituated horse—to go on. The lack of onward drive contributes to the eerie stasis of the lines

The only other sound's the sweep
Of easy wind and downy flake.

Although the first of these lines uses weak enjambment to enhance the movement on to the second, contributing some mimetic power to *sweep*, that moment of potential vigour is quickly dissipated by the adjectives *easy* and *downy* and the non-progressional form of the line (which is itself repetitive in ways that I'm not discussing here: syntactic and metrical).

The last stanza begins with a line—'The woods are lovely, dark and deep'—that at the level of the longest groups probably ought to be read as the final constituent of a group that began at the start of the poem, a group that deals with the snowy woods and—by implication—the temptation they represent to the speaker. Within that long group it stands on its own as a summary of that temptation, the underlying theme of the poem up to this point. Whether it constitutes a prolongational arrival I'm not sure; certainly in the word *lovely* something that has only been implicit is now admitted, and the unspoken desire to leave the commitments of the world to join that lovely darkness comes close to being voiced. At any rate, the emergence or near-emergence of that desire prompts an immediate counter-movement: the last three lines constitute a group that sets against the rest of the poem the demands of the human community. Within this final group, the prolongational structure is unexpected: the climactic arrival occurs in the first line, and the next two lines constitute an extension, spelling out the effect of the 'promises' which have to be kept—whether one takes the statements at face value (there are duties to be performed before the speaker can go home) or as a comment on the life that has to be lived before the dark loveliness of death can be embraced.

Even the different rhyme word that has appeared in the third line in previous stanzas is now replaced by a repetition, increasing the sense of a playing-out of what is already implicit.

But what is the effect of the repeated line with which the poem ends? It is itself a 'dead' moment, a stopping where we would expect forward motion and final arrival, contentlessness at a point where we are being reminded of the fullness of human meanings. Though it's in the place of closure, it has an effect that, as we have already noted, is characteristic of repetition: having recurred once, there is no intrinsic reason why it should not go on recurring to eternity. It's hard to see on what grounds one could call the repeated line the peak of a group or the climax of a prolongation, and yet it puts its mark on the whole poem, intensifying its suggestiveness and deepening its hitherto somewhat whimsical tone. We can read it as the expressive repetition of a dramatic speaker, as we read the repetitions of Lear and Hamlet, although it presents even greater obstacles to definitive interpretation than those examples. Is it the repetition of firm resolve? Or of a sleepy letting go that signals the defeat of that resolve? If we take it not as the representation of inner speech but as the poem's way of concluding, of playing with the idea of conclusion, we might say that the very enunciation of a forward drive—the travel that lies ahead—is caught up in the necessarily, and endlessly, repetitive structure of verse (and ultimately of language). The temptation of the dark woods—the temptation to repeat endlessly instead of moving on—has been resisted at the level of the will, but at the level of discourse it remains an essential part of what it is to promise, to speak, to think.[25]

For meaning itself is grounded in repetition; the never-before-experienced, the wholly other, is meaningless, not even available to perception. At the same time, as I think my examples have indicated, there is actually no such thing, in the temporal movement of a poem, as an exact repetition.[26] We cannot, after all, draw an absolute line between repetition and non-repetition; every apparently new appearance, if it appears, is constituted or mediated by the familiar; every repetition, repeating itself in a specific here and now, freshly contextualized, is different. The second occurrence of Frost's line is not the same as the first, most importantly in

---

[25] For an interesting consideration of the relation of repetition to timelessness, focusing on Wittgenstein's *Tractatus*, the Hindu *Upanishads*, and Kierkegaard's *Repetition*, see the final chapter of Kawin's *Telling It Again and Again*. Rimmon-Kenan also refers to Kierkegaard's *Repetition* in commenting, 'Complete repetition…is death or—if one prefers—eternity' ('Paradoxical Status', 155); and she mentions as one of the paradoxes of repetition: 'Although repetition can only exist in time it also destroys the very notion of time' (158).

[26] Rimmon-Kenan's first paradox is 'Repetition is present everywhere and nowhere' (151).

that, unlike its predecessor, it is a repeated line. (But then the first line, once we know it is about to be repeated, is no longer the same either.) Perhaps we do, after all, find exemplifications in poetry of that paradoxical event, 'equative arrival'. As I've tried to show, repetitions in literature resist many of our strategies of interpretation and constitute irreducible moments of otherness, but this is not, as I may seem to have implied, because they mark an absolute difference from the way language in the literary text usually goes about its business. On the contrary, the trouble we have with repetitions—pleasurable and perhaps profound trouble, I should add—is not ultimately distinct from the trouble we have with the cultural practice we call literature, whose statements are not quite statements, whose references do not quite refer, and whose variously drawn-out movements never allow themselves to be fully and finally mapped.

3

Rhyme in English and French

The Problem of the Dramatic Couplet

I

The history of the rhyming pentameter couplet as a medium for serious drama in English is not a lengthy one.[1] Its beginnings are usually traced to Davenant's heroic opera of 1656, *The Siege of Rhodes, Part I*, which uses a variety of rhymed metres but which may originally have been written as a spoken play in couplets, and subsequently altered because of Puritan opposition.[2] Such disguises, however, were soon rendered unnecessary by the reopening of the theatres at the Restoration, and it was Charles himself who, impressed by the French classical plays he had attended during his exile, recommended the use of the dramatic couplet to the most influential of its early exponents, Roger Boyle, Earl of Orrery. In compliance with the king's suggestion, Boyle wrote *The General* in 1661, and gave the rhymed heroic play its full form (*Dramatic Works*, I, 22–8). Among those who were impressed by Boyle's work was Dryden, who began his career as a writer of rhymed heroic drama by collaborating with his brother-in-law Sir Robert Howard on *The Indian Queen*, performed in 1663, and who initiated the theoretical debate about dramatic rhyme in the dedication (to Boyle) of *The Rival Ladies* in 1664.[3] With Dryden as its leading practitioner and defender, rhymed tragedy was soon dominating the

---

[1] It is traced in Deane, *Dramatic Theory and the Rhymed Heroic Play*, chapter 5; Prior, *The Language of Tragedy*, chapter 3; Nicoll, *A History of English Drama 1660–1900*, I, 100–31; Singh, *The Theory of Drama in the Restoration Period*, chapter 4. The favoured form for such rhymed tragedy as was written before the Restoration (mainly Elizabethan closet adaptations of Seneca) was the fourteener, though the pentameter couplet was occasionally used with an equal lack of skill.

[2] This suggestion was first made by Dent in *Foundations of English Opera* (65–8), but doubt is cast on it by Hedbäck in her critical edition of the work (lxviii).

[3] For full accounts of Dryden's theory and practice of the rhymed heroic play, see Kirsch, *Dryden's Heroic Drama*, and Alssid, *Dryden's Rhymed Heroic Tragedies*. Dryden's critical writing is conveniently collected in *'Of Dramatic Poesy' and Other Critical Essays*, edited by Watson, and page references are to this edition.

serious theatre.[4] From his somewhat tentative defence of rhyme in 1664, including the notorious attempt to adduce a native precedent in 'the tragedy of Queen Gorbuduc' (I, 5), Dryden was to reach the assurance of the 1672 preface to *The Conquest of Granada*, in which he could claim, 'Whether heroic verse ought to be admitted into serious plays is not now to be disputed: 'tis already in possession of the stage, and I dare confidently affirm that very few tragedies, in this age, shall be received without it' (I, 156). Yet only three years later he was complaining in the Prologue to *Aureng-Zebe* of a weariness of 'his long-loved mistress, Rhyme' (I, 192); and, indeed, that play was to be his last in heroic couplets. When the blank verse of *All for Love* was first heard in 1677 the tide was already turning: Lee's *Rival Queens* had appeared in that metre a few months earlier, and Otway was soon to join, and play a leading part in, the new movement. The dominance of rhymed tragedy had lasted less than two decades. Its disappearance was swift and almost total: Nicoll counts eighteen examples in the 1660s, twenty-four in the 1670s, and one in the 1680s (*A History of English Drama*, I, 100). Since then, rhyme for other than comic or burlesque purposes has not been a frequent visitor to the English stage, making only an occasional appearance for a particular dramatic purpose or in isolated scenes: one thinks of Yeats's 'heroic farce' *The Green Helmet* or of the choral and liturgical passages in *Murder in the Cathedral*. (In the past fifty years, however, there has been something of a resurgence of rhymed tragedy in English for a specific purpose to which we will come in due course.)

English literary history thus presents us with a question: why should rhyme, a powerful expressive device in much of the finest poetry since Chaucer, be so unwelcome a presence on the serious stage? If what seems more immediately puzzling is that the heroic couplet should have held the stage at all, even for twenty years, this is because its unsuitability as a dramatic vehicle is a widely accepted fact that has an air of obviousness about it; but it is a fact that needs to be explained. The brief success of rhymed drama after the Restoration has been accounted for in terms of the special aims of the heroic play, in which rhyme was an essential element;[5] but what remains to be discussed is *why* rhymed verse on the stage should produce effects which were apparently prized for this short period but seem unacceptable now. Recent translations of rhymed French tragedy will give us some examples to contemplate.

---

[4] Voices were raised in opposition, however (Buckingham's *Rehearsal* of 1672 is a notable example), and grew louder as the years passed. See Rothstein, *Restoration Tragedy*, chapter 2.

[5] See especially the discussions by Prior, Singh, Kirsch, and Alssid mentioned above.

A number of the problems arising from rhymed drama were aired in the controversy between Dryden and his erstwhile collaborator, Howard, which began in 1664 with the dedication to *The Rival Ladies* and continued, as tempers deteriorated, in the preface to Howard's *Four New Plays* (1665) and in three exchanges in 1668: Dryden's *Essay of Dramatic Poesy*, Howard's preface to *The Duke of Lerma*, and Dryden's *Defence of 'An Essay'*, prefixed to the second edition of *The Indian Emperor*.[6] The more peripheral debates over the origins of rhyme or its usefulness in circumscribing the writer's luxuriant fancy are not our concern; at the centre of the dispute, however, lie the more important questions of verisimilitude and decorum. To Howard, a poem is 'a premeditated form of Thoughts upon design'd Occasions', and rhyme is therefore appropriate; but a play 'is presented as the present Effect of Accidents not thought of', and rhyme is out of place, especially when the couplet is shared by two speakers, 'so that the smartness of a Reply, which has it's beauty by coming from sudden Thoughts, seems lost by that which rather looks like a Design of two, than the Answer of one' ('To the Reader', *Four New Plays*, sig. [a4]r). Dryden's response suggests a somewhat different conception of drama, which becomes most apparent in the *Defence of 'An Essay'*: rather than supposing a play to be 'the composition of several persons speaking *ex tempore*', we are aware that it is 'the work of the poet, imitating or representing the conversation of several persons' (I, 114). The gap between the two attitudes is not as wide as it might appear (Coleridge's 'willing suspension of disbelief' is one way of bridging it), but as far as the effects of rhyme are concerned it is Howard, not Dryden, who speaks for most English playgoers.

Howard's main argument against rhyme, however, is based on a theoretical premiss which is much weaker than his practical observations: ''Tis not the question', he claims in the preface to *The Duke of Lerma*, 'whether Rhime or not Rhime, be best, or most Natural for a grave and serious Subject; but what is nearest the nature of that which it presents.'[7] Dryden insists in reply that decorum *is* the question: if verisimilitude consisted in the exact replication of the real world, far more would have to be jettisoned than rhyme. And having driven his brother-in-law into a theoretical corner he could retire and enjoy the fruits of his victory—though not for long: soon the growing clamour against rhyme and his own change of

---

[6] The controversy is summarized by Deane (168–77) and by Kirsch (22–33), and in the valuable 'Commentary' in *Prose 1668–169* (vol. XVII of *The Works of John Dryden*), 343–8. For a more sympathetic view of Howard's part in the debate, see Oliver, *Sir Robert Howard*, chapter 6.

[7] Preface to *The Great Favourite, or, The Duke of Lerma* (1668), in Dryden, *Of Dramatick Poesie*, ed. Boulton, 119.

aims led to an admission in practice of the strength of Howard's initial position. Dryden was right in his insistence that drama involves a heightening of reality, and Howard was unwise to oppose, or appear to oppose, that position; but on the practical question of the degree to which, and the way in which, rhyme effects such heightening, Howard's instincts have the backing of over 400 years of literary history.

As we have seen, it was from France that Charles II brought one of the seeds from which English heroic drama was to grow and, although Dryden was reluctant to admit to any such influence, there can be no doubt that the works of the French classical dramatists were the most important source of the forms, and to some extent the themes, of Restoration tragedy.[8] Corneille had first appeared in an English dress as early as 1637, in Joseph Rutter's pedestrian version of *Le Cid*, and the reopening of the theatres was followed by further imitations. The best of these was Otway's *Titus and Berenice*, an adaptation of Racine's *Bérénice* which appeared in 1676, two years after John Crowne's inferior *Andromache* had introduced Racine to the English stage. As one would expect, the form most frequently used in these plays is the heroic couplet, and it is only a short step from them to the more original rhymed heroic plays of this period.[9] It is when we place side by side the French originals and the English translations and imitations that our problem poses itself in its sharpest form: why does the French alexandrine couplet succeed so admirably in the theatre when the apparently similar English heroic couplet so frequently fails? Because no other dramatist exploited the potential of the alexandrine as fully and as subtly as Racine, and because the challenge of translating his plays into English has been felt with particular acuteness during the last fifty years, it is on his dramatic verse, and attempts to refashion it in an English medium, that I shall concentrate. Most of my examples will come from the work which probably presents the translators with their most daunting challenge: *Phèdre*.

II

Before we pursue this subject into the thickets of the translations themselves, we need to survey the ground from a height, and in particular raise

---

[8] On the influence of French classical drama, see Canfield, *Corneille and Racine in England*; Eccles, *Racine in England*; and Wheatley, *Racine and English Classicism*. The current flowed in the opposite direction in the following century, when Voltaire fought a losing battle on behalf of heightened verse drama, with Dryden as one of his models: see Russell, *Voltaire, Dryden, and Heroic Tragedy*.

[9] Brooks, for example, in 'Dryden's *Aureng-Zebe*', finds echoes of *Mithridate*, *Britannicus*, *Bajazet*, *Rodogune*, and *Nicomède*.

some questions about metrical form and what determines it. Briefly, it is possible to isolate three influences on the verse forms in any language. First, there are the aesthetic tendencies which poetry shares with other art forms, either in a particular period, or, at a deeper level, running diachronically through the art of a single culture. Secondly, and more narrowly, there are the formal conventions of the particular literary tradition, creating a continuity which makes possible the appreciation of poetry of earlier periods. And thirdly, there are the conditions imposed on verse forms by the medium itself, the language whose physical substance is being shaped and patterned. The second of these influences overlaps with the first and third: specific conventions are bound to reflect wider aesthetic expectations, and are necessarily based on what the language offers; but conventions are determined in many other ways as well, by social conditions and historical change, by individual artistic achievements, by the inertia of a settled mode of apprehension, by the exhaustion of a vein, and, perhaps, by mere desire for change.

How does this general framework apply to the particular problem of metrical comparisons between English and French? We can assume that the first of these influences on verse form, that of wider aesthetic norms, has been very similar in the two traditions: whatever differences exist between the two cultural contexts are slight compared to the similarities, and although any attempt to explain why Racine was undervalued by British audiences for so long would have to invoke and particularize these differences, translation of his plays continues to be a problem in a climate much more sympathetic to the ideas of Racinian drama; indeed, the problem is highlighted when English readers with a knowledge of French have a great admiration for Racine in his own language, but find translations consistently unsatisfactory. As this notion of general aesthetic properties may seem rather vague, it will be as well to offer an example of a fundamental rhythmic pattern shared by the two verse traditions. The most elementary metrical form in English verse, the rhythmic group made up of four lines of four beats each (the basic metre of the ballad, the nursery rhyme, the popular song, and a large amount of more sophisticated verse[10]), finds an echo in what Peter France calls 'perhaps the most typical' periodic construction in seventeenth-century French tragedy: four alexandrines making up one sentence, divided, like the English four-line form, into two pairs of lines by rhyme and frequently by syntax (*Racine's Rhetoric*, 144–6). The similarity lies not just in the arrangement of lines into pairs of pairs, nor even the further subdivision of each line into equal

---

[10] See Chapters 5 and 7 for further discussion of this form.

halves, but right down to the tendency for each half-line to have two accents, creating a line with four beats. Moreover, the accents are often regularly spaced by intervening unaccented syllables, as in this example given by France (145):

. .   / . . / .   / . /
Quand aux feux les plus beaux un monarque défère,
. . / . . / . . / . . /
Il s'en fait un plaisir et non pas une affaire,
. . / . . / .   . / . . /
Et regarde l'amour comme un lâche attentat,
. .   / . . / . . . / . /
Dès qu'il veut prévaloir sur la raison d'État.

(Corneille, *Tite et Bérénice* V.i.1435)

Only at the end of the fourth line does the regular beat stutter, and the reader (especially the reader who has English as a first language) has to resist pronouncing *raison* with a stress on the first syllable. The English pentameter, too, is often characterized by four marked accents; and though in neither case can a four-beat rhythm be said to be a fundamental structural principle, it occurs as a subsidiary element often enough to suggest that even these sophisticated literary forms have a connection with the more elementary rhythmic pattern, a pattern which pervades the music as well as the popular verse of Western Europe. It is a shared relationship which could prove useful to a translator.

On the other hand, it is obvious that the second influence, the particular conventions of French and English, will produce significant differences in verse form. Whatever common aesthetic tendencies link the two literary traditions, each has been moulded by its own external and internal pressures and has acquired its own independent character, and this is undoubtedly one aspect of the difficulty of finding an equivalent for Racine's alexandrines in English verse. No metrical form in English has the pre-eminence and the associations that the alexandrine has in French: reintroduced in the sixteenth century by the Pléiade after an eclipse of two centuries, it remained the dominant metre in all forms of serious verse until the second half of the nineteenth century.[11] It therefore carries no very specific associations of genre, nor is it especially closely linked to any one author. The nearest English equivalent in terms of dramatic status, as many translators of Racine have noted in defence of their choice

---

[11] For accounts of the French alexandrine in English, see Scott, *French Verse-Art, passim*; and Lewis, *On Reading French Verse*, 43–69. Roubaud provides a detailed commentary on the fortunes of the alexandrine since the late nineteenth century in *La Vieillesse d'Alexandre*.

of metre, is blank verse; but blank verse has much more definite associa-
tions, and its use has been confined to a relatively limited range of genres.
What is more, anyone writing dramatic blank verse since Shakespeare has
found it difficult to escape his overshadowing presence, as the theatrical
attempts of all the major Romantic poets testify.

The translator who chooses rhyme, on the other hand, faces an even
greater disparity between the two sets of conventional associations. The
success of blank verse, introduced by Surrey as an equivalent of the Virgil-
ian hexameter, pushed rhymed verse into a more restricted and particular-
ized region than it occupied in France. To English ears, rhyme seems
naturally suited to verse which imitates song rather than speech, or which
displays wit rather than expressing emotion, and while these qualities can
be highly effective on the stage (*A Midsummer Night's Dream* is an obvious
example), they are seldom appropriate in tragedy. The Restoration prob-
ably offered the most auspicious moment in English literary history for
serious rhymed drama: the heroic couplet was acquiring great esteem in
non-dramatic verse (and Milton had not yet struck his counter-blow with
Paradise Lost); France's status as an arbiter of taste was an asset for a form
with French origins; and the reopening of theatres presented an opportu-
nity for a fresh start, with audiences influenced by fewer preconceptions
than usual.[12] By the mid-1670s, after a decade of rhymed tragedy, one
might have thought that a shift in conventions had been achieved, the
associations of rhyme permanently altered, and the rhymed play set fair
for an extended career. But cultural memory proved longer lasting than
might have been expected: the example of Shakespeare and his admired
successors (still appearing on the London stage during this period) re-
mained potent, and the roots of the new growth proved shallow. In es-
pousing rhymed tragedy Dryden had falsely claimed to be following an
English tradition; in abandoning it for blank verse thirteen years later
he was truly doing so, and the preface to *All for Love* makes it clear that he
was fully conscious of this: 'In my style I have professed to imitate the
divine Shakespeare; which that I might perform more freely, I have disen-
cumbered myself from rhyme' (I, 231).

But can we explain the collapse of rhymed tragedy wholly in terms of
the different place occupied by rhyme in the English literary tradition,
and the different responses it therefore evokes? Why were these associa-
tions so hard to shift, when the history of literary convention is one of
continual change? And why *did* rhymed verse come to acquire these

---

[12] There were, however, still some preconceptions to be overcome: Pepys's response to an
early performance of *The Indian Queen* in 1664 was 'the play good but spoiled with the
Ryme, which breaks the sense' (*The Diary of Samuel Pepys*, V, 33).

different reverberations in the two literatures? Was it just an accident that blank verse flourished in England and languished in France, when the shared humanist ideals made the unrhymed Latin hexameter a potent example in both countries? If there are more answers to these questions, they will be found by turning to the third major influence on verse form: the language itself.

III

Every language has its own characteristic rhythmic organization: that is to say, its own characteristic patterns of duration, pitch, and intensity, which control the speed of utterance, the rise and fall of intonation, and the placing of stresses. We learn the rhythmic configurations of our own language in childhood; but the student of a foreign language often finds that they are the most difficult things to master, the last ineradicable indication that he is not using his native tongue. These differences between language rhythms are, in part at least, the outcome of different ways of using the muscular apparatus which produces speech, and in particular the respiratory muscles which expel the bursts of air on which all speech is carried.[13] This does not mean, however, that language rhythms are purely physical phenomena which can be recorded and measured by a machine; on the contrary, what English speakers perceive is conditioned by their knowledge of English rhythms and their own re-conversion of the sounds they hear into the muscular movements that produced them. The rhythms of verse are, and can only be, created out of the rhythms of the language itself, usually by heightening whatever tendency to regularity the language already possesses. In English, this regularity is based on the occurrence of stressed syllables at predetermined places in words and sentences; and English speakers will tend, as it were, to hang the rhythm of their utterance on the stressed syllables, allowing the unstressed syllables to slip by more rapidly, and very often letting the unstressed vowels emerge as the neutral [ə], the schwa or 'reduced vowel' which is such a characteristic feature of English pronunciation. What English accentual verse does is to control the disposition of stressed and unstressed syllables in order to make this natural tendency towards accentual regularity more marked.

---

[13] The most interesting studies of this aspect of speech-production for the student of metre are those by Stetson: *Bases of Phonology* and *Motor Phonetics*, though Stetson's physiological hypotheses have been challenged. A useful summary of both the original theory and some of the criticisms is given in Allen, *Accent and Rhythm*, 40–5.

French rhythms present a different picture. Stress is not a fixed property of certain syllables, but a feature which occurs with less force and
greater freedom, gravitating to the end of the phrase, or of the word pronounced in isolation, unless it is placed elsewhere for rhetorical purposes.
The rhythmic flow of the language is determined more by the syllables
than the stresses, and vowels tend to maintain their full phonetic value
when unstressed.[14] As a result, French verse has developed on a syllabic
basis, with only a secondary role for stress, where in English it is the syllable-count which is secondary and the stress pattern which is primary.
The alexandrine keeps rigorously to its twelve-syllable structure (including the pronunciation of 'mute' *e* where it is not followed by another
vowel or at line-end), divided in its classical form into two six-syllable
hemistichs, with a syntactic break or pause of some kind in between. This
results in a stress on the sixth and twelfth syllables (in which positions the
unaccented mute *e* does not occur); but the other stresses, or *accents mobiles*, can fall on any syllable, and are often relatively weak.[15]

These differences are of the utmost importance in any attempt to translate verse from one of these languages to the other. In spite of its outward
rigidity, the alexandrine has in the freedom of its stress patterns the capacity for a type of variation of which English verse is incapable, and which
must in part account for its use in a much wider variety of genres than any
single English line. Though a distinctly heightened form of speech, its
rhythms are not insistent, and there is less danger that it will dominate the
natural movement of the language, or tire the ear with rhythmic obviousness. English dramatic verse has to use other means to subdue and vary its
rhythms; and one of the most effective is to abandon rhyme and make
liberal use of enjambment. This is one reason why rhyme in English has
an effect so different from that of rhyme in French: it emphasizes rhythmic patterns which are already prominent, where French rhyme makes it
easier for the ear to grasp a relatively unobtrusive rhythm.

Let us look more closely, however, at first the function, then the nature,
of rhyme in French. The metrical character of the alexandrine couplet is

---

[14] The distinction between stress- and syllable-timed languages was proposed by Pike in
The Intonation of American English, 34–5. Stetson offers some interesting comments on the
differences between English and French speech rhythms, based on the same distinction, in
Bases of Phonology, chapter 8, and *Motor Phonetics*, chapter 8. As a number of experiments
have shown, the distinction is not a matter of objective timing, but of the perception of
rhythmic groups and peaks. It has been suggested that a better characterization of these
differences is as a continuum from most stress-based to most syllable-based; see Arvaniti,
'Rhythm, Timing, and the Timing of Rhythm', and Reed, *Analysing Conversation*, 140–1.
[15] Useful guides to French verse written in English include Jacqueline Flescher's essay in
Versification: Major Language Types, ed. W. K. Wimsatt, 177–90; and Shaw, *The Cambridge
Introduction to French Poetry*, chapter 1.

determined by its hierarchical structure: each hemistich is made up of six syllables (often divided into smaller, balanced groups), each line of two hemistichs, and each couplet of two lines; and, though this is of less structural importance, the couplets themselves alternate between *rimes masculines* and *rimes féminines*. The keystone of this whole structure, especially when the verse is heard rather than read, is the rhyme: it signals the end of the line; it makes possible the identification of the caesura half-way between the rhymes, and subsidiary to them in the chain of pauses; and it marks the couplet as the next unit in the hierarchy.[16] Far from being an ornament, rhyme is a vital part of the metrical organization, and it was scarcely open to Racine or Molière to *choose* it as a feature of their plays in verse.[17] In English verse, however, the metrical pattern is established as the line progresses: we need only a few syllables to signal to us that a regular rhythm is being employed. Line-lengths and rhymes have important effects on the character of the rhythm, but they are not fundamental to its existence; it is possible to experience much of Shakespeare's rhythmic subtlety without perceiving where the line-ends fall. Consequently, the use of rhyme in English carries more significance than it does in French, where, as a predictable feature of the verse, it conveys less information, in the technical sense of that term. In English, rhyme brings with it a small charge of surprise each time it occurs.

The phonetic and phonological differences between French and English also make for differences in the nature of rhyme itself. The fact that the accent in French falls at the end of the word or phrase—excluding mute *e*—means that all rhymes are what would in English be called 'masculine'. (In French, the distinction between *rimes masculines* and *rimes féminines* is more a matter of sight than sound, since final mute *e* is not pronounced in this position, except in words like *perdre* or *oncle*.) This is another limitation on the use of rhyme in French for expressive purposes, since the French poet does not have the choice of the English poet, gloried in by Sidney in the *Defence of Poetry*, among masculine, feminine, or triple rhymes, and their differing associations. Such small expressive value as might lie in the choice between *rimes masculines* and *rimes féminines* is removed by building the alternation between them into the structure, thus making this aspect of rhyme another predictable element. What is

[16] To be strictly accurate, the first rhyme word presents itself as such only in potential, to be confirmed when its partner is reached; here the syllabic regularity of the hemistich is instrumental in promoting our awareness of the rhyme word, so that these two elements of form reinforce one another.

[17] In the preface to *Œdipe* (1729), Voltaire illustrated how essential rhyme is by re-writing some lines from *Phèdre* without it: see Kastner, *A History of French Versification*, 309, and the whole of chapter 12, which describes the rare attempts to write 'vers blancs'.

more important, though, is that the position of the accent makes French
a language rich in rhymes, especially as there are so many common inflec-
tional endings and suffixes which receive the final accent; added to which,
rhyming is made easier by the frequency with which final consonants are
unpronounced. Poets have responded to such an *embarras de richesses* by
imposing strict restraints on French rhyme: the mere repetition of a final
stressed vowel is regarded more as a matter of assonance than of true
rhyme, and where the English ear is perfectly happy with *flea* and *tree* a
French ear is less than satisfied with *allée* and *épée*.[18] Classifications of
French rhymes vary, but a widely accepted one is that proposed by Gram-
mont: the type just mentioned, which has only one repeated element, is a
rime faible; *rimes suffisantes* have two repeated elements (consonant and
vowel, as in *trempée/épée*, or vowel and consonant, as in *inhumaine/haine*);
and *rimes riches* are distinguished by having three or more elements in
common (*attendu/confondu, empire/respire, point* n./*point* adv.).

The constraints are not only a reflection of the ease with which rhymes
are to be found in French, but also a product of the phonetic lightness and
phonological unimportance, relative to English, of the French accent. For
if rhyme is to function as a structural element it needs a phonetic salience
which the repetition of stressed vowels alone does not have in French, and
more complex sound patterns are sought, though even the richest French
rhyme is still not as prominent a phenomenon as an ordinary English
rhyme. (It is worth noting, however, that the more desirable kinds of
French rhyme can make use of elements either before or after the stressed
vowel, giving the poet a choice between an effect somewhat analogous to
English rhyme (*jalouse/épouse*) or one which is quite different (*désolé/
parlé*).) Another reason why French rhyme is relatively unobtrusive is that
it is more frequently polysyllabic, and this too arises from the phonetic
characteristics of the language: whereas English polysyllables have to be
matched in stress pattern as well as in quality of sound, and in any case a
feminine or triple rhyme may be inappropriate, the French poet is con-
cerned only with the vowels and consonants, and can leave the stresses to
take care of themselves. On the other hand, satisfactory monosyllabic pairs
are more difficult to find in French, since a monosyllable which ends in a
vowel usually has to rhyme with a polysyllable for the sake of *suffisance*.

The phonological differences between English and French rhyme point,
however, to a more important difference in the role of rhyme in the two

---

[18] The characteristics of French rhyme are summarized in Grammont, *Petit traité de
versification française*, chapter 4, and treated more exhaustively in Elwert, *Traité de versifica-
tion française*, chapter 3. For a full account in English, see Kastner's *History of French
Versification*.

languages. Because most English rhymes involve the root rather than the inflectional ending or suffix (*looking* rhymes with *booking* but not with *liking*), the semantic contrast or parallel between the two words is more prominent than it is in French; and this aspect is emphasized by the frequent monosyllabic rhymes in English, where the semantic element and the rhyming element are both concentrated in one syllable. One might say that the characteristic function of English rhyme is to bring together in a single act of apprehension two different units of meaning and two identical units of sound. W. K. Wimsatt, in one of the most influential studies of rhyme in English, has discussed this 'wedding of the alogical with the logical', whereby the fortuitous parallel in sound contradicts or qualifies the disparity in meaning, creating a pleasurable surprise, and reawakening our consciousness of the physical quality of the words.[19] These effects are particularly pronounced in the couplet, not only because of the proximity of the rhyming words, but also because, as Wimsatt shows, the whole line is frequently involved in the parallelism. Rhyme, like the pun, can function as a kind of metaphor, bringing together two fields of discourse, and hence two different areas of experience, which the language normally holds separate.[20] And the phonetic structure of the English rhyme emphasizes this quality of sameness-with-difference: we are satisfied with a rhyme only if in conjunction with the repetition of a stressed vowel there is a *difference* in the preceding consonant; what would pass in French as desirable *rimes riches* (*spire/inspire, delight/polite, plane/plain*) strike the English ear as flat and feeble, lacking that crucial contrast which transforms an echo into rhyme.[21]

It would be untrue to say that French rhymes never function in the way described by Wimsatt. Many writers have gone to great lengths to avoid rhymes which depend on repeated morphemes, the Romantic poets in particular tightening the constraints on so-called *rimes banales*; but the most ingenious rhymes of a poet like Hugo can never have precisely the same effect as the rhymes of Keats or Byron. And when we look at Racine's use of rhyme, we find that he makes little attempt to sharpen the semantic effect by seeking contrasts or parallels of meaning.

---

[19] 'One Relation of Rhyme to Reason'. See also Hunter, 'Seven Reasons for Rhyme'.

[20] On the pun and its relation to rhyme, see Attridge, *Peculiar Language*, 188–94; and Fried, 'Rhyme Puns'.

[21] Some contemporary poets, notably Paul Muldoon, have challenged this convention and found ways of exploiting the distinctive aural properties of *rime riche*. Creaser, in an astute essay on rhyme in English poetry, instances *rime riche* being used by Spenser in conveying the deceitful harmonies of the Bower of Bliss ('Rhymes, Rhyme, and Rhyming', 457). See also McKie's valuable discussion of what he calls 'null rhymes' in 'Semantic Rhyme', 344–7.

(Pierre Guiraud has calculated that some 40 per cent of Racine's rhymes rely on grammatical forms, as opposed to only 2 per cent of Hugo's.[22]) Racine's rhymes do have a crucial part to play in the structure of the verse, and it is a part for which the French variety of rhyme is well suited; but it is not a role in which English rhymes feel most comfortable.[23]

Rhyme in English is, for all these reasons, more prominent both phonetically and semantically: it gives the physical substance of the word a particular insistence, and it draws attention to what is fortuitous or odd in the language. French rhyme, on the other hand, springs more naturally from tendencies inherent in the language itself, and has to be prevented, by the means we have observed, from slipping back into the ubiquitous and unremarked patterns of normal speech.

IV

What, then, is the translator of French rhymed verse in English to do? The decision to retain rhyme is, in view of these deeply rooted differences, certainly not an obvious one; and the problems are exacerbated when the translator is working not for the private reader but for the theatre, where audiences have expectations very like Sir Robert Howard's: the play should give the impression of people talking, not of a playwright exercising his skill, and one's attention on what is being said should not be distracted by too strong an awareness of how it is being said. Rhymed dramatic verse in English has two somewhat conflicting effects: one is to heighten the formality and stylization of the language, the other is to evoke a comic response. The artificiality of rhymed dialogue was seen by Dryden as a quality which the heroic play could take advantage of, and neither he nor Howard thought it was suitable for a 'low' form like comedy; but for most of us, the artificiality it creates is, in fact, comic. Comedy can use the particular strength of the English rhyme (its capacity to yoke incongruities together) to good purpose, and the translator of rhymed comedy may achieve effects not in the original but at least consonant with the mood of the play.[24] At its most accomplished, as in Richard Wilbur's translations

---

[22] Guiraud, *Langage et versification*, 123. The whole of Part I, 'Les Sons', is valuable, and covers more ground than the title of the work suggests.

[23] Middle English, on the other hand, did use stressed inflectional endings in rhyming. Chaucer's use of rhyme has some similarities to French practice, and is, as Wimsatt points out, noticeably different from Pope's ('One Relation', 157–62).

[24] Tony Harrison, in his translation of *Le Misanthrope*, makes use of highly Molièrean— but amusing—rhymes; and Christopher Fry takes advantage of Rostand's ingenious rhyming to produce some Byronic effects in his translation of *Cyrano de Bergerac*.

of Molière's *Tartuffe* and *Le Misanthrope*, the English rhymed couplet can convey both the formal control and the humour of French classical comedy.[25] (Wilbur's introductions to these translations set out admirably the advantages of retaining the rhymes of classical comedy.) But in aiming at tragic heightening through rhymed verse, the dramatist has to curb those features of English rhyme which make it such an apt comic vehicle; he or she has to render it less prominent, less witty, less effective in itself and more effective as an element in the larger metrical structure.

Before we examine some of the attempts to do this, it will be useful to remind ourselves of what Racine was able to achieve with the French form, and what the translator is trying to imitate. The following is part of Phèdre's painful confession of love to Hippolyte in Act II, scene v, and illustrates Racine's style at its tightest, and perhaps its closest to the style of the serious heroic couplet:

> Objet infortuné des vengeances célestes,
> Je m'abhorre encore plus que tu ne me détestes.
> Les Dieux m'en sont témoins, ces Dieux qui dans mon flanc
> Ont allumé le feu fatal à tout mon sang,   4
> Ces Dieux qui se sont fait une gloire cruelle
> De séduire le cœur d'une faible mortelle.
> Toi-même en ton esprit rappelle le passé.
> C'est peu de t'avoir fui, cruel, je t'ai chassé.   8
> J'ai voulu te paraître odieuse, inhumaine.
> Pour mieux te résister, j'ai recherché ta haine.
> De quoi m'ont profité mes inutiles soins?
> Tu me haïssais plus, je ne t'aimais pas moins.
>
> *(Théâtre 2* 222)   12

Phèdre's tragic stature lies partly in the terrible clarity and honesty with which she sees her situation, even when, as here, she is obeying the dictates of passion rather than reason. That fearful clarity is given force and precision by the firm structure of the verse, never disrupted by the strength of the emotion. In lines 2, 8, and 12 the two equal halves of the alexandrine are no mere rhetorical embellishments, but the blocked exits of a trap which makes the dilemmas in English heroic drama seem mere balancing tricks in comparison. The tightness of the couplets is increased by the relatively regular *accents mobiles*, usually falling on the second or third syllable of the hemistich, and by the quite strongly marked rhymes, all but one exhibiting the 'English' pattern of a contrasted consonant

---

[25] Ranjit Bolt has perfected the use of the four-beat rhymed couplet in his translations of French classical comedy, a form in which the rhymes are even more prominent than in pentameter couplets.

before the stressed vowel.[26] (The exception is *passé/chassé*, which is in a way even more like an English rhyme in that the two words differ only in their initial consonants.) The rhyme between *célestes* and *détestes* is further emphasized by the assonance of the first syllable, and the opposed connotations produce a bitter irony of the sort more commonly encountered in English couplets. Yet the balanced structure does not settle into stasis, and Phèdre never becomes a mouthpiece for neat verbal symmetries; the different units of the metrical scheme are used to achieve an onward motion and a variation in pace that is rare in English heroic couplets, which have a tendency to come to a halt, in movement and meaning, at the rhymes. For example, the passage opens with a sentence filling a couplet; then follows a four-line group which traces a rising wave of emotion through expanding units beginning, with obsessive insistence, 'Les Dieux' (half-line), 'ces Dieux' (one-and-a-half lines), and again 'Ces Dieux' (two lines). The two longer units drive over the medial and final pauses, reaching a climax on 'une gloire cruelle', and subsiding into the helplessness of 'une faible mortelle'. In this third couplet the rhymes are only part of a larger parallel between the final hemistichs, which make identical use of mute *e*'s to slow down the line, but which exhibit a chiastic pattern of syntax; the effect is once more to underline the contrast between divine power and human weakness, yet emphasize the strength of the links that join them.

This passage marks only one stage in the mounting intensity of Phèdre's emotions, and it can be usefully compared with a speech by the heroine at the limit of her suffering (Act IV, scene vi), in which she imagines herself dead, and being judged by her father, Minos:

> Ah! combien frémira son ombre épouvantée,
> Lorsqu'il verra sa fille à ses yeux présentée,
> Contrainte d'avouer tant de forfaits divers,
> Et des crimes peut-être inconnus aux Enfers!   4
> Que diras-tu, mon père, à ce spectacle horrible?
> Je crois voir de ta main tomber l'urne terrible,
> Je crois te voir, cherchant un supplice nouveau,
> Toi-même de ton sang devenir le bourreau.   8
> Pardonne. Un Dieu cruel a perdu ta famille:
> Reconnais sa vengeance aux fureurs de ta fille.
> Hélas! du crime affreux dont la honte me suit
> Jamais mon triste cœur n'a recueilli le fruit.
>
> (*Théatre 2* 241–2)   12

[26] Taken as a whole, Phèdre's speeches to Hippolyte in this scene show a more frequent use of this type of rhyme than is characteristic of the rest of the play, well over twice as many as any other type. This may be coincidence, but it does suggest that such rhymes, with their emphasis on phonetic contrast, are especially suited to a controlled antithetical style.

Within the strict limits of Racinian style, the use of the alexandrine couplet has changed markedly (and it is because of those strict limits, of course, that the slightest changes are so effective). To convey this final summit of agony, the despair at the end of the last route of escape, Racine makes little use of the line with balanced hemistichs, and often runs over the caesura, sometimes breaking the line after an initial exclamation instead. In place of clear, antithetical structures, we find syntactic inversions which maintain a grammatical tension until the end of the line, where the noun we have been waiting for ('l'urne terrible', 'le bourreau') comes with a violence which its function as a clinching rhyme serves to increase. In lines 11–12 the same technique extends over two lines: after the subordinate clause in the first line we have to wait until the final syllable of the couplet to reach the noun which it qualifies, and to understand the terribly human thought that gives the final twist to the vice. The metrical structures are in conflict, therefore, with the rhetorical and syntactical structures; in fact, the opening of lines 6–7 suggests a two-line unit which counterpoints the couplet structure, so that the conjunction of *terrible* and *nouveau* almost has the jarring effect of a failure to rhyme. There is little trace of rhymes functioning as semantic contrasts; if one is alerted to the sense at all it is because of an echo rather than an opposition (*terrible/horrible, famille/fille*), and rhymes like *épouvantée/présentée* and *terrible/horrible* are of the phonetic type which minimizes the impression of sameness-with-difference.

In the earlier passage we examined, the skilful rhetoric is to some extent Phèdre's own, part of the complexity of her confession to Hippolyte lying in the fact that she is, for all her distress, trying to move and persuade her hearer; but in this speech there are no such ulterior aims. It is an unpremeditated expression of her tormented thoughts, and the consummate handling of language and metre is all the dramatist's. If the rhetoric were to draw any attention to itself, if the balance of the couplets seemed at all clever, or the rhymes at all obtrusive in sound or sense, the effect of spontaneity would be lost. But the firm structure of the alexandrine is still present, of course, conveying the sense of a world where nothing happens by chance,[27] maintaining the impression of a human dignity which even this extremity of feeling cannot destroy, and suggesting to the end the terrible lucidity with which Phèdre understands both herself and the rigorous moral universe that is destroying her.

---

[27] Scott describes the effect of Racine's use of rhyme as follows: 'It is precisely the function of rhyme in French neoclassical tragedy to imply that all has already been thought of, that the accidents and spontaneities of speech are an illusion, have already been foreseen as part of a preordained design' (*Riches of Rhyme*, 158).

V

No one familiar with Racine's drama would dispute that the alexandrine couplet is an important source of his power, and these examples illustrate only a small part of its range and flexibility in his hands; but they provide sufficient indication of the translator's problems.[28] The safest course is probably to use blank verse, as the great majority of Racine's translators have done:[29] it has the virtue of familiarity on the stage, and is associated with tragedy; it is a flexible metre not too far from the spoken language; and it avoids all the pitfalls of rhyme. One of its weaknesses as a medium for translating Racine, however, is that English audiences have come to associate it with the rich, image-laden, linguistically heterogeneous style of Elizabethan drama, and it can make the severe purity of Racine's language seem mere colourlessness. This is a product, too, of the loss of the tight metrical organization of the alexandrine couplet; the freer movement of the unrhymed pentameter encourages proliferation and diversity whereas the closed, firmly structured alexandrine couplet can, in Racine's hands at least, transform a seemingly prosaic sequence of words into a precise and unforgettable poetic expression. Two blank verse attempts at the first four lines of Phèdre's speech to Hippolyte, quoted above, will be sufficient illustration:

> I wished you to think me odious, inhuman.
> More surely to resist you, I sought your hate.
> What have my useless efforts profited?
> You hated more, I did not love you less.
>
> (Dillon)

---

[28] Some of these problems are discussed, for the most part in a rather ad hoc fashion, by Knight, 'On Translating Racine'; Stewart, 'Racine's Untranslatability'; Wheatley, Introductions to Racine, *Complete Plays*, translated by Solomon; Knight, Introduction to *Phèdre*; Adams, *Proteus, his Lies, his Truth*, 127–32; Swinden, 'Translating Racine'; Gervais, 'Racine Englished'; and Tonkin, 'Translating a Trapped Tiger'.

[29] These include Abel Boyer, *Achilles, or Iphigenia in Aulis* (1700); Ambrose Philips, *The Distrest Mother* (1712), a version of *Andromache*, which, unlike most of these translations, was highly successful in the theatre; Charles Johnson, *The Victim* (1714), adapted from *Iphigénie*; William Duncombe, *Athaliah* (1722); R. B. Boswell, *Dramatic Works* (1889–90), for a long time the standard translation; John Masefield, *Berenice* (1922); Agnes Tobin, *Phaedra* (1958); Kenneth Muir, *Five Plays* (1960); George Dillon, *Three Plays* (1961); Margaret Rawlings, *Phèdre* (1961); John Cairncross, *Iphigenia, Phaedra, Athaliah* (1963) and *Andromache, Britannicus, Berenice* (1967); R. C. Knight, *Phèdre/Phaedra* (Edinburgh, 1971); Eric Korn, *Andromache* (1988; with occasional rhyme, mostly at the end of scenes); and Edwin Morgan, *Phaedra* (2000; translated into Scots). C. H. Sisson, *Britannicus, Phaedra, Athaliah* (1987) uses an eleven-syllable, four-stress line without rhyme. The best known German translation, Schiller's *Phädra*, is also in blank verse.

I strove to seem to you inhuman, vile;
The better to resist, I sought your hate.
But what availed my needless sufferings?
You hated me the more, I loved not less.

(Cairncross)

The strictly end-stopped lines retain some of Racine's metrical precision, but without the larger architecture of the couplet, the effect is of flat, isolated lines, only the slight 'poeticisms' producing a somewhat uneasy heightening ('What have my useless efforts profited?'; 'I loved not less'). Some translators have kept closer to the norm of English blank verse, with frequent enjambment (Boswell, Muir, Rawlings) or a wider and more concrete vocabulary than Racine's (Tobin, Knight); the result is often more appealing, but the danger is that Racine is made to sound like a second-rate Shakespeare. Of all the blank verse translators perhaps only John Masefield, in a few of the lines of his otherwise tepid version of *Bérénice* (1922), has been able to convey emotional intensity by means of simplicity and directness. It is true, of course, that blank verse allows the translator much greater freedom in all the other decisions he or she has to make, and this pragmatic advantage may be felt to be an overriding one.

But the challenge of rhyme, and more generally of the concentration and power of Racine's form, continues to lure the translator away from the well-trodden fields of the unrhymed pentameter. Attempts at rhymed alexandrines in English have not met with much success; the uncomfortably long line tends to break in two, becoming a somewhat jerky variant of the standard rhythm of popular song and verse, and the six beats are not equivalent to the usual four accents of the French alexandrine.[30] The four-stress English line, on the other hand, is even more insistent in its rhythm than the pentameter, and hence further from Racine's line— though Craig Raine, in a version of Racine's *Andromaque* entitled '*1953*', overcomes this problem by choppily alternating between rhyming four-beat lines and longer lines without regular metre. So the problem resolves to this: can anything be done with the rhymed pentameter couplet to create an effect for English audiences comparable to the effect of the alexandrine for French audiences? Nearly all the attempts at a solution date either from the period of heroic tragedy or from the past fifty years, and some examples of each will serve at least to highlight the difficulties, if not

---

[30] See William Packard's and Robert David MacDonald's translations of *Phèdre*, and W. McC. Stewart's version of a speech from the play in 'Racine's Untranslatability', 241–2. Neil Bartlett has translated *Bérénice* into rhymed syllabic couplets: each line has twelve syllables, without attention to stress placement. The result is a curious mixture of an informal, speech-like rhythm and chiming line-ends (usually end-stopped).

to provide an answer. *Phèdre* was not translated into rhymed verse in the earlier period,[31] but we do have a version of *Bérénice* by one of the most skilled Restoration dramatists, Thomas Otway, and Dryden's aims by the time he wrote *Aureng-Zebe* (1675) were sufficiently close to those of the English followers of Racine to make his handling of the heroic couplet at this period equally instructive.

Although he championed the heroic couplet as a heightening device, Dryden was also conscious of the need to lessen its formality and obtrusiveness; in the *Essay of Dramatic Poetry* he betrays this dilemma when he notes the usefulness of enjambment and the occasional short line in 'making art and order appear as loose and free as nature' (I, 84). In practice, he secures further variation by the use of triplets and alexandrines (though these do nothing to diminish the prominence of rhyme), and he seldom allows his rhymes to draw attention to themselves by their ingenuity or their semantic function.[32] Although the couplet lends itself to debate and argument, and its suitability for antitheses, paradoxes, and parallels is a boon to the translator of French alexandrines, Dryden at his best keeps this tendency under control, recognizing that a tragic hero should not manifest his sufferings through wit and argumentative display. Two short speeches from *Aureng-Zebe* will demonstrate some of the qualities of Dryden's dramatic couplet style at its most mature: the first, Arimant's admission to himself of his love for Indamora; the second, Aureng-Zebe's reply to his father's offer to spare his life if he yields Indamora.[33]

> Oh! Indamora, hide these fatal eyes;
> Too deep they wound whom they too soon surprise:
> My virtue, prudence, honour, interest, all
> Before this universal monarch fall.
> Beauty, like ice, our footing does betray;
> Who can tread sure on the smooth slippery way?
> Pleas'd with the passage, we slide swiftly on:
> And see the danger which we cannot shun. (II.31)
>
> Life, with my Indamora, I would choose;
> But, losing her, the end of living lose.
> I had consider'd all I ought before;

[31] Edmund Smith, the first English translator of *Phèdre* (as *Phaedra and Hippolitus*, 1707), moves between blank verse and rhymed couplets, in a wordy version that does very little justice to Racine's steely lines. See Swinden, 'Translating Racine', 210–12.

[32] For a comparison of Dryden's dramatic and non-dramatic couplet versification, see Alssid, *Dryden's Rhymed Heroic Tragedies*, II, 315–54.

[33] John Dryden, *Four Tragedies*. I have modernized spelling and punctuation in earlier quotations for ease of comparison.

> And fear of death can make me change no more.
> The people's love so little I esteem,
> Condemn'd by you, I would not live by them.
> May he who must your favour now possess,
> Much better serve you, and not love you less. (III.282)

The diction is straightforward, the rhymes unassertive, the rhythm formal but varied, the rhetorical structure firm. The couplet-by-couplet progression is perhaps too stiff, and the second half of the first speech begins to wander into poetic generalization: both weaknesses to which the heroic couplet is rendered susceptible by English rhymes. Although the first passage is the more striking by virtue of its imagery, the second, with its austere phrasing and unwitty antitheses, is perhaps the more Racinian. Having said this, one must admit that Dryden comes nowhere near achieving Racine's dramatic power, and one of the reasons is that rhymes, though subdued by comparison with those of the non-dramatic couplet, inevitably deflect some of the feeling by their neatness: too often the second word offers some semantic connection with the first in the characteristic English way, either by complementing it (eyes which surprise; all that fall) or by contrasting with it (I choose, I lose; before, no more). Where Phèdre in the face of death involuntarily gives voice to her thoughts, Aureng-Zebe makes a touching speech.[34] And in the play as a whole there are still too many pretty speeches, too many dilemmas, debates, resolves, and renunciations, to create anything like the rising wave of intensity that gives *Phèdre* its remarkable cohesion.

Dryden was obviously not aiming at such a simple outline (and had not read *Phèdre*, which was first performed just over a year later than *Aureng-Zebe*), but Otway, for his attempt to Anglicize Racine, chose a play whose plot and pattern of emotion are distilled to a purity even greater than those of *Phèdre*. Critical opinion of *Titus and Berenice*,[35] first performed in 1676, has varied, depending partly on whether it is compared with the original or with other attempts to translate French classical tragedy. The latter comparison is generally favourable to Otway; although the play is compressed and the action given a little more spice for English tastes, many threads in the web of tensions and conflicts remain unbroken, and the language, if not distinguished by many positive qualities, seldom jars. Otway has an advantage over Dryden in his rhymes: whether

---

[34] This is no doubt partly what prompted Eliot's comment: 'The great French tragedy is classical in the sense that it is strongly *moral*. Now Dryden's plays are emphatically not "moral" in this way; they are diversified, certainly, with fine, if not very profound *moralising*, but that is not at all the same thing' (*John Dryden*, 39).
[35] *The Works of Thomas Otway*, I.

through deliberate seeking of a more muted effect or through lack of skill, he is less strict in his matching of vowels, and the many off-rhymes which result help to subdue the resonance of the couplets. The following speech, Otway's rendering of Berenice's unhappy contemplation of a life without Titus, represents his use of the couplet at its best:

> Now I believe't, enough I've heard you tell,
> And I am gone—eternally, farewell:
> Eternally—Ah, sir, consider now
> How harsh that word is, and how dreadful too.
> Consider, oh, the miseries they bear,
> That are forever robb'd of all that's dear.
> From this sad moment never more to meet:
> Is it for day to dawn, and day to set,
> In which I must not find my hopes still young,
> Nor yet once see my Titus all day long? (III.88)

Something like Racine's controlled intensity survives in Otway's simple style, so unlike the rant of most heroic plays of the time, and the couplets help convey the heroine's dignified mastery of grief, assisted, as in the original, by rhetorical repetitions (for Berenice, like Phèdre in the first of the passages quoted above, is not just expressing her grief, but attempting at the same time to sway the vacillating Titus). Dryden would probably have produced something smoother, avoiding the clumsiness of the fourth line, for instance, but he might not have come so close to Racinian verbal purity as Otway has done.

The degree of Otway's, or Dryden's, success should not be exaggerated, however; set-pieces like these lend themselves to couplets, but the rapid exchange of dialogue is, as Howard was aware, another matter. Moreover, in extended dramatic use the features of English rhyme that we have noted produce a persistent chime that rapidly tires the ear. Otway was soon to abandon rhyme for blank verse, a change of allegiance which arose, ironically, from the same liking for sentiment that underlay his sympathy with Racine. His influence in this respect was felt by Dryden, who, notwithstanding the harsh comments on *Phèdre* in the preface, created a more Racinian plot in *All for Love* (1677), echoing in particular the situations, and sometimes the language, of *Bérénice*.[36] The decision of both dramatists to use blank verse for the new mode of sentimental tragedy reflects their awareness that the regular rhyming couplet that had emerged in the seventeenth century, whatever its suitability for the large-scale conflicts and epic pretensions of the heroic play, was incapable of conveying

[36] See Wheatley, *Racine and English Classicism*, 266–7.

the subtle inflections of unpremeditated speech or tracing the delicate currents of human feeling.

VI

The great loosening of verse forms that began with the Romantic poets and has continued ever since has made it possible for writers to treat the couplet with a freedom rare in the Restoration, when the taste of the time and the model of French prosody encouraged a fixed syllable-count, masculine rhymes, and end-stopped lines. But it is only in the last half-century that the rhymed couplet has re-emerged in workable translations of Racine, including versions of *Phèdre* by Robert Lowell (*Phaedra*, 1963); Tony Harrison (*Phaedra Britannica*, 1975); and Richard Wilbur (*Phaedra*, 1986). The year 2010 saw the initiation of an ambitious rhymed *Complete Plays* translated by Geoffrey Alan Argent.[37] Partially rhymed translations have been made by Samuel Solomon (Racine, *Complete Plays*, 1967) and by Derek Mahon (*Racine's Phaedra*, 1996), and provide a useful foil against which to set these bolder experiments.[38]

Lowell recognizes the drawbacks of the English dramatic couplet, and although he claims that his metre is based on that of Dryden and Pope he makes free use of run-on lines and various kinds of off-rhyme to lessen its insistence. Especially interesting in the present context is his rhyming of stressed with unstressed syllables (*die/blasphemy, limb/victim, son/abandon*), and of two unstressed syllables (*executioner/murderer, Hippolytus/ venomous, loyally/minority*), creating an effect closer to French rhyme than is usual in English. The result is a loose couplet which is successful in its own terms, achieving, for the modern ear, a balance of heightening and naturalness that offers a way out of Dryden's dilemma. The following is Lowell's re-creation, and expansion, of the first six lines of Phèdre's speech to Hippolyte quoted above:

> I wished to hate you, but the gods corrupt
> us; though I never suffered their abrupt
> seductions, shattering advances, I
> too bear their sensual lightnings in my thigh.

---

[37] An earlier translation in rhymed pentameter couplets of *Phèdre* and other plays is Lacy Lockert's *Best Plays of Racine* (1936); the stilted archaic diction and too-prominent rhymes make this version unperformable and well-nigh unreadable.

[38] Perhaps the most successful unrhymed translation of *Phèdre* is Ted Hughes's, first performed in 1998; it uses Hughes's characteristically energetic free verse to create an un-Racinian but nevertheless powerful psychological drama.

> I too am dying. I have felt the heat
> that drove my mother through the fields of Crete,
> the bride of Minos, dying for the full
> magnetic April thunders of the bull.
> I struggled with my sickness, but I found
> no grace or magic to preserve my sound
> intelligence and honour from this lust,
> plowing my body with its horny thrust. (44)

I am concerned only with the metre and sound-texture of this passage, though it is perhaps worth taking note of the way in which Lowell, no doubt recognizing the impossibility of achieving Racinian intensity by Racinian methods, has substituted his own extravagant style, creating a totally different character, but endowing her language with more expressive power than any other English Phèdre. Most of the time he breaks down the couplet and tames the rhymes by run-on lines, even to the extent of a monosyllabic *rejet* (*us*) and *contre-rejet* (*I*); however, when he wishes to he can give great emphasis to a rhyme (*lust/thrust*). Hearing these lines one is aware of a shifting pattern of sound-repetitions rather than of couplets; note, for instance, how the vowel of the first pair of rhyme words also occurs in *us*, *suffered*, and *seductions*, or how that of the second pair recurs in *lightnings* and *dyings*, and reappears two lines later (after *heat*, *fields*, *Crete*) in 'the bride of Minos, dying'. The rhyme words are not left high and dry, standing out from a verbal background unremarkable in its sound-texture, but become only one element in a continued play of vowels and consonants; and, in this respect at least, Lowell preserves some of the distinctive quality of the original.[39]

The same cannot, however, be said for most aspects of his imitation, including its verse form: Lowell has created a couplet style that works on stage, but in a manner so different from Racine's immaculate metrical architecture that it is more a skilful evasion of the problem than a solution. Samuel Solomon's translation of the *Complete Plays* is a more judicious attempt to naturalize Racine without losing too many of his distinctive qualities, and although one frequently trips over painfully inappropriate words and phrases, the method adopted has much to commend it. The basic metre is regular blank verse, but rhyme is used for particular effects, which seems to be an acknowledgement that its function in English is more expressive than structural. Where it is used continuously for several lines, as happens from time to time in most of

---

[39] Ricks is sensitive to Lowell's manipulation of sound-echoes, and find much to praise in his translation ('Racine's "Phèdre"'). For a discussion of rhyme that emphasizes the role of the sound-texture of the whole line, see Jarvis, 'Why Rhyme Pleases'.

Solomon's translations, it exhibits all the failings that we have already observed, and increases the likelihood of ineptly chosen diction; but in the translation of *Phèdre* it is limited to the occasional couplet, which gives a different character to the verse. Solomon, too, is conscious of the 'alliterative and onomatopoeic challenge' he is facing,[40] and, though his verbal music is a little thin compared to Lowell's, he does sometimes catch the charged simplicity of a Racinian line. Two short extracts from the speeches we have been looking at will demonstrate some of the merits of his approach:

> I did not flee, I drove you off;
> I wanted you to think me hateful, heartless;
> To resist you better, I aroused your hate.
> Of what worth have my vain precautions proved?
> The more you hated me, the more I loved. (II.v.684)

> Ah, how his stricken ghost will start and shudder,
> When he beholds his daughter come before him,
> Compelled her trembling trespasses to tell,
> And crimes perhaps unheard of even in Hell!
> What will you say, my father, at this horror?
> I see the urn of terror fall and crash;
> I see you, seeking some strange penalty,
> Yourself becoming butcher of your blood! (IV.vi.1281)

The first example shares much of the drabness of the blank verse translations quoted earlier, though the diction and syntax are under firmer control and, while remaining formal, avoid uncomfortably 'literary' language. The final near-rhyme, although it is achieved at the expense of accuracy, imitates the original in its suggestion of closed options. Even without rhyme, the strict end-stopped pentameters have something of the firm shapeliness of Racine's alexandrines, though their cumulative effect does not become apparent from a few lines. In the second example rhyme is employed successfully to point a climax within the speech, and the whole passage shows the same increase of emotional intensity over the earlier one that was evident in the original. Solomon's use of sound effects can be too obvious ('compelled' echoes the rhymes too self-consciously), but it does provide some compensation for the loss of continual rhyme, helping to bind the lines together and to give some sense of inevitability to the language; note, for instance, the succession *shudder, daughter, father, horror, terror,* and (its culmination) *butcher.* There are hints here that the difficulties of translating Racine may not be totally insuperable.

---

[40] See the 'Translator's Note' in volume I, xlvi–xlix, and Solomon's review of Lowell's *Phaedra.*

We may compare the second of these examples with the same passage in Mahon's translation, which also treats rhyme with some freedom: many of the rhymes are imperfect, there are frequent sequences without rhyme, and couplets are sometimes replaced by quatrains. As this example indicates, Mahon's deployment of the pentameter is also very free, a far cry from Racine's metrical strictness (the fourth line and last lines offer a considerable challenge to the performer).

> Oh, how his ghost will look up in surprise
> when his own daughter comes before his eyes,
> forced to confess to every kind of vice
> including some never before known in that place.
> Father, what will you say to such a sight?
> I can just see you drop the urn in fright;
> I can just see you, my inquisitor,
> dreaming up some new torture for me there. (54)

This seems to me less successful than Solomon's version: the rhythmic looseness is matched by an uncertainty of register (colloquial in 'I can just see you' and 'dreaming up', formal in 'comes before his eyes' and 'my inquisitor'), and the rhymes remain inert, providing neither an unbending structure, as in Racine, nor expressive emphasis, as in Lowell.[41]

Where Lowell evades the problems, and Solomon and Mahon attempt a compromise, Tony Harrison and Richard Wilbur meet the challenge of the couplet head-on. Harrison, transferring the play to nineteenth-century British India, follows Lowell in employing a highly coloured language teeming with images, and spreads his lexical net to take in Indian and Anglo-Indian vocabulary, deployed in a wide range of styles from past and present. It is a method which makes for amusement and admiration in his updated version of *Le Misanthrope*, but is hardly suited to the world that Phèdre inhabits. Here is part of his treatment of the speech by the heroine, now called 'Memsahib', to Thomas, the Hippolytus character:

---

[41] One of the most successful versions of a play by Racine in rhyming pentameter couplets is Douglas Dunn's *Andromache*. Dunn uses run-on lines freely, and often rhymes stressed with unstressed syllables, yet retains a good deal of Racine's formal economy. Argent's translations—so far of *The Fratricides* (2010), *Bajazet* (2011), *Iphigenia* (2011), and *Athaliah* (2012)—reveal the unwanted prominence of rhyme in English by end-stopping most lines. Here is Antigone in Act II scene iii of *The Fratricides*: 'No, from his memory I've been blotted out; | Now shedding blood is all he cares about. | Don't seek in him that prince who, at one time, | Showed such a noble horror of all crime, | Whose soul was sweet and generous and true, | Who cherished me and who respected you' (53).

I call on India to testify
how one by one she bled my family dry,
the gods of India whose savage glee
first gluts itself upon them and now on me,
my mother and my sister, now my turn
to sizzle on love's spit until I burn.
You know very well how much I tried
to keep my distance, O I tried. I tried.
Keeping my distance led me to devise
a barrier of hate built up of lies—
I faked hard-heartedness, I cracked the whip,
filled you with hatred for her Ladyship,
was everything they say stepmothers are
until the Memsahib was your bête noire. (24–5)

Ignoring the bizarre mixture of registers, the uncertainty of the syntax, and the veering tone, I want merely to remark on the way the rhymes draw attention to themselves, not only because they are inappropriately ingenious (*are/noire*), or emphasize a word or phrase which already sounds strained (*testify/glee*), or seem to be there only for their own sake (the bathetic 'until I burn'; the unlikely 'her Ladyship'). The characteristics of English rhymes that we noted earlier, both semantic and phonetic, are underlined by Harrison's style, and not only the reader but the hearer, too, is continually conscious of the couplets. On the other hand, there is very little attempt to imitate Racine's use of the metrical structure to achieve balance and concentration, nor any of his subtle handling of sound-texture, which is not the same thing as obvious alliteration. It is, in fact, very difficult to see what the couplet structure is for; its formality is at odds with the colloquialism of much of the syntax, its strictness with the catholicity of the diction, and its comic artificiality with the tragic intensity of the emotion.

Wilbur also uses run-on lines from time to time, observing in his introduction that 'too long a sequence of end-stopped English lines, especially if rhymed, can sound like the stacking of planks in a lumber-yard' (xv). However, even in Wilbur's accomplished hands, the chiming of the rhymes has an insistence that detracts from the powerful emotions being expressed. Here's Phaedra to Hippolytus again:

The gods could tell how in this breast of mine
They lit the flame that's tortured all my line,
Those cruel Gods for whom it is but play
To lead a feeble woman's heart astray.
You too could bear me out; remember, do,
How I not only shunned but banished you.

> I wanted to be odious in your sight;
> To balk my love, I sought to earn your spite.
> But what was gained by all of that distress?
> You hated me the more; I loved no less.
> And what you suffered made you still more dear.
> I pined, I withered, scorched by many a tear. (45)

Not only do the rhymes have the prominence characteristic of the English language, they often seem to dominate the unfolding of the line. 'My breast' becomes 'this breast of mine' so a rhyme can be set up for 'line'; 'do' is added to the instruction 'remember', making Phaedra's speech sound momentarily like a Tin Pan Alley lyric; 'many a tear' is pure padding to eke out the pentameter and reach the rhyme.[42]

The translations and imitations of Racine over the past three centuries testify to the gulf between the two superficially similar verse forms we have been considering, confirming what is suggested by a comparison of the two languages and literary traditions. The failure of the English dramatic couplet is not to be seen as a mere accident of literary history, and an unlucky blow to the translators of Racine, but more as the extinction in the evolutionary struggle of a species unfitted for its environment. This does not mean that the heroic couplet is totally and permanently unsuited to the tragic stage; for a brief period its artificiality and extraversion were precisely the qualities required of dramatic verse, and there is no reason to assume that its potential as a dramatic medium has been exhausted. What has to be acknowledged, however, is that the English rhyming couplet, like any other formal entity in poetry, carries with it a rich set of associations, proclivities, and possibilities, rooted in the traditions of English literature and in the nature of the English language itself, and shared by all those who are familiar with those traditions and that language. Any writer who ignores this fact runs the risk of severing the forms chosen for the work from their source of life.

---

[42] For a discussion of Wilbur's translation that defends his use of heroic couplets, see Shaw, 'Phaedra in Tact'; for a critical view, see Ricks, 'Racine's "Phèdre"'.

4

Sound and Sense in Lyric Poetry

The role of sound in lyric poetry is one of the most fundamental and most discussed questions in theoretical and practical poetics, yet there is no sign of a consensus on this issue among those who write about poetry (including those who write poems themselves). The comments by Helen Vendler and Tom Paulin on the sounds of Yeats's poetry that I discussed briefly in chapter 1 are not at all untypical in their shortcomings, which are a measure of the difficulty of the terrain rather than of any exceptional deafness on the part of these critics, who have contributed importantly to our understanding of the workings of language in poems. This is not the place to attempt a summary of the long history of the debate about the contribution of the sound of words to sense, a debate whose beginnings lie at least as far back as Plato's Cratylus; instead, I want to examine two striking, and strikingly opposed, attempts by contemporary poets to establish solid ground in this swampy area, both carried out partly by attending closely to the findings of linguistic science. My hope is that this examination will both throw a little light on the problem and reveal some of the poetic consequences of holding a particular view of the relationship.

Contemporary British poetry is sometimes seen as consisting of two schools with very different aims and methods: on the one hand, 'mainstream' poetry—also termed, usually by its opponents, 'conservative', 'traditional', and 'populist', and sometimes given the synecdochic label 'Faber poets'—and on the other, 'innovative' or 'experimental' poetry—also known as 'Poundian', 'modernist', 'radical', or, rather more pejoratively, 'postmodernist', and sometimes referred to, again synecdochically, as 'Cambridge poets'. It is, of course, far too broad a categorization to be very profitable for anything but the crudest cultural history, but it will give us a starting point for our discussion because the two poet-critics who have written challengingly on our topic represent with particular transparency each of the two schools. Their representativeness cannot be doubted: Don Paterson has taken up the cudgels for Mainstream poets (his upper case) against the Postmoderns (ditto) in a very public manner,[1] and J. H. Prynne, though he would never stoop to the same kind of name-calling, has often been hailed by his followers as a standard-bearer of the innovators. To take one example of the way in which the two poets have been set in opposition, here is Ian Brinton, in his introduction to a collection of essays on Prynne:

> Randall Stevenson's suggestion in volume 12 of *The Oxford English Literary History* that Prynne's 'full significance for the period's poetry began to be realised only at the end of this century' seemed wildly at odds with Don Paterson's comment...: 'The Norwich phone book or a set of log tables would serve [readers] as well as their Prynne, in which they seem able to detect as many shades of mind-blowing confusion as Buddhists do the absolute'.[2]

My purpose is not to weigh in on either side of this debate—there is good and not so good poetry in both camps, and much that doesn't fit easily into either—but to use the arguments of these two poets to further the discussion about poetic sound.

I

Don Paterson is primarily known as a poet: he is one of today's most lauded poets in English, the author of, among many other publications, four highly praised collections (*Nil Nil*, 1993; *God's Gift to Women*, 1997; *Landing Light*, 2003; and *Rain*, 2009) and an accomplished set of translations of Rilke's *Sonnets to Orpheus*. He has won virtually all the important poetry prizes awarded in Britain, some of them twice.

Less well known is the fact that Paterson is also the author of two remarkable long double essays on the techniques of lyric poetry. The first, entitled 'The Lyric Principle', is on questions of sound and appeared as two articles in *Poetry Review* in 2007; it is also available in a slightly different form on Paterson's personal website.[3] The second, 'The Domain of the Poem', which examines the operation of meaning in lyric poetry, also appeared in *Poetry Review* in two parts, in 2010 and 2011. Some of the arguments in these two essays surface in the course of Paterson's commentary on all of Shakespeare's sonnets in a hefty—and controversial—volume, *Reading Shakespeare's*

---

[1] See, for example, Paterson's article 'Rhyme and Reason' and his testy Introduction to the poetry anthology he edited with Charles Simic, *New British Poetry*.

[2] Brinton, ed., *A Manner of Utterance*, 7–8; the comment by Paterson is quoted from the article mentioned in the previous note.

[3] See <http://www.donpaterson.com/files/arspoetica/2.htm>. The two parts of the essay will be referred to here as 'I' and 'II'. Some of the points he makes in the essay are developments of ideas expressed in his T. S. Eliot Lecture of 2004, 'The Dark Art of Poetry', also available on his website.

Sonnets. (That they don't surface as often as one might expect in his commentary is no doubt owing to the embarrassed, and sometimes a little embarrassing, stance he adopts towards any technical matters that might be considered the province of the poetry 'anorak'—a category within which he apologetically includes himself.) It's not unusual to find a poet attempting to articulate in prose some aspects of the craft of poetry, but it *is* unusual to find it done with such thoroughness, exactingness, and forthrightness. It's also rare to read a poet's account of poetry that, for good or ill, is so willing to turn to the findings of science for evidence and support.[4]

It is the earlier essay, which has two parts entitled 'The Sense of Sound' and 'The Sound of Sense', that is relevant to our topic. In 'The Sense of Sound', Paterson, having discussed the role of silence and the importance of connotation in poetry, moves on to the familiar claim that sound and sense are inseparable; however, he is willing to go further than most recent and contemporary poetic theorists in interpreting this claim. He starts with a thoroughly Cratylist view of language: dismissing the notion of the arbitrariness of the sign—a 'monstrous dogma' 'which poets know to be sheer madness' (I, 67)—he asserts that there are two processes at work in creating the language-user's feeling that 'words sound like the things they name'. The first is the phenomenon of phonesthemes—a sound or sound-cluster shared by a group of words linked also by meaning, such as *glisten, glare, glow, glint, gleam, glitter, glance*—and the second is a view of the origin of language which claims that 'the shapes of sounds in the mouth formed naturally as physical analogues to the shapes of real things and processes in the world' (I, 68).[5] The term was coined (as 'phonaestheme') by J. R. Firth in 1930, marking an advance, as Paterson notes, on older

---

[4] Paterson postpones a discussion of rhythm and metre to a later moment—perhaps the *Ars Poetica* in book form that he has promised. There is, however, a short note on metre at the end of the book on Shakespeare's sonnets which provides some background to an impassioned plea during the course of an earlier disagreement—one of many—with Helen Vendler over Sonnet 126. Vendler's claim is that the sonnet 'falls into trochaic and amphibrachic pattern, not iambic' (*The Art of Shakespeare's Sonnets*, 535), and Paterson comments, 'This is the sort of nonsense that can arise when you proceed with a great ear but only a partial understanding of how metre actually functions. There are no feet in English verse, only metrical patterns. ... Can everyone please stop marking in the feet, and imagining caesurae where there's no punctuation to indicate a pause? I know it's fun. But they're just not there, folks.' (*Reading Shakespeare's Sonnets*, 377). I too will stay away from the topic of metre here, as it is discussed in several chapters of this book, though to separate questions of rhythm from questions of sound is, of course, entirely artificial.

[5] Interestingly, Paterson's first example of a phonestheme is also the combination of sounds made much of by Jacques Derrida in *Glas*. Leslie Hill summarizes Derrida's account of *gl-* as follows: 'simultaneously a gurgling and a gargling, a gagging and a glugging, a clogging and a clearing, a clenching and an unclenching, a rocking to and from constriction to release and back again' (*Radical Indecision*, 297). In drawing attention to the movement of tongue and throat in the pronunciation of *gl-*, Derrida makes its association in English with light and sight seem to run counter to any possible natural analogy.

notions of onomatopoeia that focused on words like 'thump' and 'clatter', and the phenomenon has often been discussed in the literature on phono-semantics. The second process, sound-symbolism as the origin of language—what linguists since Max Müller in the nineteenth century have called the 'ding-dong theory'—has received less support than the theory of phonesthemes, which may well play a part in the way languages develop: as Paterson points out, new coinages often gravitate towards phonesthemic nodes. (He has an interesting discussion of the word *blog*.) Though Paterson's examples are from English, these observations on language are clearly meant to be universally applicable.

In stressing the close relation between sound and sense Paterson is not indulging in the kind of mystified view of language that poets sometimes fall into (and perhaps need to believe in order to do what they do); he's perfectly well aware of the arguments against motivation in language, but like Derrida in his analysis of Saussure's account of arbitrariness in *Of Grammatology*, he finds the refusal to accord any role to iconicity contrary to the evidence of our own linguistic habits and suppositions. The 'iconizing engine', as he calls it (I, 71), is clearly at work in a great deal of language-use, from slogans to speeches to song-lyrics.[6] It's possible to disagree with Paterson over his suggestions regarding the origin of language while finding his account of the way we *use* language, and the assumptions that govern that use (however mistaken we might be in those assumptions), compelling. We detect a certain appropriateness when close, front vowels (like [ɪ] in 'little') are used in the representation of small, high sounds and tiny objects, or open, back vowels (like [aː] in 'large') are used in the representation of deep sounds and vast objects—though there are plenty of counter-examples, like 'big' on the one hand and 'particle' on the other, that show this to be a rather weak correspondence.[7] More importantly, Paterson announces as a principle: 'Words are so *indivisibly* part-sound and part-sense that the patterning of sound alone can generate sense *as if it constituted a syntactic relation* (I, 71).' This is a version of Jakobson's famous assertion that 'the poetic function projects the principle of equivalence from the axis of selection into the axis of combination': sound-relations, which in non-poetic language function paradigmatically between a given sound and the other possible sounds in that position, take on meaning in poetry as a result of echoes and contrasts along the linear chain of language.[8]

---

[6] This phrase itself, with its alliteration and final increase in word-length, is an example of the preferences operative in language-use. I would have been less likely to write 'from song-lyrics to mottoes to speeches'.

[7] See Jakobson and Waugh, *The Sound Shape of Language*, chapter 4, 'The Spell of Speech Sounds'.

[8] Jakobson, *Selected Writings*, 27.

Here then, according to Paterson, we have the linguistic resources from which lyric poets draw their power to move and please through the medium of sound: a tendency in language towards an association between certain categories of sound and certain categories of meaning (I would say a weak tendency; Paterson would no doubt say a strong tendency), and a willingness, almost a wishfulness, on the part of speakers of the language, to believe that sound is not an arbitrary shell around meaning but an inherent part of meaning itself. The task of the lyric poet is to create a verbal artefact in which that desire is fulfilled, and meaning—and with it emotion—is made to emerge from the sounds of words as much as from their sense. This project may not be a feature of all poems in all languages, and we shall shortly examine an alternative view of the linguistic resources exploited by the poet; however, it is surely an animating principle in a great deal of poetry in many cultures.

It's in Part 2 of the double essay that Paterson's most original contributions to the discussion of sound and sense in poetry occur, and it's here that he appeals to the properties of sound as detected by acoustic science in order to ground poetic practice in something outside the vagaries of culture and history. Paterson borrows the term 'pink noise' to argue that both music and poetry, at their most effective, betray in their progress from one item to the next a relation analogous to that found in a category of noise called 'pink' to distinguish it from other types of noise given other colour names, most significantly 'white' noise and 'red' noise, the latter also given the adjective 'Brownian', or sometimes just 'brown'. I'm not competent to judge the accuracy of Paterson's scientific borrowings—samples of these different noises can easily be found on the internet, and they all sound rather similar, though pink noise, in which lower frequencies have more power, has a distinctive throatiness—and therefore his rather grandiose claim that the sounds of successful lyric poetry correspond in their mathematical relations to quasar emissions, river discharge, sunspot activity, and DNA sequences had better be left to one side.[9] What the argument boils down to, in its application to poetry, is that a completely *random* relation between one element and the next—or, putting it

---

[9] The key paper for the argument that music from several cultures is characterized by pink noise appears to be Voss and Clarke, '"1/f Noise" in Music'. A useful summary, with comments on the extension of pink noise to several other domains, can be found at <http://asmir.info/lib/Fractals_Chaos_Music.htm>. For samples, see the Wikipedia entry for 'colors of noise'. Pink noise is even more ubiquitous than Paterson indicates: other instances include almost all electronic components, all semi-conducting devices, all time standards from the most accurate atomic clock to quartz oscillators to the sand flow of an ancient hourglass, the speed of ocean currents, and the yearly flood levels of Nile (measured over the last 2,000 years). One suspects that this is just too familiar a phenomenon to be very useful in analysing poetry.

differently, one surprise after another—results in the dullness of constant novelty, whereas a completely *predictable* relation results in the dullness of total familiarity. The ideal balance between randomness and predictability is right in the middle, just as pink noise, we are told by Paterson, is half-way between white noise and Brownian noise.[10]

Summarized in this way, it seems a rather straightforward and uncontroversial point. But it gets more interesting when Paterson applies it to one of his cardinal focuses in lyric sound: the contrast between vowels and consonants. He starts with a somewhat tendentious distinction between the way vowels and consonants work:

> In the human voice, the vowel carries the bulk of the feeling in its complex tonal and quantitative discriminations, while the consonants which interrupt that breath make the bulk of the sense.... Vowel fills the word with its fairly uniform stuff, while the consonant carves it into recognizable shapes. (II. 59)

We only have to turn to one of the phonetic charts provided as an appendix to the online version of Paterson's essay to raise doubts about this distinction: one chart, for example, includes the words *bead, bid, bayed, bed, bad, bard, bawd, bode, booed, bud, bird, bide, bowed*, and the name *Boyd*, demonstrating vividly that vowels are far from uniform and function just as importantly as do consonants in distinguishing between the series of sounds that constitute different words. A more satisfactory distinction could be made between the role of vowels and consonants in intonation and stress: much of the emotional (as well as some of the semantic) force of an utterance is conveyed by rises and falls in pitch and increases and decreases in stress (the two phenomena being in fact inseparable), and it is the vowels that carry these distinctions. (Strictly speaking, other voiced continuants—in English, the phonemes represented by *l*, *r*, *n*, and *m* in particular—can carry intonation and stress: think how many different ways '*m-m-m-m-m-m-m*' could be pronounced.) Paterson also suggests that speakers of a language carry an awareness—usually unconscious—of the grouping of consonants into various types, allowing poets to draw on connections between different members of the same group. Thus, for example, the English plosives, represented by the letters *p*, *b*, *k*, *t*, *d*, and the so-called 'hard' *g*, can substitute for one another 'for compositional purposes', as can the various fricatives, affricates, nasals, and approximants.

---

[10] The association of Brownian noise with absolute predictability is somewhat puzzling, given that Brownian motion, after which it is named, is precisely the unpredictable motion of individual particles whose behaviour is subject only to statistical probabilities in a mass. My thanks to Dominic Lash for clarifying this in personal communication.

With these materials at hand, Paterson can state his basic rule, articulating the manner in which the poet achieves in the sounds of a poem the equivalent of pink noise, the ideal equilibrium between predictability and surprise, the fulfilment and the thwarting of expectation: 'In English poetry, the feeling that a piece of writing is 'musical' usually means that it quietly exhibits two kinds of phonetic bias.... The first is the deliberate variation of vowel-sounds; the second is consonantal patterning' (II, 58). Thus for Paterson a stretch of poetry perceived as 'beautiful' or 'musical' or perhaps 'lyrically effective' (these terms all raise further questions, of course) is likely to have, on the one hand, many different vowel-sounds and, on the other, frequently repeated consonants, or repetitions from within one of the consonant groups. By contrast, an equivalent stretch of workaday prose, or poetry of a different, non-lyrical, kind, will not display any significant relationship between variation and repetition of vowels and consonants. In order to achieve vowel variation, Paterson argues, poets also reduce the frequency of unstressed syllables, and especially of the vowel-sound schwa (the vowel used, for instance, in the first syllable of *above* or the last syllable of *sofa*, whose frequency in English we noted in Chapter 3), a reduction that our habits of verse reading encourage as well. In handling consonants, by contrast, he suggests that poets tend to create what he calls a 'consonantal signature' for every line or group of lines. (Alliteration is the most obvious form of this consonantal patterning, but Paterson is dismissive of what he calls this 'loud' effect.) Of course, if this happens it does so without conscious deliberation; it's what is summed up in the notion of a poet's 'ear'—though one wonders whether Paterson's extraordinary awareness of the workings of phonetic detail is something that, when composing, he has to make an effort to expunge from his consciousness.

There's an obvious objection to Paterson's argument, and he neatly circumvents it. Rhyme, such a central element in so many poetic traditions, is based on *vowel* repetition combined with prior *consonant* variation: just the reverse of Paterson's fundamental principle. But it turns out that rhyme is all the more effective *because* it is an exception: 'A normative shift towards vowel heterophony and consonantal homophony creates the unconsciously experienced "lyric ground", above which the more consciously-registered saliences of rhyme, assonance, alliteration and anomalous consonants can cleanly stand' (II, 58–9). And then there is pararhyme, of which Paterson the poet is very fond (and the inventive use of which he greatly admires in Paul Muldoon's poetry): here we do have the required repetition of consonants and variation of vowel. Some examples from *Rain* are *tell-until, home-him, ship-shape.*

(As Paterson points out, this is a principle on which some Semitic languages, such as Arabic and Hebrew, are built.) He also frequently uses weaker rhymes in which the vowel and its preceding consonant are varied but the final consonant is repeated, as in *dream-whim, apart-dirt, trapeze-days*. However, we don't hear too much about rhyme in the essay, since, as Paterson notes, it would require another essay to accommodate it. (See Chapter 3 for some suggestions about the operation of rhyme in English.)

Paterson is discussing more than just the pleasing effects of sound here; we must not forget the guiding principle from Part I of his essay: sound and sense in poetry are inseparable. One way in which sense enters the poet's composition process is the resistance provided by the need to achieve the appropriate disposition of vowels and consonants: our sense-making must adapt to these demands, and 'this way we end up saying something better than the thing we intended' (65). Thus the subtle requirements of vowel variation and consonant patterning function, for Paterson, in the same way as the more overt requirements of rhyme and metre, taking the poet into realms of meaning and emotion that would otherwise be closed off. 'If writing a poem isn't a way of working out what you mean, then I don't know what it is', remarks Paterson in a telling footnote (II, 73 n. 27).

In the final section of his second essay, Paterson mounts a forceful challenge to the kind of advice frequently given to neophyte poets: make it concrete. Let me quote him again: 'We have—correctly—perceived a bored and dwindling audience, and have instituted a manic attempt to keep them awake through data-reward, through the brain-sweets of image and anecdote. To get the air flowing in our poems again, we require the bravery of showing ourselves to be engaged in thought while in the *act* of writing' (II, 69). This 'over-concretization of the poetic voice' has been a musical disaster, he comments. Musical poetry, in the sense that Paterson expounds and applauds, is also the poetry of thinking aloud.

II

J. H. Prynne is also a poet with a considerable reputation, though of a very different kind from Paterson's, and his statements about poetry, including the role of sound in poetry, are equally uncompromising. Although Prynne hasn't won the big prizes, and chooses to publish with small presses dedicated to innovative poetry (whereas Paterson publishes with Faber),[11] he is regarded by many as Britain's most important living poet; it's not unusual to find statements such as Rod Mengham and John Kinsella's in their short introduction to his poetry: 'J. H. Prynne is possibly the most significant English poet of the late twentieth century.'

Prynne has not published critical or theoretical writing of any substantial length, but his shorter essays, letters, and other prose works amount to a considerable body of commentary, no less challenging and thought-provoking than Paterson's.[12] In many respects, his views on poetry and the process of poetic composition chime with Paterson's, though his language is very different. Here, for instance, is a comment on the way formal constraints are productive for the poet, all of which except the very last phrase would surely meet with Paterson's approval: 'The focus of poetic composition, as a text takes shape in the struggle of the poet to separate from it, projects into the textual arena an intense energy of conception and differentiation, pressed up against the limits which are discovered and invented by composition itself' ('Poetic Thought', 596). And Paterson's emphasis on thinking in verse has some affinities with Prynne's notion of poetic thought, though it lacks the latter's insistence on the non-subjective nature of the thinking process.

Prynne's most important engagement with the question of poetic sound is a talk entitled 'Mental Ears and Poetic Work' given at the University of Chicago in 2009 and subsequently published in the *Chicago Review*. The concept of 'mental ears' is designed to counter the dominant understanding of poetry, and lyric poetry in particular, as having to do with the work of real ears. A footnote establishes clearly this opposition: having asserted that the domain of the poem is 'textuality', Prynne adds:

It is indifference to the alterative effect of textuality that causes Derek Attridge to write, following the consensus, that 'Poems are made out of spoken language' (*Poetic Rhythm: An Introduction* (Cambridge, 1995), 2). I believe this statement to be decisively not true, unless it is also to be believed that tables and chairs are made out of living trees. (144)[13]

---

[11] In 1999, however, Prynne published an almost complete collection with a rather more visible poetry publisher, Bloodaxe Books, and followed this with an updated collection in 2005. Bloodaxe was only the secondary publisher, however; the primary publisher, in keeping with Prynne's support for small operations, was the Australian Fremantle Arts Centre Press.

[12] See the remarkably thorough *Bibliography of J. H. Prynne*, compiled by Nate Dorward and Michael Tencer, <http://prynnebibliography.wordpress.com/>, which lists over eighty items of published prose. The bibliography of secondary materials runs to two or three hundred items, providing a clear indication of the extent of the 'Prynne industry'.

[13] The term 'alterative' is a puzzle: commonly used of medicines that alter bodily processes, it presumably suggests that textuality produces changes in the way language functions.

The comment about wood is, I suppose, intended to emphasize the series of transformations that lie between the growing plant and the finished article of furniture, just as the spoken language is transformed when used in a poem, a proposition with which it would be hard to disagree. But the rhetorical force of the note is clear: Prynne wishes to distance himself from a way of talking about poetry that takes vocal utterance as central. In the following footnote he takes issue with Gerald Bruns's statement that a poet 'plays' the uses of language 'by ear in the literal sense that the poet's position with respect to language is no longer simply that of the speaking subject but also, and perhaps mainly, that of one who listens' (*The Material of Poetry*, 30). Prynne comments: 'This "literal sense" is instructive by being almost entirely alternative to the argument about "mental ears" that is advanced here' (144).

Prynne's account of poetic textuality is presented in his characteristic dense and mannered style. It proposes two 'reductions' of the actual speech of human utterances (128–30). The first involves the use of the 'specialized audition' he has named 'mental ears' to effect the disintegration of 'the real-time sounds of speech and vocalized utterance' into 'sublexical acoustic noise'; this is then 'transposed into a textual constellation in which compositional purpose begins to remake the anecdotal variety of human speech'.[14] In this way 'the sociology of utterance-occasions is part-replaced by the textuality of a language domain'. In other words, linguistic sound in poetry leaves behind the utilitarian functions it serves as the material of the sentences we use in our daily lives and becomes available as sound, 'by analogy with the striking clatter of real work in the material world'. Prynne quotes a comment by Bruns which he is willing to accept as 'somewhat comparable' to his own position; for the reader wrestling with the essay's prose, Bruns offers a much more accessible version:

Poetry is made of language but is not a use of it—that is, poetry is made of words but not of what we use words to produce: meanings, concepts, propositions, descriptions, narratives, expressions of feeling, and so on.... Poetry is language in excess of the functions of language. (144)

Bruns's comments here help to make clear that what is at stake not sheer sound as material phenomenon, but sound which, though it is still the

---

[14] Prynne, like Paterson, sees composition as happening *between* a human agent and an external mechanism or power, hence 'compositional purpose' rather than 'poet'. ('Textuality' he defines in an earlier note as 'the conceptual manifold of writerly script in production format of projection beyond the confines of compositional selfhood'.) 'Anecdotal variety', it would seem, is a dismissive way of referring to the merely human, occasional uses to which we put language in talking to one another.

sound of language, is no longer that of the quotidian employment of language, the merely 'anecdotal' use of words we familiarly engage in all the time.

The second reduction made by the mental ears of the poet is described as the imposition of 'selection constraints with the purpose to define and empower the mode of a distinct and distinctive poetic textuality'. These constraints 'are not only or primarily those of prosody or versification; they comprise a re-modelled schedule of speech-sounds and performance features within the constrained language itself' (129). The word 'schedule' is somewhat perplexing here: it's evident that prosody and versification impose constraints on the language being used (including line-breaks and disposition on the page, which are very important in Prynne's own poetry), but this statement gestures towards other, unspecified, constraints, perhaps patterns of assonance or echoing syllabic units, though how these constraints operate 'within the constrained language' is not easy to fathom.

More importantly for the discussion that follows, Prynne adds the following extension to his account: 'Mental ears also permit reconstruction of raw phonetic data, in particular across precedent historical eras, so that the alert poet as reader can "tune in" to earlier schedules [that word again] of poetic composition.' Thus mental ears are, we are told, 'evolutionary by retroflexive recognizance'. After acknowledging that there may be something in the common idea that it is 'the rhythmical deployment of sense carried into sound' that 'gives poetic discourse its special power', he offers his own approach as an 'alternative (if also complementary) mode of reckoning'; an approach via 'the methods of descriptive and historical phonology'. These are the tools whereby the reader or critic is able to analyse 'the language-use of actual poems'. The appropriate methodology, argues Prynne, is that of phonology not phonetics, since 'the sounds poems make' are to be treated not as straightforwardly acoustic phenomena that a machine might record but as 'semi-abstract representations of relations and orderings between and across sounds, within a textual domain'. What Jakobson called the 'delivery instance', therefore, the specific performance of a poem (by its author or someone else), is of no interest to Prynne. What he is after is what he calls 'base-level rule patterns and their historical evolutionary forms': mental ears allow the reader to achieve a kind of hearing by means of which 'the mere anecdotalism of sonic variety in speech sounds and phrasal accent-contours is brought into diagnostically understood formalization' (132). Once again, poetry is regarded as a means of giving substance to the ephemeral sounds of quotidian experience—a highly traditional view, of course, even if the means of achieving it are unfamiliar.

This account of the importance of historical phonology in 'hearing' the words poets use is intriguing but, until Prynne turns to an example, it is hard to deduce what it might mean in poetic or critical practice. Awareness of earlier meanings of words can, of course, play an important part in poetic understanding, but awareness of earlier *pronunciations* is perhaps another matter. The example Prynne chooses is a passage from Wordsworth's 'Tintern Abbey', and the first line he examines closely is the familiar:

> Felt in the blood, and felt along the heart.

In a flamboyant display of philological scholarship (the notes to this essay are longer than the essay itself), Prynne draws attention to the 'word-final stops, plosive (*t* and *d*) and nasal (*ng*)' (*felt, blood, felt, along,* and *heart*) and 'reverse-traces' the morphology of the verb and nouns, finding that *felt* is derived from *feel* and *blood* from *bleed*, and that *heart* goes back, via Middle and Old English, to proto-Germanic **hertan-*. This enables him to conclude that these words 'demonstrate conditions originally continuing, chiefly in tense structure systems, that have been clipped or stopped and thus marked as concluded, so that they shift out of immediately present knowledge into recognition by retrospect' (135).

Unfortunately, Prynne does not clarify his phonological terminology, making it rather difficult to follow the argument. In phonological description, the term 'stop' is usually used as an alternative for 'plosive'; that is, as both names suggest, it refers to consonants produced by blocking the flow of air and suddenly releasing it. Thus *t* and *d* are alveolar stops, made by placing the tongue against the ridge behind the teeth, allowing pressure to build up, and then removing it. The sound indicated by *ng*, however, is a nasal continuant rather than a stop, as the sound continues until the speaker ceases to produce it.[15] When Prynne says that *feel* is not 'end-stopped', somewhat confusingly borrowing a term from versification, he must mean that the ending on *l* (a lateral rather than a plosive or a nasal) has a different quality for the hearer, that it is somehow more 'open', although why this should be so (for him, at least) remains mysterious. Also mysterious is the assertion that *heart* has been 'word-final end-stopped throughout its evolutionary history', when the Old English and Middle English forms given by Prynne both end in *e*. The claim that Wordsworth's line conveys, through the history of its significant words, a

---

[15] Phonologists are not unanimous in the classification of these sounds, however, and nasals are sometimes called 'nasal stops'; they are also sometimes regarded as non-continuant, because the mouth cavity is blocked. See, for example, Skandera and Burleigh, *A Manual of English Phonetics and Phonology*, 20–5.

shift from 'immediately present knowledge' to 'recognition by retrospect' is unproven, to say the least.[16]

A similar commentary is applied to the words *trust, mind, gift, burthen,* and *blessed* in the passage from which this line comes, all of which, apart from 'burthen', are, in Prynne's idiosyncratic terminology, 'end-stopped'. The puzzle as to what 'end-stopping' means only deepens, as one might have expected *burthen* to be included, ending as it does on a nasal, like *along*. (That it's not a matter of stress is made clear by the inclusion of *blessèd*, indisputably disyllabic and stressed on the initial syllable, among the end-stopped words.) *Gift*, as the 'finite outcome of open giving', is, it appears, end-stopped where *give* is not (so ending on a fricative is not end-stopping); *sublime* has a 'word-medial stop' (this is presumably *b*; but why is the nasal *m* not an end-stop?); *blessing* is 'unstopped' in spite of the earlier end-stopping of *among*.[17]

In a further brief study—a booklet entitled *Stars, Tigers and the Shape of Words*—Prynne, in order to demonstrate that Saussure's principle of the arbitrariness of the relation between sounds and meanings doesn't hold for poetry (a demonstration with which Paterson would be wholly in sympathy) examines the workings of phonemes and syllables in the nursery rhyme 'Twinkle, Twinkle Little Star' and in Blake's 'Tyger'. Here, although there are scholarly notes tracing etymological connections, it is less the history of the words that is foregrounded, since Prynne is imagining a child reader or listener, than their divisibility and polysemy. Thus *twinkle* is said to contain the word *ink* and in this way to suggest 'the dark blue of the sky' even before the sky is named; and before we reach the word *light* in the second stanza we have been given its past participle in *lit-tle*.[18] (Saussure's work on anagrams in Latin poetry is called on as supporting evidence for this procedure.) When Prynne turns to Blake's poem, it is the *letters* on which he focuses his attention. His main claim is that the words *tiger* and *bright* at the start and finish of the first line present

---

[16] This view of the role of sound in poetry is summarized by Prynne in 'Poetic Thought': among what he calls the 'fingertip energies of a language' is the 'sonorous echo-function from auditory cross-talk and the history of embedded sound values in the philological development of a language system' (598). He appends a page-long note with a somewhat scattershot list of phonetic and phonological studies, from reconstructions of Indo-European and handbooks of phonology to studies of ancient and modern Chinese and accounts of rhyme (604–5).

[17] In another commentary on the poem, 'Tintern Abbey, Once Again', Prynne offers an account of the operation of sound that sounds more like Paterson, referring to 'the lapping sound-plays across "oft/soft/tuft" and the dispersed presence of "oft" and "soft" within the letters of "frost" itself'. The use of 'letters' rather than 'sounds' or 'phonemes' suggests, however, that mental ears, or perhaps eyes, are at work here too.

[18] Tom Paulin would approve of this analysis, presumably; see Chapter 1 section II.

reversed forms: *t*—*g*—*r*/*r*—*g*—*t*; and that the first three letters of the first word are contained within the letters of the last word. (Bafflingly, given his historical scrupulousness, Prynne uses the modern spelling of *tiger* with an *i* rather than Blake's spelling with a *y*, which would have undermined the argument.) Since the *g* of bright is not a sound that is heard, it seems that we are dealing only with the printed or written word here—though we are also told that the /r/ of *bright* can be equated with the /r/ of *tiger* if the latter is a 'vocalic /r/' (as in an American accent and many regional British accents), so sound does appear to matter after all. (Prynne uses the conventional slashes to indicate a phoneme rather than a letter.)

In both these discussions of linguistic detail in poetry, what Prynne seems to be aiming at is an account of the working of sound that ascribes to it a significant contribution to the richness and effectiveness of poems *without* making use of the traditional arguments about musicality or iconicity.[19] The astute poet will exploit the history of words, the patterning of phonemes, and the embedding of shorter words within longer words to enrich and complicate the semantic and referential dimension of the poem, and the alert reader—working as much with the poem on the page as the poem in the ear—will respond accordingly.

Where Paterson, and most other commentators on sound in poetry, examine the operation of the sonic dimension of words in a purely synchronic manner, then, Prynne sees it as inseparable from the history that has produced the words; they are apprehended, therefore, not simply as sounds but as dense sedimentations of historical processes. 'These features', Prynne states,

are by no means instances of adventitious sound symbolism, or association of semantic values with surface features; they are within the structure and history of English as an evolved system, and furthermore they are selected here for a mutually reinforcing, if latent, prominence: in other words, they are *motivated*. (137–8)

The account of the temporality of 'Tintern Abbey' that Prynne derives from this somewhat suspect phonological analysis is compelling, even if Prynne's most radical suggestion, concerning the morphological history

---

[19] In his longest critical work, *Field Notes*, a 134-page analysis of Wordsworth's 'Solitary Reaper', Prynne barely mentions sound or letter effects. One mention is in a traditional mould—the word *overflow* as containing a 'sonic self-echo', like *murmur* as used in 'Tintern Abbey' (43)—while others are more fanciful, like those in *Stars, Tigers—single* is 'latently' *singing*, *alone* is 'latently' *all one*, *lass* is 'maybe' 'part-way to *last*, even to *alas!*' (26), and, in a bilingual visual pun that Joyce would have liked, *vale* 'is by latent play of meaning a place of tacit, ancient leave-taking (Latin *vale* = farewell)' (76).

of words, remains unconvincing. Words don't carry their former incarna-
tions with them, and neither poets nor readers can be expected to possess
the kind of philological knowledge that Prynne displays in his analysis.
The broader argument that poetry involves a special kind of hearing,
using 'mental ears' rather than just bodily ears, alert to sound patterns
that operate independently of the language's quotidian uses, carries more
weight—but is not, of course, a position with which Paterson would be
likely to disagree. Both poets would take issue with the view that sound
in poetry is purely mimetic of the sounds of ordinary speech or the sounds
of the world, and both are attempting to make explicit the unconscious
rules that have governed the writing and reception of poetry for centuries.
That reception, for Paterson, is primarily a matter of an ear sensitive to the
patterns of linguistic sound, whereas for Prynne it is a matter of a mind
furnished with philological knowledge and attuned to the letters on the
page as much as it is to the sounds in the air.

III

Both Paterson and Prynne are, to my mind, fine poets. Although I have
expressed reservations about both their accounts of sound in poetry, it
would be a cheap shot to say that they write better poems than they do
poetic theory: I don't mean to suggest that their theoretical accounts are
anything other than bold, original, thought-provoking, and well worth the
effort of engaging with. Now I want to ask what happens when we turn to
examples of their poetry with these theoretical accounts in mind. Short
specimens will be most useful. Here is a poem by Paterson from his collec-
tion *Rain*:

> *Correctives*
>
> The shudder in my son's left hand
> he cures with one touch from his right,
> two fingertips laid feather-light
> to still his pen. He understands
>
> the whole man must be his own brother
> for no man is himself alone;
> though some of us have never known
> the one hand's kindness to the other. (16)

Although the subject is a serious one—the otherness of the self to the self,
the body's self-healing capacity, the surprising benefits of physical frailty—
the poem comes across as light and deft. This is partly due to the metre
and stanza form—Tennyson's *In Memoriam* stanza (a form praised by

Paterson in his essay on lyric)—but that is not our topic. It's also partly due to the transparently clear progression, from specific description in the first stanza to generalization in the opening of the second to an unexpected coda, but that is not our topic either. Nor are we concerned here with the diction—for instance, that menacing word 'shudder' right at the beginning of the poem, which is drained of its threat by everything that follows—or with the effects of syntax—notably the inversion that highlights the object of the poem's first verb—or with the tone—the sense of intimacy that begins with 'my son' and runs through to the end, where it is seen to exist between one part of the body and another. We are concerned only with the organization of sound.

The first stanza in particular, I think most readers would agree, possesses the quality of lyric musicality; we would probably also agree that the third line is especially effective in its articulation of sound: 'two fingertips laid feather-light'. And here is exactly the kind of 'consonantal signature' that Paterson identifies with the lyric at its most winning: three consonants dominate the line, and are deployed in a subtle pattern: *t—f—t—l—f—l—t*.[20] And these are the three consonants of a word in the poem's first line that plays a central role in its semantic unfolding, the word for what is most often the weaker side of the body: 'left'.

If we examine the stanza as a whole, though, it's not evident that consonantal repetition is particularly marked. There are slightly more plosives than fricatives, with a sprinkling of nasals and liquids (I'm using Paterson's terminology here), and one affricate (*ch*). If we turn to the vowels, on the other hand, we find just what Paterson says we *shouldn't* find: striking patterns of repetition and echo. That potent word *shudder* starts us off, its short *u* sound ([ʌ] in the IPA alphabet) almost immediately echoed in *son's*, and then doubled in the next line in *one touch*—successive stresses taking two of the line's four beats, thus coming across as rhythmically as well as semantically salient. The sound then seems to disappear, but returns once more in the last line of the stanza, in *understands*. Playing against this sound is the short *i* ([ɪ]), first heard unremarkably in *in* in line 1, then picked up in the first and last syllables of *fingertips*, and finally in the important verb *still*. (I'm examining only the vowels that take a beat, since the others are much less prominent; the further instances of [ɪ] in the two occurrences of *his*, for example, don't carry much weight.) The stressed [ʌ] and [ɪ] words (leaving out *in*, which

---

[20] One might be tempted to add to the three *t*'s the 'th' of 'feather', though this belongs to the fricative group rather than the plosive *t* and is thus closer to the *f*'s. Paterson is very alert to the misleading properties of English orthography.

is an unstressed syllable carrying a beat through promotion) constitute a kind of skeleton for the stanza: *shudder—son's—touch—fingertips—still—understand*. Then there are the rhymes *hand* and *understands* [æ] and *right* and *light* [aɪ], and one other pair in *feath-* and *pen* [ɛ]. Only one vowel carrying the beat has no partner, the vowel (or glide-plus-vowel) in *cure*; perhaps it receives some emphasis from this fact. (Interestingly, it begins with a consonant whose only echo is in the crucial word of the poem's last line, *kindness*.) If we include demoted stressed vowels—i.e. those that don't carry a beat—we have another short *e* ([ɛ]) in *left*, the vowel [u:] in *two*, and the diphthong [eɪ] in *laid*. They play a much less prominent part in the sonic texture of the stanza.

The feeling that sound plays an important role in our response to this stanza, then, is a product of the patterning of *both* vowels and consonants. Paterson is correct to the extent that the effect of vowel repetition and patterning is different from that of consonants; the second stanza seems to me less musical in sound, and this is probably because the consonants are more varied. There is a certain musicality about it, though, which we can ascribe largely to the vowels: listen to the sequence *whole—own—no—alone—known*, which introduces a new sound into the poem, played against a continuation of the [ʌ] sound of the first stanza in *must* (though it's not clear if this takes a beat), *brother*, *some*, and, at the climax, *other*. Although this is one very small example, it does suggest that the simple formula of vowel variation and consonant patterning is insufficient to account for lyrical beauty in language. The equivalent of pink noise in poetry is perhaps a degree of patterning in both consonants *and* vowels that is not so great as to overwhelm the sense and emotional quality of the poem.

There is no space to examine any other whole poems, but here are a number of endings—the final two, three, or four lines—of poems in *Rain*. These are examples of the heightened lyricism with which Paterson's shorter poems often end (as is the case with a significant proportion of the lyric poems in the tradition). Vowel-sounds occurring more than once in syllables that take the metrical beat are shown in bold type:

> They were tr**ee**s, and tr**ee**s don't w**ee**p or ache or sh**ou**t.
> And tr**ee**s are all this poem is ab**ou**t.
>
> ('Two Trees', 3)

> and th**i**s is wh**y** we f**i**nd
> however deep we l**i**sten
> that the sk**ie**s are s**i**lent.
> ('The Error', 4)

I gave the empty seat a push
and nothing made a sound
and swung between two skies to brush
her feet upon the ground
                                        ('The Swing', 7)

look at the little avatar
of your muddy water-jar
filling with the perfect ring
singing under everything
                                        ('The Circle', 11)

I turned and shut my eyes and lay
my head against the growling glass
and waited for the train to pass.
                                        ('The Rain at Sea', 13)

So the whole world blooms continually
within its true and hidden element,
a sea, a beautiful and lucid sea
through which it pilots, rising without end.
                                        ('The Bathysphere', 35)

In all these examples, two or more vowel-sounds are interlaced to produce a pattern of assonance that, whether the reader or listener is consciously aware of it or not, contributes to any sense of concluding rightness that may be experienced.

In *Reading Shakespeare's Sonnets* Paterson comments as follows on a line of Sonnet 18: 'Rough winds do shake the darling buds of May': 'The vowels are fat, which inflates the line, but also carefully varied, which means it's great fun to wrap your mouth round, and enact the distinct shape and sense of each word in turn' (57). This is one of the rare moments in the book where he alludes to his principle of vowel variation. 'Fat vowels' are presumably low, back vowels ('winds' is the exception); by 'inflates the line' I guess he means that these vowels are, as we've noted, suggestive of largeness, in an appropriate context. But one might want to argue that the sense of the line's phonetic rightness comes also from the assonance that marks the conclusion of the two parts of the line: *shake* and *May*. (Paterson would insist, rightly, that there's no caesura here, but one of the most common rhythmic articulations of the pentameter, as I've argued elsewhere, is into a two-beat, slower section, and a faster three-beat section.[21]) There is also the chiming of *rough* and *buds*—although the former word doesn't carry a beat, it is surely as strongly stressed as any of the other words

---

[21] See *The Rhythms of English Poetry*, 142–3 and 352–3. See also my discussion of the English Sapphic, which is closely related to this form of the pentameter, in Chapter 7 section V.

of the line. By contrast, there is relatively little consonantal patterning; apart from a repeated /d/ the consonants are marked by their variability. Once again, the sense of an effective marriage of sound and sense is due at least as much to vowel repetition as it is to consonantal repetition.

IV

For comparison I've chosen a poem by Prynne that is also in two four-line stanzas with rhyme (though not, in this case, the *In Memoriam* stanza). It is untitled, and is from the 1993 collection *Not-You*:

> Their catch-up is slow and careful
>   to limit levels in thick shade
> fallen there but untouched yet
>   by the hot slants which fade
>
> Both coming and going. On a stair
>   or quickly the defined
> several inlays make a breath
>   of so much ascent, in mind.
>
> (*Poems*, 396)

Of course, this can't be claimed to be a 'representative' Prynne poem, just as 'Correctives' can't be said to be a 'representative' Paterson poem; but it will enable us to examine the workings of a small sample of his work that is surely not untypical.

It's not my purpose to examine the fitfulness with which sense gleams through the resistance to sense here—we're in a different poetic world from that of Paterson, whose poems, though often oblique and allusive, read as if we *ought* to be able to extract some paraphrasable content—but to focus on the sounds of the poem. (John Wilkinson, in 'Counterfactual Prynne', has undertaken a heroic analysis of the sequence from which this poem comes, though the meaning which he succeeds in extracting is less interesting than the struggle to elicit it: like all poems, this one is not a paraphrasable statement but an event.) Paterson, in the online version of 'The Lyric Principle', makes a strong claim about the sounds of Prynne's poetry after having carried out his own analysis:

Prynne's default music runs *directly counter* to all the norms of the English lyric tradition. In every aspect we find him doing what we might caricature as 'the opposite of Heaney': lots of schwa—partly a result of his love of jargon and poly-syllabic words—lots of 'bound' words with the vowel firmly opened and closed, often by unrelated plosives, and so on. However the impressive thing was that these features occurred with far more frequency than normal conversational speech would ever exhibit; in other words, the verse appeared to work on a deliberately *anti-lyric* principle. It was interesting to discover a project was so rigorously defined in the negative. Which made me think rather better of it, as a) at least it had a clear signature music, however ugly I might have found it, and b) its brutal rejection of even conversation-level lyric patterning made the sense even more jaggedly discontinuous that it would have been: as we know, Prynne's poetry is notoriously discontinuous. (<http://www.donpaterson.com/files/arspoetica/2.htm>)

Let us look again just at the first stanza, testing it against Paterson's comments. The alliteration in the opening line—*catch* and *careful*—invites us to listen for further consonantal echoes, and there is one, at the end of *thick*; the final sound of *catch*, too, is echoed in *untouched* and *which*. The other phoneme repeated in the first line is /l/—*slow* and *careful*—and this is even more fully echoed in *limit levels* in the second line, and again in *fallen* and *slants* in the following lines. Meanwhile, the fricatives (/ð/ and /θ/—*th* voiced and unvoiced—/s/, /ʃ/—sh—/f/, and/h/) have been prominent: two in the first line, three in the second, two in the third, and five in the last. (This is far less than in 'Correctives', though, where the count is 6, 5, 4, and 5.) The rhyme, of course, provides another consonantal echo. Turning to the vowels, we find something closer to the Patersonian ideal of constant variation than in his own poem's first stanza: there are ten different stressed vowels, only three of them repeated, including the rhyme, and only one of those more than twice (*care-*, *lev-*, *there*, and *yet*—and to many ears, there would be two different vowel-sounds here). It seems that in this stanza at least, Prynne is following, rather than countering, what Paterson presents as the lyric norm.[22]

If we turn to the endings of Prynne's poems, we again find a degree of vocalic and consonantal patterning, in many cases no different from what we would expect from a specimen of prose, though there are occasional marked repetitions of one or other type. There is no clear evidence of a resistance to the Patersonian model of patterned consonants and varied vowels. The following are the final sentences of the poems in the sequence 'The Kirghiz Disasters'[23] from *Brass* (a 1971 collection often taken to be the turning point in Prynne's poetic career to a more radical poetics); I have again indicated repeated stressed vowels by bold, and given some examples of chains of repeated constants (or related consonants) after each quotation:[24]

---

[22] The second stanza is somewhat less Patersonian: seven different stressed vowels, and four of them repeated; not so much consonantal patterning, though it is perhaps noteworthy that there are eleven nasals, two of them in the last word.

[23] Prynne, *Poems*, 155–8.

[24] My aim, I should stress, is not to make any statistical claims about Paterson's or Prynne's poetry; it is to ask, by means of a few examples, how sonic patterning relates to the reader's perception of 'musicality'.

> The fire is an **un**real
> **mix**ture of sm**o**ke & damp; the **rea**son for
> **thi**s is **un**musical, in st**o**ic **si**lence by the door.
> *n—m—m—m—n—n—m—n; z—s—s—z—s—z—z—s—s—s*

(Although there is an approximation of rhyme between *for* and *door*, the lack of stress on the first of these words means that the sonic echo is not pronounced.)

> **O**therwise the **re**st is **ju**st
> **a**bsolute; **ri**ght down at the **fo**ot of the **bu**ttress a mark
> of wasted a**ff**ection **li**es a**wry**, a**ll fa**lling apart.
> *t—t—t—t—t—t—t—t—t; last line: f—f; l—l—l*

> The **con**tinent will of
> course embrace us: we wound only, reluctant to kill.
> *k—k—k; l—l—l.*

> What **e**lse is there: the **cap**tain orders the sight
> of land to be erased from the log, as well he might.
> *t—t—t—t—t; l—l—l—l*

> **Swea**r at the **lea**ther by the knee-joint
> shouts Jerome, crumbs **rea**dy as a favoured bribe.
> *n—m—m*

> The
> tribe inflates and
> each **mu**scle sh**u**ts.
> *No significant consonantal patterning.*

> How c**ou**ld it be
> as we turn quickly round and l**oo**k at what you s**ee**.
> *k—k—k—k*

> She n**ex**t stuffs her little crown **in**to a
> bag and runs daintily up**s**t**ai**rs, she nauseates everyone.
> *n—n—n—n—n—n—n; st [in –xt]—st—st—ts*

What can we conclude from these examples? If Prynne's poetry seems to lack the quality of musicality or lyric beauty that much of Paterson's writing possesses—and I suspect most readers (or listeners) would agree that this is the case, whether or not this is seen as a failing—the reason is not that it is wholly lacking in the kind of vocalic and consonantal patterning that the other body of poetry manifests.[25] The perceptible

---

[25] Prynne's poetry has been praised for its sound-textures: thus one of his best critics, John Wilkinson, points out the 'skilful vowel and consonant patterning' ('Counterfactual Prynne', 7) of the first poem of *Not-You*, and states that the whole collection is 'bound strongly by sound-patterning' (20). While Wilkinson makes no claims about musicality, Nigel Wheale asserts that 'there is a specific kind of music, of poetic beauty, to Prynne's

difference between the experience of sound provided by the two poets must derive from the inseparability of sound and sense. To the degree that the sense is faint and flickering, the sound effects—unless they are produced by extreme phonetic patterning—will be muted. In Prynne's poem from *Not-You*, the phrase that strikes me as having greater salience and memorability than much of its surrounding language is 'hot slants'; I could say that this is due to the consonantal patterning (it contains an almost chiasmic sequence of *fricative—plosive—fricative—liquid—nasal—plosive—fricative*), the vowel variation, and the successive stressed monosyllables, or I could say it is due to the semantic suggestiveness of the two words in combination and the unusual use of *slants*, apparently as a noun (rays of the sun, perhaps?). But I would prefer to say that it is both: that the patterned sounds invite attention to the meaning, and the semantic surprise invites us to savour the sound. Returning to the line of 'Correctives' I drew particular attention to, 'two fingertips laid feather-light', we might ask how much work the sounds alone would do without the semantic suggestiveness of *fingertips* (not just fingers), of *laid* (with its connotations of gentleness, as in the laying on of hands), and of *feather-light*, which underlines powerfully all the suggestions that have come before. Perhaps not a great deal. The indivisibility of sound and meaning can be understood as implying that the former alone can convey little, rather than suggesting that sound by itself possesses semantic properties.

If we are to assess Prynne's 'Their catch-up is slow and careful' according to his own critical practice, we should not, as I have been doing, concern ourselves with the ways in which sounds might be thought to contribute to the experience of musicality or to activate, echo, emphasize, or counter meanings; we should attend to the complex history that underlies the words, whose sounds are the outcome of a long process of change, and we should look for patternings of phonemes that, through repetition, reversal, or embedding, work semantically by linking distant words. To explain the salience of the phrase *hot slants* we could follow up the word *slant* in the *OED* to find that it can mean 'a slight breeze, or spell *of* wind, etc.'—thus giving us a more fitting sense—and that *slant* used in this way is a late form of *slent*, which comes originally from Old Norse *sletta*, 'to dash, throw, etc.' Perhaps here, too, the loss of the final vowel gives the sound of *slant* a feeling of abbreviation, of cutting off. Then there is the inversion of many of the sounds of *slant* in *inlays*, s—l—n

---

lyricism'—though he goes on to suggest that it may be 'pointless to continue thinking of it as "lyric" at all' ('Crosswording', 169), so it is clear he's not thinking of music, beauty, or lyricism in a traditional manner.

becoming *n—l—s*, and the repetition of the *s—n—t* of *slant* in *ascent*. Thus, perhaps, the sliding down of *slant* is reversed in an upward motion, on inlaid stairs.

I can't say I have convinced myself with this analysis, and I'm not sure that readers without the *OED* to hand or a Saussurean interest in anagrams would be convinced either. In a sense, both Paterson's and Prynne's approaches provide tools that are too powerful to offer any kind of reliable guide to the reader: many a passage of dead prose could be shown to possess the types of repetition and variation preferred by Paterson or the etymological and literal cross-referencing espoused by Prynne.

V

Where does this leave the question of sound and sense in lyric poetry? Many years ago, in a discussion of Joyce's *Ulysses*, I tried to formulate an account of the working of onomatopoeia: we experience this effect, I asserted, 'when a more than usually powerful semantic evocation of a suitable physical property is achieved in words that constitute a more than usually patterned phonetic sequence (whether or not that patterning involves anything that could be deemed specifically appropriate to the properties in question)' (*Peculiar Language*, 151). In other words, there's very little inherent in the sounds of *f, l,* and *t* that makes them appropriate to the action of gently placing two fingers of one hand on the other; but the vividly evoked meanings of this line enhance and are enhanced by the patterning of the consonants. (The principle may hold beyond the fairly limited realm of onomatopoeia, in which case it would not be a matter only of a 'suitable physical property' but any property, emotional or intellectual.) As Paterson shows in his essay, the operation of phonesthemes may require some modification of this account, since they provide, within a given language, a certain degree of existing sound–meaning connectivity that may be exploited by the poet (though the suggestiveness of phonesthemes can always be annulled by the sense—there's no hint of light in, for instance, *gloom* and *glum*). And poets can, and do, exploit the weak correspondences between some categories of sounds and some categories of meaning I alluded to earlier. A further possibility is that a kind of nonce-phonestheme may be set up by a poem: an example would be the combination of the sounds of *l, f,* and *t* in the line we have looked at, which create the temporary impression that these words, and the way they relate to the earlier word *left*, represent a genuine cluster in the language highly appropriate to the meanings of the words in which they occur.

This account of the working of sound in poetry does not represent, any more than Paterson's or Prynne's theoretical claims, an algorithm which would enable us to program a computer to produce, or identify, poetry of the highest quality—if only because the notion of 'quality' is inseparable from the specific cultural context within which it is formed. Each of us brings to the poems we read a complex of information, memories, habits, expectations, fears, associations, prejudices, emotional tendencies, and physical inclinations that we have inherited and absorbed from the culture or cultures we have lived in as well as from the specific encounters that have shaped us, and our experience of the words we read takes place in, and makes a difference to, that internal complex. What we find worth attending to in a poem, what delights and moves us, will depend in part on what we have imbibed from those whose theories and judgements we trust and learn from; both Paterson and Prynne, as teachers in print and in speech, have undoubtedly enriched the poetic experiences of many readers of their own and others' work—and have done so in part because of their intolerance of opposing views. The danger in such intolerance is that, while enhancing the enjoyment and understanding of one kind of poetry, it will limit the appreciation of other kinds. I'm not suggesting that an all-embracing universal appreciativeness is possible, but I am suggesting that, as poetry readers (and perhaps as poetry writers too), we can benefit from attending carefully and generously to the many voices in the continuing conversation, including those that make what we feel to be exaggerated and one-sided claims.

PART II

RHYTHM AND METRE

5

Rhythm in English Poetry

Beat Prosody

I

Here is the opening stanza of a poem that I have enjoyed reciting for as long as I can remember; its title is 'Disobedience':

> James James
> Morrison Morrison
> Weatherby George Dupree
> Took great
> Care of his Mother,
> Though he was only three.
> James James
> Said to his Mother,
> 'Mother', he said, said he;
> 'You must never go down to the end of the town, if you don't go down
> with me.'

The poem, which goes on to tell of the horrible fate of parents who don't pay sufficient heed to their children's warnings, comes from the collection by A. A. Milne entitled *When We Were Very Young* (30–3), first published in 1924 and reprinted at regular intervals ever since. (My two-year-old replacement copy is the 85th reprint.) I suspect that the reasons why this poem has been a favourite of mine and of many other listeners and readers extend further than its revolutionary sentiments and the wonderfully impossible name of its young hero. The word that most of us would use to characterize its special quality would probably be 'rhythm'. Thousands, perhaps millions, of parents, children, and others—very few of them literary specialists—have opened the book at this page and begun to read, their voices almost immediately adopting the same slightly sing-song contours and heavy stresses as they shape the words into a distinctive temporal pattern.

Neither the traditional terms of academic prosody, based on the foot-scansion of classical verse, nor the more recent linguistic models of metre lend themselves to a description of this rhythmic pattern, partly because these approaches have had as their major focus the verse forms of high culture. Yet without an understanding of rhythm as it operates in popular forms—children's verse, nursery rhymes, rap, ballads, advertising, and so on—we can't hope to achieve a clear appreciation of its working in the more rarefied domain of the poetic tradition. This isn't because rhythm is necessarily a more *simple* presence in these popular forms—it frequently isn't—but because it plays a more dominant role in the complex interplay of linguistic features that constitutes all verse, and because in so doing it reveals more clearly the sources and characteristics of the rhythmic pleasure so central to our experience of poetry. What is needed, then, is an approach that begins not with the abstractions of metrical feet or grids of weak and strong positions, but with the psychological and physiological reality of the sequences of rhythmic energy pulses perceived, and enjoyed, by reader and listener alike.

One immediately striking feature of the example we're considering is the speed with which a forceful rhythm imposes itself upon the reader, and communicates itself to the hearer. Here's the beginning again:

> James James
> Morrison Morrison
> Weatherby George Dupree

Simply a string of names, yet by the time we've reached the end of it the brain, and the muscles of the vocal organs, have already been programmed to give a distinctive rhythmic shape to the material that follows, if this proves to be at all possible. As indeed it is:

> Took great
> Care of his Mother,
> Though he was only three.

This immediate establishment of a strong expectation suggests that the poem employs a rhythmic organization that is both familiar and instantly recognizable. There's one structure that, above all others, possesses these qualities, and it's one that occurs everywhere in popular verse and song (and not just in English): a pattern of four beats repeated four times.[1] (I'll

---

[1] 'Structure' is not a very satisfactory term for a recognizable rhythmic entity, suggesting as it does something spatial and fixed, but the alternatives—'form', 'pattern', 'arrangement'—are just as misleading in this respect, and don't convey the sense of potential multi-levelled complexity in the way that 'structure' does. The language lacks a term for a

return to the word 'beat' later, but I think in this context its meaning is obvious enough—a rhythmic pulse that we seem naturally to mark by a movement of the hand.) If rhythmic structures can be said to vary in the degree to which they are 'natural' or 'cultural', this one is obviously one of the most natural, and has been found in children's verse in several languages on several continents.[2] Here is the stanza set out to make this structure clear:

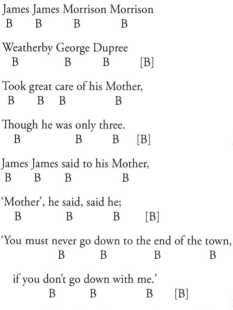

James James Morrison Morrison
B   B   B   B

Weatherby George Dupree
B   B   B   [B]

Took great care of his Mother,
B   B   B   B

Though he was only three.
B   B   B   [B]

James James said to his Mother,
B   B   B   B

'Mother', he said, said he;
B   B   B   [B]

'You must never go down to the end of the town,
        B   B   B   B

if you don't go down with me.'
    B   B   B   [B]

There are two groups of four four-beat units here, and I have indicated the occurrence of beats by means of a 'B' under the appropriate syllables.[3] If we read the poem out aloud as we would to a young child, we find that the intonation contour we use produces a familiar melody on these beats that signals very clearly the four separate units in each of these groups, as

repeatable organization created out of energy fluctuations through time (other than 'rhythm').

[2] See Burling, 'The Metrics of Children's Verse'; Attridge, *The Rhythms of English Poetry*, 81–4 and *Poetic Rhythm*, 53–7; Arleo, 'Counting Out'; and Dufter and Hanna, 'Natural Versification'.

[3] For a table of all the scansion symbols used in this book, see the Appendix. The symbol is placed below the vowel of the syllable (or the first vowel in a diphthong), in recognition of the nature of English speech rhythm. As Reed puts it, 'Rather than claiming that in stress-timed rhythm speakers place stressed syllables at regular intervals, it is more correct to say that they place the *vowels in stressed syllables* at regular intervals' (*Analysing Conversation*, 143).

well as the sense of temporary closure at the mid-point of the group (after two lines) and the cohesion of the whole eight-unit structure, which ends with a falling pitch on the last beat that gives a powerful feeling of finality.

One thing that is immediately noticeable is that not all the beats are actually realized by means of a spoken syllable; I have indicated the points at which there is no verbal substantiation of a beat by [B]. However, the rhythmic pulse at these points can be easily felt in a strongly regular reading, such as the poem clearly invites. If the stanza is read aloud by a group of English speakers in chorus, without anyone taking a leading role, the group rhythm that establishes itself by common consent will show these beats very clearly—that is, there is a tendency to pause at the ends of the second and fourth lines of the four-line span which doesn't occur at the ends of the first and third lines. And if the members of the group are asked to nod their heads on the beats, there will be many nods in the middle of that pause (as well as a nod *after* the last word of the poem). These 'unrealized' pulses, experienced but not sounded out, I have termed *virtual beats*.[4]

This pattern, which we may label as the 4.3.4.3 stanza, is found very commonly in English verse and song, from hymn-tunes (where it's called 'common measure') to ballads (it's often referred to simply as the 'ballad stanza') to poems by Jonson and Donne, Blake and Wordsworth, Dickinson and Browning, Auden and Frost, and a host of other writers. The one-beat gaps that occur after every seven beats function as highly effective rhythmic articulators; they mark the mid-point and end of the group, and augment whatever structuring is effected by the poem's rhymes and by its syntactic and semantic segmentation. A virtual beat of this kind gives a strong sense of finality to the previous beat, which is the one on which the rhyme regularly falls; when this pattern occurs in songs, the virtual beats are usually manifested as held notes, prolonging the previous syllable over the second beat and heightening the feeling of closure.[5] I'm emphasizing the role of virtual beats because they demonstrate vividly that the rhythms of verse—at least of verse in regular metres—are not simply produced by the configurations of the language; there's a continu-

---

[4] Virtual beats are not confined to verse; Reed gives an example of a recorded conversation which includes 'a *silent beat*, that is, a beat which receives no vocalization' (151).

[5] Some writers on prosody advance the idea of a 'silent stress' in various positions (for instance, at the end of a pentameter as well as at the end of three-beat lines). Such a notion is very different from that of virtual beats, since stress is a feature of language, not rhythm. My contention is that virtual beats occur only in regular verse (and, of course, music) once a strong rhythmic pattern has been established, and that the conditions under which they occur are highly circumscribed.

ous interaction between the rhythmic habits we've learned as speakers of a given language and those which we've acquired through our wider experience of rhythm, much of it prior to and independently of our acquisition of language.

The use of a commonplace underlying form explains why we latch on to the rhythms of 'Disobedience' so immediately, but it doesn't explain why its rhythms are so distinctively jaunty, to infant and adult ear alike. To begin to understand this, we need to pay attention to what happens *between* the beats, where the necessary slack phase is either occupied by one or more unstressed syllables or left empty. (A beat is constituted not just by the energy pulse that creates it, but also by the relaxation that occurs before and after it; these phases of relaxation are *offbeats*.[6]) There are three common types of offbeat in English, the commonest being a *single syllable*, which aligns verse rhythm most closely with the rhythmic tendencies of ordinary spoken English. An offbeat made up of *two syllables* inclines the rhythm toward a triple or ternary movement, especially if it occurs frequently in a line. The third possibility is an offbeat which occurs *without* the aid of a syllable, experienced only as the weakening of energy between two successive stressed syllables and usually manifested in pronunciation by a prolongation of the first of these; these unrealized offbeats are *implied offbeats*. In 'Disobedience', we find all three types. The first three beats are separated by unrealized offbeats: 'James—James—Mor'. This is an unusual beginning, because readers of English verse tend to treat three stressed syllables in a row as a beat, an offbeat, and a beat: 'Out, brief candle!' occupies two, not three, beats of its pentameter. But Milne has chosen to start this poem with one of the few situations in which all three syllables must be pronounced with the same degree of stress: a sequence of given names. (Imagine if the stanza began with the words: 'Take great care...': here we'd be inclined to weaken 'great'.) And just in case we're still tempted to weaken the second syllable in order to produce the usual alternating rhythm of English, he makes it the *same* as the first and so very difficult to pronounce differently.

---

[6] In music, these terms are used somewhat differently, since 'beat' refers to all rhythmic pulses, not just the strongest ones in the pattern. But musical analysis does make a distinction between strong beats and offbeats (or weak beats) which is similar to that between beats and offbeats in verse. Virtual beats, strong or weak, are common in music, where they are produced by syncopations and held notes; they can also, of course, occur on rests. Because of the essentially hierarchical nature of regular rhythm, these terms are all relative; what are perceived as measures (that is, groups of beats) in a piece of music played at one speed will become beats when the piece is played much faster, or phrases (groups of measures) when played more slowly. Four-beat verse often possesses similar characteristics, as we shall see.

There is another type of unrealized offbeat, in which the pause be-
tween stresses is aided by punctuation; this is the *virtual offbeat*. In
Chapter 7 I discuss a poem that begins with a line whose metricality
depends on such virtual offbeats, Tennyson's 'Break, break, break, | On
thy cold gray stones, O sea'. There is no hard-and-fast distinction between
the two types of unrealized offbeat, but it is helpful to maintain the two
terms since the presence of punctuation results in less disruption of
rhythmic regularity.[7]

When we turn to the third, fourth, fifth, and sixth beats, we find that
they are separated by *two* unstressed syllables: 'MORrison MORrison |
WEAtherby GEORGE'. Two syllables now occupy the same rhythmic slot
as none did to begin with, retrospectively confirming our sense of a slow
rhythm with marked beats at the start of the poem; and the rhythm is
briefly shifted into something approaching a triple metre. This dancing
movement is halted by the next offbeat, however, which consists of a single
syllable, and which steadies the rhythm at a concluding point: 'GEORGE
DuPREE'. Thus over the first seven words we've already had all three ways
of filling the slack between beats. We can show this as follows:

James James Morrison Morrison
B   ôB   ô B -o-   B -o-

Weatherby George Dupree
B   -o- B   o B [o B]

Here, ô indicates an implied offbeat; o a single offbeat; and -o- placed
between the two syllables to which it refers—a double offbeat. (Note that
both an offbeat and a beat are unrealized at the end of the second line;
successive beats are, by definition, separated by an offbeat—if they were
not, there would be only one beat.) The result of this variety is not, as one
might expect, to create a weak and disordered rhythm, but to strengthen
the salience and periodicity of the beats, and to subdue the weak syllables
into compliance with that overriding rhythm. The fact that all we've had
so far is a string of proper names increases the prominence of the rhyth-
mic pattern, for the absence of a syntactic or semantic framework means
that no subordination of one word to another is possible, except perhaps
for an added emphasis when we finally reach the stressed syllable of the
last name.

Once this version of the four-beat rhythm is established, the rest of the
poem moulds itself to its demands. 'Took great care' would, as I've said,

---

[7] In *The Rhythms of English Poetry* I used the term 'implied offbeats' for both types of
unrealized offbeat. For fuller discussion, see Chapter 6.

usually be read as a realization of two beats: 'He TOOK great CARE to LOCK the DOOR'. But here we allow 'great' its own beat so that the rhythm will echo 'James James Morrison'—and we thereby, perhaps, emphasize the magnitude of the young boy's sense of filial responsibility, as well as imitating a child's way of talking (or is it an adult's way of talking to a child?). The whole of this four-beat unit, and the next one, follow the first two very closely in rhythm.

Took great care of his Mother,
B ô B ôB -o- B o

Though he was only three.
B -o- B o B [o B]

The second half of the stanza begins identically with the first half and sustains the same rhythmic pattern through the first two four-beat units, verbal repetition encouraging a strong alternation between beats and off-beats (first 'he SAID', then 'said HE'):

James James said to his Mother,
B ôB ôB -o- B o

'Mother', he said, said he;
B -o- B o B [o B]

Then there occurs the poem's rhythmic surprise: where in the first part of the poem we had 'Took great care of his mother', with that exaggerated, marked articulation enforced by implied offbeats, we now have a run of double offbeats, beginning even before the first beat:

'You must never go down to the end of the town,
-o- B -o- B -o- B -o- B

This is still a highly regular four-beat rhythm, but now with a full-blooded triple movement, and a rapid passage of syllables—twelve of them moving by as the rhythmic equivalent of seven. The triple swing carries on to the beginning of the last four-beat unit (there is of course no virtual beat to slow the rush from one unit to the next), but then an effect of closure, of determination, perhaps, is achieved by the rhythm's settling down again into the simplest available form: alternation of single beat and single offbeat:

if you don't go down with me.'
-o- B o B o B [o B]

Milne's exploitation of the syllabic freedom allowed by a strong four-beat rhythm is evident in this stanza. It's not merely a matter of sprinkling different kinds of offbeat among the beats, however. The following lines don't have the same strong and catchy rhythm, though they have the same words and can be scanned as four-beat verse in the same way:

James Morrison George Dupree
B   B   B   B

Weatherby James Morrison.
B   B   B   [B]

This is not just a matter of losing the lilting quality encouraged by the repetitions in 'James James Morrison Morrison'; the lines now lack the steady pacing and resounding climax produced by the particular disposition of stressed and unstressed syllables in the original. The perceptual laws governing what we hear in such patterns have never been worked out in detail, but the effect of these laws is something we all readily respond to. A. A. Milne certainly didn't know them as explicit rules, but his ear would have been familiar with them, no doubt primarily from his own nursery days, but also from the verse of W. S. Gilbert, Kipling, Chesterton, and many other poets popular in his time. In Chapter 7 I discuss the long tradition of this strongly rhythmical metrical form, with its variation in types of offbeat and exploitation of the possibilities of the virtual beat in the four-beat line, to which the name dolnik has been given.

One aspect of four-beat verse capitalized on by all these poets in their use of unstressed syllables between the beats is its capacity to fall into larger rhythmic groupings, thus giving the rhythm an even more potent swing. There's a hint of this larger structure in the rhymes of our example: the whole stanza is made up of four segments rhyming in -*ee*. This larger structure can be achieved in recitation by deliberately emphasizing the quadruple rhythm that underlies the alternating one—that is to say, the odd beats have the potential to be stronger than the even beats (and not the other way round: for one thing, several of the even beats are unrealized). Such a reading can be shown as follows, with a bold **B** indicating the stronger and a normal B the weaker beats:

James James Morrison Morrison Weatherby George Dupree
B   B   **B**   B   **B**   B   **B**   [B]

Took great care of his Mother, though he was only three.
B   B   **B**   B   **B**   B   **B**   [B]

James James said to his Mother, 'Mother', he said, said he;
B   B   **B**   B   **B**   B   **B**   [B]

'You must never go down to the end of the town, if you don't go

      B   B   **B**   B   **B**

    down with me.'

    B   **B**   [B]

Read with some rapidity and with the main emphasis falling only on the syllables marked with the bold **B**, the stanza becomes a single four-times-four-beat structure, the even beats functioning at this level as offbeats. Although no reader paying attention to the meaning of the words would be likely to adopt this pattern (we've already seen that the opening encourages an even stressing of beats), its latent existence plays a part in the character of the rhythm, and distinguishes it from other four-beat verse from which this quadruple possibility is excluded—and from five-beat verse, which doesn't lend itself to such a strongly hierarchical rhythm.[8] (As a way of demonstrating the hierarchical nature of four-beat rhythms, it is possible to read the stanza even faster, with primary stresses spaced out over the double the span of the quadruple beats, yielding two four-beat structures.) I believe that an aspect of the complexity of rhythm is that we can respond to a potential organization that isn't in fact activated, and the quadruple underswell of much four-beat verse is one example.

II

What, then, do I mean by 'rhythm' when I use the term to talk about this specimen of verse? And is it a natural or a cultural phenomenon? As my use of the term 'beat' might suggest, I don't believe it's possible to discuss rhythm without relating it to the movements of the human body. A poem like 'Disobedience' actually seems to invite not just a regular reading but a beating of the hand or a nodding of the head—and this phenomenon occurs not because a rhythmic structure, such as a melody, has been *imposed* upon the language, but because the language, read aloud, produces a rhythmic organization that encourages regular muscular movement. The explanation for this lies in the spoken language of English, which, like every spoken language, involves a distinctive use of the body's musculature to produce a sequence of sounds of differing qualities and durations. The muscles controlling the lungs expel air in regulated bursts which are modified by the larynx and the higher speech organs of the mouth to emerge as recognizable syllables. This production of syllables

---

[8] What I am calling a 'quadruple' metre is often called 'dipodic'—i.e. 'two-foot' metre.

tends, like all repeated muscular activities, toward temporal regularity. (It's much easier to do keep-fit exercises if you employ regular movements, which is why it helps to do them to music). What's important for the experience of regular rhythm is not exactly equal durations but the psychological and physiological *experience* of periodicity, what has been called 'stress-timing' (in contrast to 'syllable-timing' in certain languages).[9] Where English differs from many other languages (and here, of course, we have a cultural factor) is in the coexistence, in some degree of tension, of *two* series of energy pulses in speech—those that produce the syllables, and those that augment certain syllables with stress, that is, with an additional peak of muscular energy. Both these series of pulses incline toward rhythmic repetition, but in the random syllabic arrangements of prose, neither can be fully satisfied.

In our example, a combination of factors rapidly establishes the supremacy of the second rhythm—the stress rhythm—over the first—the syllabic rhythm—to produce strongly marked beats falling at regular intervals. These factors include the particular sequence of stressed and unstressed syllables that allows all stresses to function as beats;[10] the arrangement of those beats, through syntactic and rhetorical grouping, into a highly familiar rhythmic structure; and, of course, the cultural association of this type of verse with a chanted recitation. What we have, therefore, is a 'natural' basis, both in the rhythmic production of language by the speech musculature and in the psychological preference for certain simple rhythmic structures, overlaid by cultural factors: the particular ways in which the English language harnesses those muscular capabilities and those rhythmic forms, the tradition of English popular verse, and the expectations associated with children's poetry.

III

While popular verse in its many varieties overwhelmingly makes use of four-beat metre, whether in full four-beat lines or in versions with unrealized beats, much literary verse is designed to avoid the forceful

---

[9] See Cooper, *Mysterious Music*, 16–24, for a survey of the debate about stress-timing in English.

[10] It is common in English verse to find stressed syllables functioning as beats (as in my earlier example, 'He TOOK great CARE to LOCK the DOOR', where 'great' can be stressed in the reading but will be perceived as an offbeat), as it is to find unstressed syllables functioning as beats ('JIMmy MORRiSON is YOUNG', where the last syllable of 'Morrison' can be given very little stress while functioning as a beat). These variations, 'demotion' and 'promotion', occur only under very determined conditions, however (see Attridge, *The Rhythms of English Poetry*, 164–72, *Poetic Rhythm*, 70–7 and 109–14, and Chapter 6 section III).

rhythm created by the doubling process that gives rise to groups of two and two, four and four. The commonest way of doing this is to base the line on a sequence of five beats, which can be neither divided nor conjoined to produce a four-beat rhythm. The result is a rhythmic shape that allows for a great degree of flexibility: internal divisions are determined by the words and syntax without any pressure from the metre to break the line at a certain point; one line can flow more easily into another, and as a consequence rhyme is optional rather than obligatory; and the rhythms of English speech can be given greater prominence. I shall discuss the rules governing what is by far the most common type of five-beat verse, the iambic pentameter, in the next chapter, but here I would like to examine a specimen of this metre to illustrate its variety and suppleness even when it occurs in a particularly strict form—and to demonstrate some of the uses of beat prosody in analysing it.

This description of 'Timon's villa' is from Pope's 'Epistle to Richard Boyle, Earl of Burlington: Of the Use of Riches':

> Lo, what huge heaps of littleness around!
> The whole, a labour'd Quarry above ground.
> Two Cupids squirt before: a Lake behind
> Improves the keenness of the Northern wind.
> His Gardens next your admiration call,
> On ev'ry side you look, behold the Wall!
> No pleasing Intricacies intervene,
> No artful wildness to perplex the scene;
> Grove nods at grove, each Alley has a brother,
> And half the platform just reflects the other.

> (*Poetical Works*, vol. III, 191–2)

Although Pope is following the constraints of the strictest form of iambic pentameter, he finds ways of continually varying the movement of these lines. Two of them are examples of what I've called *sprung pentameters*, where the line pivots around an implied point of articulation after two strong beats, followed by a three-beat section that moves more quickly—usually as a result of the use of an unstressed syllable in the position of the central beat—to produce the effect of a forceful opening yielding to a lighter continuation. Because of the difference in weight of the two parts of the line, the rhythm has some of the character of the four-beat line, divided two and two, without actually falling into that alternative pacing. We can see this in the first line, where the accumulation of stresses at the start of the line (barely containable by the metre—I indicate one of a number of possible scansions) gives way to a quicker tempo thanks to the regular alternations and the succession of three unstressed syllables:[11]

> Lo, what huge heaps of littleness around!
> B   -o= B |o B o b   oB

The sound here—or rather the rhythm, moving from clogged to rapid— is clearly, as Pope might have put it, an echo to the sense. The ninth line also stands out as a result of its complex rhythmic orchestration:

> Grove nods at grove, each Alley has a brother
> B   =o- B |o   B o   b o B o

Here the idea of mirroring formal elements in the garden is itself mirrored in the rhythmic mirroring of the two parts of the line; as in the first line of the quotation, the surplus of stresses in the initial part is matched against the shortfall in the second part. (It would, certainly, be possible to stress *has*, but there is no rhetorical necessity to do this, and, to my ear, it weakens Pope's shapely management of sound.)

Another type of pentameter with only four fully realized beats is the *balanced* line: here, too, there is a point of articulation after two beats, but it is the middle beat of the line that falls on an unstressed syllable. The result is something closer to an equality of rhythmic weight on each side, as there is no temptation to speed up the second half:

> Improves the keenness of the Northern wind
> o B   o B   o |b o B   o   B

> No artful wildness to perplex the scene
> oB o B   o |b o B   o B

These lines run more smoothly than the two I have just discussed, and perhaps their smoothness can be related to the tameness of the prospect being described. However, it is probably more accurate to say that they contribute to the variety of the poem's rhythms while conveying the assur- ance of impeccably controlled language. The last line of the extract is an- other example of this type of pentameter, unless we choose to stress 'just', in which case it is an equally smooth continuous pentameter, with five realized beats and no marked break.

There are moments when Pope's rhythms pull against these paradig- matic patterns; when, for instance, the five beats are divided three and

---

[11] The symbol –o= indicates a double offbeat in which the second syllable receives a stress, b indicates an unstressed syllable that carries a beat; and | indicates the point of articulation—not necessarily a pause or, more technically, a caesura, but a transition from one kind of rhythm to another.

two, providing less equilibrium to the line than the two–three division. The ugliness conveyed by the second line is emphasized by this lack of balance:[12]

> Two Cupids squirt before: a Lake behind
> O B o   B   oB ¦o B   oB

The strong run-on—unusual for Pope—adds to the unseemliness of the movement. In line six, the final two beats close up the pentameter in an appropriate firm arrest after the initial run of three:

> On ev'ry side you look, behold the Wall!
> o B oB   o   B ¦o B   o   B

And we may note finally how the second line labours—to quote *The Essay on Criticism*—as it encounters a break after the first beat, then struggles to fit the word *above* into the alternating rhythm (I show two possible scansions):

> The whole, a labour'd Quarry above ground
> o   B ¦o B o   B obo   B
>   -o- B ô B

Pope's critique of the over-formal, overweening architecture and horticulture of Timon, although it is couched in one of the most formal varieties of English metrical verse, finds in the iambic pentameter all the resources it needs.

IV

Here is another poem; by John Ashbery, it's entitled 'Crazy Weather':

It's this crazy weather we've been having:
Falling forward one minute, lying down the next
Among the loose grasses and soft, white, nameless flowers.
People have been making a garment out of it,
Stitching the white of lilacs together with lightning
At some anonymous crossroads. The sky calls
To the deaf earth. The proverbial disarray
Of morning corrects itself as you stand up.
You are wearing a text. The lines
Droop to your shoelaces and I shall never want or need

---

[12] The upper-case O indicates a stressed syllable functioning as an offbeat: that is, demotion. It is a means of slowing down the movement of the line.

Any other literature than this poetry of mud
And ambitious reminiscences of times when it came easily
Through the then woods and ploughed fields and had
A simple unconscious dignity we can never hope to
Approximate now except in narrow ravines nobody
Will inspect where some late sample of the rare,
Uninteresting specimen might still be putting out shoots, for all we know.

(Houseboat Days, 21)

When we speak of the rhythm of a poem like this, we clearly mean some-
thing rather different from the rhythm of 'Disobedience': here the move-
ment of stressed and unstressed syllables promotes no familiar pattern
that has the power to organize the words of the poem and to simplify their
accentual and temporal relations. It would not be appropriate to use the
terms 'beat' and 'offbeat' in talking about this poem, since that particular
psycho-physical phenomenon doesn't occur. Instead, the syllables retain
all the variety of weight and duration that they have in ordinary speech,
and all the freedom to fall into any kind of sequence that may arise.
There's much more freedom for the reader, too, in choosing how to read
the poem, and there would be no such agreement about the placing of
strong stresses and the pacing of the language as there is in the case of
'Disobedience'. If there's a principle at work in the rhythm, it's a principle
of avoidance: the regular patterns of metrical verse are kept at bay by
the constant changes in the configuration of stresses and the refusal of the
syntactic units to match familiar metrical structures. Thus the occasional
regular sequence, such as

> You are wearing a text. The lines …
> -o-   B   -o- B   o B

(which matches a run of syllables in 'Disobedience'), is followed by a less
regular sequence, 'Droop to your shoelaces and I shall never want …' If
we desire a somewhat narrower term than 'free verse', which is used of a
wide range of rhythmic styles, including some that play much more in
and out of traditional metres, we can call this 'non-metrical verse'.

To attempt to characterize the rhythm of this poem, then, is not to
specify the traditional rhythmic structure which it evokes, and to detail its
distinctive use of that structure, but to note the general features of syllabic
movement that it displays, and to point to particular examples of rhyth-
mic allusion or expressiveness. It's still in part a matter of the reader's
experience of the movement of language through time, articulated
by stresses of different strengths (no longer basically two), but it's not an
experience of a sequence of beats and offbeats. The poem's rhythmic dis-
tinctiveness (which it shares with much of Ashbery's writing) lies in its

changeable, unpredictable movement, seldom seeming to dominate the language or to pursue its own semantic or emotional course. Such rhythmic periodicity as it possesses is for the most part that of the English language, enhanced by the cultural associations of 'poetry'—a rather deliberate reading, with careful attention to the sounds and movements of language. And the rhythm of Ashbery's poem, therefore, is more the product of a specific culture than that of Milne's or Pope's; one can't imagine non-English speakers obtaining much sense of its rhythmic character merely from hearing it read, and its status as poetry is acknowledged only within a narrow circle.

In an example like this, it's clearly not possible to get very far without including a discussion of the other aspects of language with which rhythm interrelates, and which a wider definition of rhythm must include. The most obvious of these is syntax, which plays an important part in all verbal rhythm: I've already noted that one reason for the exceptionally regular pulse of the opening of 'Disobedience' is the syntactically unsubordinated relationship of the first seven words. In verse like Ashbery's, syntax tends to have a more dominant role, since there are few rhythmic expectations influencing our sense of movement. The unhurried pace of 'Crazy Weather', the lingering over each moment as it occurs, is in part due to the loose sentences, which show very little tendency toward the suspense-and-resolution model of periodic organization: a statement is made by means of a complete syntactic unit, and then is followed by qualifications or additions which extend it further and further.[13] The most striking example in this poem is the extremely long last sentence which keeps seeming to be ready to stop, but keeps revealing that it has more in reserve. It is in fact grammatically complete after three words, but it continues for another seventy-three:

The lines droop—to your shoelaces—and I shall never want or need any other literature than this poetry of mud—and ambitious reminiscences of times when it came easily—through the then woods and ploughed fields—and had a simple unconscious dignity—we can never hope to approximate now—except in narrow ravines—nobody will inspect—where some late sample of the rare, uninteresting specimen might still be putting out shoots—for all we know.

Compare this with the relentless drive of the second part of the opening stanza of 'Disobedience' toward its final word: 'me'.

---

[13] As noted in Chapter 2, Richard Cureton presents an analytical method which makes it possible to represent the part played by syntactic and semantic considerations in the experience of rhythm, prominence, and anticipation (see his *Rhythmic Phrasing in English Verse*). What such an approach reveals about this poem is the extraordinary difficulty of deciding which are the dominant and which the subordinate elements at every level of analysis.

Meaning and tone are fully involved in Ashbery's rhythms, too: the uncertainty about the status of the objects, individuals, and actions in the poem, and about the attitude of the speaker (if there is a speaker) toward them, limits the opportunities for moments of semantic emphasis which would function as rhythmic nodal points. The rhythm of Ashbery's poem, like Milne's and Pope's, is a psychological and physiological experience: not, in this case, of a coming together in energetic pulses but of a dispersal of energy—energy remembered, glimpsed, hoped for, abandoned.[14]

IV

I have been discussing the subject of rhythm so far as if it were a purely aural phenomenon (insofar as this is possible in a printed book), and this coincides with the traditional understanding of rhythm: we tend to think of the use of the term to refer to visual experience as merely a metaphorical extension. Yet for an early twenty-first-century reader, the typical encounter with a poem—in spite of the increasing popularity of poetry-readings as public events over the past twenty years—is reading it from a page, an experience that is simultaneously visual, oral, and aural.[15] In reading a poem to ourselves, that is, we see it, say it, and listen to ourselves saying it. If the reader proceeds silently with only a mental semi-realization of the poem's oral qualities, the role of sight is of course even more important.

The obvious limitations of my discussion of the rhythms in 'Crazy Weather' spring at least in part from this temporary willed phonocentrism. Much of the rhythmic work of Ashbery's poem—the attention drawn to movements of words, the pacing of the language, the emergence of regularities within the free variations—is achieved by the lineation. The immediate visual appearance of the poem has an effect in itself: the solid block of lines of roughly similar length, starting with initial capitals and going most of the way across the page, establishes a connection with a long tradition of English poetry: although there's just sufficient raggedness at the right-hand margin to signal that we're not in the domain of regular metre, the look of the poem invites the same full attention to sound and sense demanded by blank verse. The spoken voice, that is to say, and not song, is the model evoked by this first glimpse.

---

[14] See Chapter 9 for a discussion of the development of free verse in the history of English poetry.

[15] In what is a pun only in the spoken language (appropriately enough), I will use the somewhat awkward combination 'oral/aural' to bring out the simultaneously vocalized and heard character of rhythm in this typical mode of reading.

The visual segmentation of the poem into lines is impossible to convey with complete accuracy in a purely spoken rendition (unless one were to use some arbitrary convention—different from the pauses and intonation contours that mark syntactic features—to indicate line-ends); but it is this segmentation that does much of the work of heightening attention to the movement of language, whether it crystallizes a single syntactic unit into a visual unit as in the first line, or cuts across a syntactic unit to create a moment of drama, as in 'The sky calls | To the deaf earth.' The final sentence presented as prose would be a scarcely intelligible block of verbiage; the line-divisions, although they correspond to no divisions of grammar or sense, allow the reader to move sequentially in measured phases, concentrating on the words at hand while the words to come remain a mystery. We may even have in the poem as it appears on the page in *Houseboat Days* an accidental feature that contributes to the poem's closure: the final phrase, part of the last, unusually long line, appears visually on its own, as a short coda, qualifying the already qualified statement that precedes it, summing up the poem's atmosphere of half-glimpsed but immediately ironized revelation:

> ... some late sample of the rare,
> Uninteresting specimen might still be putting out shoots,
>   for all we know.[16]

In this case, then, rhythm isn't entirely an oral/aural matter; Ashbery's poem, like most of what we call free verse, belongs to a print culture, and the changing pace of the language, the expectations and fulfilments or disappointments that draw us through the poem, are the product of the interaction between sight and sound. The common association of free verse with 'nature' or 'spontaneity' and regular verse forms with 'artifice' is itself a wholly cultural phenomenon, reflecting our post-Romantic situation; it could be argued on the contrary that free verse, with its reliance on the properties of print, is more artificial than verse derived from the rhythms of spoken English and the common rhythmic forms that verse shares with music. But that would be to presuppose a greater artificiality in the printed language than in the oral, which would itself be another cultural assumption. Moreover, it's not only free verse that relies on the page for its rhythmic identity; as I argue in Chapter 9, as soon as blank verse was introduced into English there existed a form of poetry which did not signal line-endings with a simple aural device. True, the use of syntactic and semantic units that coincide with rhythmic groupings made

---

[16] In Ashbery's 1985 *Selected Poems*, the last four words form part of the final line (221)—a loss, it seems to me.

it possible to retain strongly marked subdivisions; but the growing free-
dom in the use of run-on lines, beginning in the drama of the Renaissance
and entering the tradition of printed poetry with Milton, together with
less strict adherence to regular metrical alternations, meant a growing role
for the visual aspect of rhythm in the seventeenth century. Nursery
rhymes, by contrast, remain primarily oral/aural. There's no 'authentic'
way of presenting, say, 'Little Jack Horner' on the page, and it preserves
its strong rhythm through a number of visual permutations. Its words are
transmitted orally, and lodged in the brain on the basis of its memorable
rhythmic form, in much the same way that a tune is lodged.

It might seem that 'Disobedience' is a similarly oral/aural artefact.
However, we must remember that it's a poem written by a single author
and published in a printed book in 1924, and while it—or at least its
opening stanza—may exist in many memories as a verbal sequence with-
out a specific visual organization, its appearance on the page is not with-
out importance to its rhythm. In discussing its rhythmic structure earlier
I quickly abandoned the layout which Milne chose, and it should be rein-
stated again:

> James James
> Morrison Morrison
> Weatherby George Dupree
> Took great
> Care of his Mother,
> Though he was only three.
> James James
> Said to his Mother,
> 'Mother', he said, said he;
>   'You must never go down to the end of the town, if you don't go down
>   with me.'

One's immediate response to this visual image is likely to be very different
from one's response to the Ashbery example: here is an odd, wayward
poem, with both exceptionally short and exceptionally long lines.
Humour, a lightness of tone, not colloquial speech but a heightened de-
livery of some kind, are thus signalled. Looking at the difference between
the way the poem is set out here and my version set out in four-beat
rhythmic units, we may observe that the first and third four-beat units are
presented by Milne as two two-beat lines, giving the second and fourth
units—the ones with virtual fourth beats—a stronger quality of resolu-
tion, since they now appear not as *shorter* lines but as *longer* ones: 'James
James | Morrison Morrison | Weatherby George Dupree.' This pattern is
repeated in 'James James | Said to his mother, | "Mother", he said, said he';
but then the last two four-beat units, with their additional syllables, are

all run together as one extraordinarily long line that limitation of space forces into two lines on the page. Reading from this printed text, the rhythmic saliencies of the stanza are all the more marked: the strong beats, one per syllable, with which the poem opens, the exaggerated carefulness of 'Took great | care …', and the climax of the rapidly moving syllable-thronged utterance in which the crucial injunction is uttered. (We might note the nice reversal whereby there is *no* rhyming between the two-beat lines, creating a little fragment of poetic modernity, while the only section of the poem that *is* rhymed in two-beat units is presented as a single line—'You must never go **down** to the end of the **town** if you don't go **down** …') Another result of the short lines is the further blocking of the quadruple or dipodic potential I mentioned earlier: we're likely to award as many full beats as possible to such a minuscule unit.

The importance of the visual aspect continues to the end of the poem; indeed it increases as the poem progresses. (And I'm not referring to the deft E. H. Shepard illustrations which, by punctuating the sequence of stanzas, further heighten the poem's visual interest.) After the mother predictably disobeys her son's edict in stanza 2, the third stanza presents in large capitals and some boldface type the notice put up by King John announcing her disappearance, and the next two stanzas make use of italics for emphatic stresses that give a slightly different balance to the rhythm. The final stanza—after all hope for the mother is given up—allows print to take command. (We might recall that this poem was published two years after *The Waste Land* and *Ulysses*.) Here we have words on the page revelling in their status as visual image, yet claiming to be nothing but instructions for an oral performance ((*Now then, very softly*)). That performance is obliged to reduce the rhythmic pattern to an even more basic skeleton, allowing the names of single letters in many cases to carry a beat, before expanding to the last, long, and now even more rapid, filial instruction:

(*Now then, very softly*)
J. J.
M. M.
W. G. Du P.
Took great

C/o his M*****
Though he was only 3.
J. J.
Said to his M*****
'M*****', he said, said he:
'You-must-never-go-down-to-the-end-of-the-town-if-you-don't-go-down-
with ME!'

In some places, this is less different from the other stanzas when read aloud than when seen on the page. Notice, for example, how the skeleton of the third line retains the essential rhythmic qualities of the full version: 'Doubleyou gee Du pee' has the same stress pattern as 'Weatherby George Dupree'. But at several points the reciter has to improvise: how, for instance, do we pronounce the asterisks of 'M*****'? As for the word 'three' that becomes the figure 3, I can think of no way in which that change could be vocalized, just as the occurrence of figures instead of words in Molly Bloom's chapter of *Ulysses* exist only on the printed page we read, not in the internalized speech they are supposed to represent.

V

It will have been observed that I've used the term 'metre' only rarely, preferring in most cases the term 'rhythm'. This is not because the latter has more positive connotations in current literary discourse, suggesting vibrant life as opposed to dead mechanism; it is because I think of metre as a system, enshrined in a particular culture, that has arisen because of its power to elicit and finesse something basic to human movement and perception. That basic human propensity is rhythm, the principle of alternation—of tension and relaxation—that governs such muscular activity as breathing and walking. We also use the term 'rhythm' to name the subtle variations played by the particular words of a given line, often in tension with the regularities of the metre and their source in this fundamental rhythm. Possibilities for confusion arise, therefore; and it's useful when necessary to distinguish between 'basic' or 'fundamental' rhythm and 'surface' or 'local' rhythms.

I don't, however, wish to make too rigid a distinction between the two terms. In the mass of writing on this subject, 'rhythm' and 'metre' have been used in such different ways, and with such different relationships to one another, that it's probably unwise to try to make the distinction do too much work. Henri Meschonnic used it fruitfully in parallel with a whole set of other oppositions, between language (or more strictly, *langue*) and discourse, between structure and system, space and time, individual and subject, and so on; but in this case the meaning and function of the distinction are built up by virtue of all the other associated oppositions, not by an appeal to the history of the two terms or to a current consensus about their use.[17] Meschonnic still runs the risk of reinforcing a common

---

[17] Meschonnic, *Critique du rythme*; see also the interview with Meschonnic published in *Diacritics* in 1988.

prejudice in literary circles against generalization and in favour of con-crete particulars, a prejudice which at its worst can issue in sub-Romantic sloganizing, impressionistic description, and a refusal of careful analytical work.

When it comes to examining poems, the danger of laying too much emphasis on the opposition of rhythm and metre, it seems to me, is that a dualistic model of poetic movement is produced, in which the actual contours of the poem are regarded as being in constant tension with a Platonic (or Pythagorean) ideal. As I noted in the Introduc-tion, on this model the reading of regular verse becomes a process of relating the concrete example to an abstract universal, rather than an activity that occurs wholly in the real world of time and space, of mental and physical experience. I should make it clear that my indi-cation of the beats in 'Disobedience' is not meant to imply an abstract schema from which the actual words are felt to depart. The Bs mark syllables which actually take on a particular physical and psychologi-cal quality by being perceived as rhythmic beats, and this in turn generates an expectation for further beats and therefore modifies the production and perception of the words that follow. Where the expectation is defeated or its realization delayed, we can legitimately speak of 'tension' or 'irregularity'—but this is not felt as a metronome ticking away in the brain while the poem itself performs an intricate dance around it.

Rhythm, then, can refer to any movement through time which pos-sesses some tendency toward perceptible periodicity, whether this be the insistent regularity of the four-beat structure that dominates A. A. Milne's poem, the varied but controlled periodicity that animates Pope's couplets, or the heightened version of the typical patterns of English speech that characterize Ashbery's. It can refer to the quality of a particular verse tra-dition, or a particular poem, or a particular performance of a poem. In-stead of imposing its own definition on the term 'rhythm', as so many theories of versification do, this strategy allows it all the laxity it has in common usage. We can justifiably talk about the rhythm of spoken Eng-lish, or any other language, because all living languages—produced as they are by the muscles of the body—have some tendency toward perio-dicity. (Dead languages tend to be spoken with the rhythmic features of the speaker's native language.) This is not, I should emphasize, to suggest that rhythm is a matter of actual durations in time, measurable by instru-ments: it's the *perception* of periodicity that is crucial, and this involves muscular empathy more than the ear's calculation of temporal equivalences.

VI

My first and third examples represent extremes within the realm of English poetry, in terms of cultural function as well as rhythmic organization. Rhythmically, of course, I might have chosen even more extreme examples: such as a simple nursery rhyme with a primarily oral/aural existence, and a prose poem, where there is even less contact with the tradition of rhythmically regular verse (though the rhythms of prose poems are, of course, not as dependent on visual appearance as those of free verse). The range in between these extremes is enormous, and different types of verse draw in different ways on both the 'natural' origins of rhythm—in the repetitions of muscular activity—and the 'cultural' tradition of metrical form. The major tradition of regular English verse represented by Pope's 'Epistle to Burlington'—the accentual-syllabic tradition—derives its unique character from its use of the two sources of rhythmic regularity in spoken English that I have already mentioned, the sequence of syllables and the sequence of stresses. By controlling both the number of syllables *and* the number of stresses in a metrical unit, it brings the two rhythmic resources into harmony; but it's an unstable accord, and the strength and variety of accentual-syllabic metre spring from its exploitation of that instability. Within the realm of accentual-syllabic metre, any given metrical form will have a certain relation both to speech rhythms and to the regularities of rhythm understood as a psychological phenomenon. A falling rhythm, for example (one that tends to group into units beginning with a beat) will have a stronger rhythmic beat and will impose more upon the spoken rhythms of the language than a rising rhythm. Because spoken English has a tendency towards an alternation of stressed and unstressed syllables—noticeable, for instance, in the stress patterns of polysyllabic words—a duple rhythm will dominate the language less than a triple rhythm. As we have seen, a five-beat line is a much weaker rhythmic Gestalt than a four-beat line, and is the simplest way of avoiding the much stronger rhythmic drive of four-beat verse. Adding all these features together, it is not difficult to understand why four-beat falling and triple metres are furthest from spoken English (and nearest to song), and that the line which would most closely emulate the rhythms of speech, while retaining a distinctively regular movement, is five-beat rising duple verse or iambic pentameter.[18]

---

[18] The following two chapters examine some of the properties of these two types of verse, Chapter 6 focusing on the iambic pentameter, Chapter 7 on one of the commonest forms of four-beat metre.

There are, of course, forms of verse in English which don't draw upon the rhythms of spoken English: verse which is purely visual, for instance, scattering letters across the page, or purely oral/aural, uttered in a way that parts company with the norms of English pronunciation. Anything can become a poetic device, if a culture deems it so; there's no inherent 'poetic' property that renders some phenomena available for poetry and rules others out of court. To say the same thing in a different way, there's no guarantee that a cultural category like 'poetry' will retain its identity over time. But in the history of versification in English, and in all the languages that I'm familiar with, the dominant practice of poetry has involved building upon the particular use made by the language of the speech apparatus. Phonological studies over the past thirty years have shown a much closer link than had been suspected between the traditional forms of English verse and the complex rules that govern English pronunciation; it's appropriate that this work goes under the name 'metrical phonology'.[19] To the extent that verse rhythm has a natural or biological origin, it is in the ways I have sketched; there's no need for the misty speculation about biology that mars some discussions of metre, such as the introduction to an anthology of contemporary American verse in traditional forms, *Strong Measures*, edited by Dacey and Jauss, where we are told once more that the iamb is the rhythm of the heartbeat, and that the pentameter is favoured because the heart beats, on average, five times to a breath (5).

The rhythms of English poetry are perhaps more alive today than they have been for a long time. Anyone who has listened to the handling of language by a rap artist will know that it involves a complex and original harnessing of those rhythmic properties of English that I've been discussing, particularly remarkable in that rhythm takes centre stage to the virtual exclusion of melody and harmony; while other areas of popular music show a similar sophistication in dealing with the relationship between the irregularities of speech and the regularities of musical metres. The video explosion has accustomed viewers to a complex interaction of visual and aural rhythms. Children still learn the characteristic rhythms of their language at an early stage, and can respond to patterns of beats and offbeats as sensitively as the most advanced student of prosody. But there's a huge divide between, on the one hand, the skilful deployment and subtle appreciation of rhythm to be found in many areas of popular music and home-grown linguistic play and, on the other, the feeble attention now given to rhythmic matters in the academic study of literature. One cause

---

[19] See, for example, Hayes, *Metrical Stress Theory*; and Hogg and McCully, *Metrical Phonology*.

of this enfeeblement has been the rise of non-metrical verse in the twentieth century, with its associated rhetoric of freedom from ancient bondage—it's typical that no less a work than the *Oxford Companion to Literature* in its 1985 revision, edited by Margaret Drabble, should end its article on 'metre' with this single-sentence paragraph: 'Verse in the 20th Cent. has largely escaped the straitjacket of traditional metrics' (644).

We're also in a phase in the history of literary studies—perhaps near the end of this phase, as I suggested in Chapter 1—dominated by *content*: literature is valued for its political efficacy, its ethical significance, its historical illumination. A critical stance which attempts to do justice to the distinctiveness of the 'literary' in our culture (a highly complex question which can hardly be said to be resolved) is regarded by many as irresponsible, even if, like deconstruction, it's capable of posing the most difficult historical and political questions about literature without losing sight of the fact that a literary text is never simply a historical document or a political tract. Another reason for the dwindling attention to rhythm is the decline in memorization as an exercise and an art; to know poems by heart now smacks of a discredited pedagogy, but even if it emphasizes the mechanical learning of form at the expense of deep familiarity with content, it's an unrivalled way of becoming intimate with the variety of rhythms and metres into which one's language can be moulded.[20] Notwithstanding the increasing popularity of poetry as an art of the spoken word, reading aloud is, I would guess, much less common now than fifty years ago, and poetry may be gradually becoming a largely visual art. If this does occur, the irony will be that this has come about at a time when the easy availability of recordings and recording devices has given the human voice a cultural centrality it hasn't had since printing became the dominant representation of language.[21] Whether English poetry as an art of the voice, and, through the voice, the body, is rejuvenated by influences from other cultural forms, and from other cultures, or dwindles to a diversion or scholarly pastime of the very few while newer cultural practices thrive, there can be little doubt that rhythm will continue to play a vital part in that realm of social and cultural experience in which human beings exploit the inseparability of formal urgings from their most insistent concerns and durable pleasures.

---

[20] As I write this, in 2012, the British government has announced proposals for a revised syllabus for primary education which includes the memorization of poetry. Whether this marks a genuine return to learning poems by heart remains to be seen.

[21] See Durant, 'The Concept of Secondary Orality'.

6

Rhythm and Interpretation

The Iambic Pentameter

I

In a pair of essays whose very titles played a part in the achievement of a certain notoriety, 'What Is Stylistics and Why Are They Saying Such Terrible Things About It?', first published in 1973, and 'What Is Stylistics and Why Are They Saying Such Terrible Things About It? Part II', first published in 1980, Stanley Fish assailed the practitioners of a stylistic criticism which sought to ground interpretative and evaluative commentary in objective linguistic analysis.[1] Though Fish's argument shifted somewhat between the two essays, the aim of the onslaught in each case was the same: to show that any claim of objectivity in stylistic commentary is spurious, because what is presented in the guise of a neutral description is necessarily already informed by an interpretation. This has to be the case, Fish argues, since there is a multitude of possible relations between formal properties and meanings, and these can be limited only through the operation of such a prior interpretative act. Fish's summary, in the second of these essays, of the two-stage procedure of stylistic analysis and the difficulties it produces for the analyst will have to serve as a token of the more elaborately presented case:

First, formal features and patterns are discovered by the application of some descriptive apparatus, and then they are found to be expressive of, or to reflect or mime, a meaning or a content which stands apart from them and which could have been expressed (or reflected or mimed) by some other pattern, or which could have been packaged in formal patterns that did not reflect it at all, but merely presented it.... It is here at the heart of stylistics that one feels the contradictory pull of two demands. Only if forms are separable from the meanings they encase and adorn can there be said to be a choice between them, and a question for stylistics to answer (what is the relationship between this form and that

---

[1] The essays were reprinted in Fish's *Is There a Text in This Class?* as chapters 2 and 10.

meaning?). But only if the relationship of the form to the meaning can be shown to be necessary (indeed inevitable) will its demonstration escape the charge of being arbitrary, of being capable of assertion in any number of directions. (*Is There a Text*, 248–9)

The study of the rhythmic features of poetry is as susceptible to this kind of attack as any formal and linguistic analysis of literary texts, and as someone who has brought into the world unasked a theory of English metre I feel obliged to submit my own stylistic apparatus to these questions. The issue is of importance in dealing with poetic texts of any period, but the sixteenth century, as the period in which the major metrical forms of Modern English were established, offers particularly interesting scope for discussion. What I wish to do is to offer a possible metrical analysis of a single Renaissance sonnet, and then comment on that analysis in the light of the Fishian critique.

II

When Edmund Spenser was engaged on the sonnets to be published in 1595 as *Amoretti* he had already written thousands—perhaps tens of thousands—of English iambic pentameters; we can take it, then, that these poems are the product of a mind and ear completely at home with this metrical form, and that it is fair to regard them as representative of the assured centrality of accentual-syllabic metre in the later English Renaissance. I have chosen to look at Sonnet viii, addressed, as becomes evident in line 3 through a rhetorical denial, to the beloved's eyes:

> More than most fair, full of the living fire,
> Kindled above unto the Maker near:
> No eyes but joys, in which all powers conspire,
> That to the world nought else be counted dear.   4
> Through your bright beams doth not the blinded guest
> Shoot out his darts to base affections wound:
> But angels come to lead frail minds to rest
> In chaste desires on heavenly beauty bound.   8
> You frame my thoughts and fashion me within,
> You stop my tongue, and teach my heart to speak,
> You calm the storm that passion did begin,
> Strong through your cause, but by your virtue weak.   12
> Dark is the world, where your light shined never;
> Well is he born, that may behold you ever.[2]

---

[2] *Shorter Poems*, 605–6. I have modernized the spelling.

The rhythmic shape of this poem is easily perceived as a repeated fivefold alternation of strong and weak pulses—beats and offbeats—per line; any native speaker of English familiar with the verse tradition will be able to bring this out by an exaggerated recitation, most easily in the case of lines like 10 and 11:

> You **frame** my **thoughts** and **fashion** me **within**,
> You **stop** my **tongue**, and **teach** my **heart** to **speak**.

Insofar as lines like these represent a norm, it can be seen that the reader's expectation will be for an initial weak pulse or offbeat, and a final strong pulse or beat; and for each beat or offbeat to be realized by one syllable. In such a chanted reading, it is clear that the rhythmic Gestalt being perceived is, in part at least, a temporal one: the beats come out at what are perceived as equal intervals in time. In a normal reading, this equal-timing, or isochrony, need not be manifested, but for a line to be called metrical (or regularly rhythmical) it may not move too far away from it.[3]

Just how far lines may move from the paradigmatically regular alternation of pulses is the central issue in any English metrical theory. In *The Rhythms of English Poetry* I tried to formulate a set of simple rules which specify the major limitations which the exigencies of metrical form place upon the free composition of English sentences or word-strings, though I would always insist that the number of factors operating in any specific metrical context is such that definitive rules are impossible. A rule, in this sense, is simply a statement of a regularity observable in the work of a number of poets; thus it is a rule that the Shakespearian sonnet (of which this is an example) ends with a couplet. There is no single way of representing these regularities: one can try to capture in fine detail all possible variants, or one can aim at generalizations which omit a certain amount of detail but which capture what many different metrical examples have in common; one can integrate one's formalizations closely with those of phonology, or one can attempt to devise symbols that are immediately accessible to those without any linguistic training. Linguists engaged in the study of metre are often aspiring to a universal statement that will apply to all metres in all languages, and are less interested in the singularity of individual poems or poetic traditions. My main aim is to enhance the reader's understanding, and therefore enjoyment, of this dimension of particular poems, without assuming a knowledge of phonology or phonetics. What follows is a set of rules and conditions which state the basic features of the iambic pentameter as it is used by Spenser in the *Amoretti*, which is to say as it is used by most poets from Chaucer to the present

---

[3] See Chapter 5 section II on the argument that English is a 'stress-timed' language.

(though with variations from period to period in degrees of strictness). These rules and conditions are also observed by poets employing strict accentual-syllabic verse in other line-lengths, with the appropriate modifications being made to the first rule governing the number of beats and the way the lines may begin and end.

1. *The line has five beats and begins with an offbeat; there is an optional offbeat at the end.*

If the line doesn't have five beats, as determined by the conventions of the form, it is in another metre. It is part of the definition of a beat that it is separated from an adjacent beat by an offbeat. One eventuality the rules of the iambic pentameter are designed to prevent is a slide into a four-beat metre, which, because of its insistent rhythm, is always lying in wait as a possibility—which is another way of saying poets writing pentameter verse down the centuries have intuitively avoided arrangements of stressed and unstressed syllables which encourage the emergence of a four-beat rhythm. This is not to say that verse which is basically pentameter can't vary the metre with shorter or longer lines: the Spenserian stanza, for instance, ends with a six-beat line.

2. *A stressed syllable may realize a beat.*

This is the fundamental rule of English metrical practice, associating stresses with rhythmical beats (an association which has a straightforward phonological and physiological basis). But note that a stressed syllable does not *have* to realize a beat.

3. *One or two unstressed syllables may realize an offbeat.*

Offbeats, as weaker rhythmical pulses which exist only in relation to beats, are naturally associated with unstressed syllables (let's call them non-stresses); but whereas the single burst of energy that constitutes a beat cannot be divided between syllables, the slack period that constitutes an offbeat can be shared between two syllables. Such an offbeat is termed a 'double offbeat'. Again, unstressed syllables do not necessarily realize beats.

4. *An unstressed syllable may realize a beat when it occurs between two unstressed syllables, or at the end of a line after an unstressed syllable. This is termed* promotion.

5. *A stressed syllable may realize an offbeat when it occurs between two stressed syllables, or at the beginning of a line before a stressed syllable. This is termed* demotion.

These two rules specify the conditions under which the opposite relation to that specified in the first two rules may hold between beats and offbeats on the one hand and stresses and non-stresses on the other. A sequence of three stresses will thus usually produce the rhythm beat–offbeat–beat, while a sequence of three non-stresses will usually produce the rhythm offbeat–beat–offbeat. A non-stress at the end of a line that occurs after another non-stress may function as a beat; while an initial stress before a stress may function as an offbeat. The two rules are clearly parallel, and are a formalization of the fundamental tendency towards an alternating rhythm in spoken English. Note that they are not prescriptions for a certain kind of reading, therefore; they represent the perceptions of a native English speaker in responding to the underlying rhythmic tendencies of the language. (Occasionally in five-beat verse one of two syllables in a double offbeat may carry a degree of stress, and thus be demoted, a variation that produces some disruption to the alternating rhythm—Pope's lines quoted in the previous chapter contain examples. In the following chapter, we shall examine a four-beat metrical form in which the restriction doesn't apply.)

6. *An unrealized offbeat may occur in a pause between two successive stressed syllables.*

Unrealized offbeats in the iambic pentameter are places where we feel a slack interval between two stressed beats, though there is no syllable to give vocal representation to that interval. Sometimes the stresses are divided by a syntactic break, usually signalled by punctuation; in which case the unrealized offbeat coincides with a naturally occurring pause and the regular rhythm of the line recovers quite quickly from this disruption. This is a *virtual* offbeat. If there is no such break, the offbeat is less strongly felt, and the disruption to the line is greater. In this case, we have an *implied offbeat*, several examples of which we noted in Milne's 'Disobedience' in the previous chapter.[4] Because unrealized offbeats constitute the most disruptive departure from the norm of alternation, they are strictly controlled: they occur only under certain metrical conditions, the first of three such conditions which govern the operation of the rules. These conditions also ensure that the line always contains ten syllables (or eleven in the case of a feminine ending), or, putting it another way, in order to preserve the syllabic count poets have limited the use of unrealized offbeats to situations in which the absence of a syllable is made up for elsewhere in the line.

The three conditions are as follows:
Condition 1. An unrealized offbeat may occur only when it is immediately preceded or followed by a non-final double offbeat.

---

[4] See also the discussion of unrealized offbeats in the previous chapter. As I noted earlier, in *The Rhythms of English Poetry* I didn't distinguish between these two types of unrealized offbeat, but I have since come to think that they have such a different rhythmic feel to them that they ought to be kept separate—though it would be more accurate to say that there is a gradation from one type to the other.

The missing syllable is thus compensated for by an extra syllable in a neighbouring offbeat.

Condition 2. The initial offbeat may be omitted only if the first beat is immediately followed by a double offbeat.

This is the familiar phenomenon of 'initial inversion', very common in iambic verse throughout its long existence. It is so called because it is the result, in effect, of a switching of the first two syllables, so the pattern non-stress–stress becomes stress–non-stress, giving rise, of course, to a double offbeat.

Condition 3. A double offbeat may occur only in observance of Conditions 1 or 2.

In the strictest forms of iambic verse, that is, double offbeats occur only in the rhythmic formations already handled by the first two conditions; it is necessary to state this as a specific condition since in freer forms of the metre *any* offbeat may be realized by two unstressed syllables.

All the rules and conditions function as a kind of filter to allow only certain sequences of words out of all the possible sequences in the English language to count as realizations of the basic iambic pentameter metrical pattern. A scansion of a line will indicate by which rules this metrical pattern is realized in the actual words of the line.

III

Turning now to Spenser's sonnet, we can observe the operation of these rules as they relate the stress-contour of the words as they would be spoken to the metrical pattern.[5] If at any point it proved impossible to do, we would have to conclude that at that point the line was unmetrical, since the rules encapsulate all the ways in which the metre, with its five beats, may emerge from the normal pronunciation of the line. (If, on the other hand, such a line sounded acceptably metrical to someone familiar with the language and the verse tradition, this would of course constitute a challenge to the metrical theory I've outlined.)

---

[5] Of course, we can't be certain how Spenser or his contemporaries would have spoken lines of verse, though what evidence there is suggests a quite strong emphasis on the metrical pattern. (See, for example, John Thompson, *The Founding of English Metre*.) However, my starting point is the fact that we find Spenser's poetry rhythmically successful *now*; it seems likely, therefore, that there are significant similarities between our way of reading and that of the sixteenth century. My discussion does not depend on the existence of such similarities; it is not an exercise in historical reconstruction.

Promotion occurs, for example, in line 4, where the first three monosyllabic words can be read as unstressed syllables without any damage to the metre. (I use the symbols explained in the previous chapter: lower case o indicates an offbeat, and a promoted syllable is shown by lower case b.)

> That to the world nought else be counted dear.
>   o   b   o

There is no implication here that the syllable in question need be pronounced with additional emphasis; to do so would move the reading towards a chant, which is not currently in fashion as a mode of poetry recitation (though it might once have been and perhaps one day will be again).

Demotion is less common, but still a frequent occurrence in duple verse; it has the effect of slowing the line down, whereas promotion speeds it up. Line 7 contains a clear example, indicated by the upper case O occurring between beats realized by stressed syllables:

> But angels come to lead frail minds to rest
>   B   O   B

'Frail' may be pronounced with its usual weight, but will function in the sequence as if it were an unstressed syllable, and will not destroy the experience of rhythmic alternation.

A *virtual offbeat* occurs in the first line, between the beats on 'fair' and 'full', the break between the two phrases that make up the line—signalled by a comma—allowing a temporal space for the unrealized offbeat to be felt. It is shown by square brackets around the o:

> More than most fair, full of the living fire,
>   B[o]B

This sequence satisfies the *unrealized offbeat condition* by coming immediately before a double offbeat (-o-), 'of the':

> More than most fair, full of the living fire,
>   B[o]B -o-

Taken together, the implied and double offbeats exhibit another form of inversion, highly typical of the tradition of iambic verse: the regular sequence of *stress–non-stress–stress–non-stress* is replaced by *stress–stress–non-stress–non-stress*, the emphasis on the middle two syllables being switched. Notice how the second part of this rhythmic figure produces a pattern that is the same as that of inversion at the start of a line. We may call this type of inversion *falling*, as it moves from stressed to unstressed syllables.

The inversion may occur the other way round, as in line 3 (at least in one possible reading):

No eyes but joys, in which all powers conspire,
        -o-   B ô B

Here the double offbeat of 'in which' is followed by the successive beats of 'all powers', which are separated only by an implied offbeat (ô); this is rising inversion.[6] (We can assume the common monosyllabic pronunciation of 'powers', since the metre requires it. A similar contraction—a regular one in Elizabethan English—happens with 'heavenly' in line 8.)

The operation of the *initial inversion condition* is obvious in the first two and the last three lines of the poem:[7]

More than most fair, full of the living fire,
B   -o-   B
Kindled above unto the Maker near:
B -o- B
Strong through your cause, but by your virtue weak.
B   -o-   B
Dark is the world, where your light shined never;
B -o- B
Well is he born, that may behold you ever.
B -o- B

Here the expected initial optional offbeat does not occur, producing something of a hiatus between the lines, but this absence is compensated for by the double offbeat that follows in each case. It's a very common alternative opening to the iambic line, and it produces rhythmic tension only if one of the syllables of the offbeat takes some degree of stress. This type of tension occurs in the opening of the poem, where the word 'most' seems to demand a degree of semantic emphasis not quite consistent with its metrical position. (Compare the statement 'Jane is most fair', in which 'most' is a conventional modifier and carries little weight; in Spenser's poem, however, there is a hyperbolic contrast between 'More' and 'most'.) The result is that the poem opens with a kind of suspended rhythm; true alternating regularity is achieved only with 'living fire'.[8] It's almost as if

---

[6] An alternative reading would refrain from stressing 'all', thus allowing 'which' to take a beat through promotion (and also perhaps a slight emphasis). Although this makes for a more regular line, it fails to acknowledge the importance of the adjective to the sense of the line.

[7] Line 6 could be read with initial inversion—'**Shoot** out his **darts**'—or without—'Shoot **out** his **darts**'.

[8] The reader may also wish to give some emphasis to the word 'your' in the opening of line 12, which would have the same effect, but the contrast between 'cause' and 'virtue' suggests that the two occurrences of the personal pronoun have little stress.

the poem starts again on 'full', this time as a very normal pentameter beginning with an inversion.

There are other syllables which allow the reader some choice, but where the rhythmicality of the line is not affected. Thus the initial 'You' of lines 9 to 11 could be unemphatic, giving a normal offbeat, or emphatic, giving an offbeat by demotion—a perfectly ordinary way of beginning an iambic line:

> You frame my thoughts and fashion me within;
> o   B
> O   B

As with many of these metrical variations, the framework established by the metre allows for a variety of pronunciations, all of which are acceptable. At other points, alternative readings produce alternative scansions, as in the opening of line 5: one can emphasize 'your' (as opposed to all other eyes), to produce three stresses in a row and the demotion of 'bright', or one can throw the emphasis onto 'bright' to yield a rising inversion, as shown in the lower scansion:

> Through your bright beams doth not the blinded guest
> o   B   O   B
> -o-   B   ô B

It might have been noted that every line has some degree of a syntactic break after two beats, marked by punctuation in lines 1, 3, 8, 9, 10, 12, 13, and 14, and implied in the others. (Elizabethan treatises on prosody commonly recommend a caesura in this position.) In some cases, the disposition of stresses produces a sprung pentameter, examples of which we also observed in Pope's verse in Chapter 5. This way of organizing the line associates it with the older and in some sense more fundamental four-beat line; for example, it wouldn't be too distorting to read line 9 as follows (the occurrence of the rare triple offbeat is shown by -o-):

> You frame my thoughts and fashion me within
> o   B   o   B   o   B -o-   B

However, it's important not to exaggerate the assimilation of the five-beat line to the four-beat line, as some commentators have done; this rhythmic pattern doesn't turn the former into the latter, it merely endues the pentameter with a movement that draws on the liveliness of the four-beat form, encouraging the reader to speed up in reading the second part of the line.[9] In another version of the two–three division, it is the fourth and fifth beats which are stronger, creating a balanced line:

---

[9] In Chapter 7, we shall consider the English Sapphic, which takes this process a step further. See Chapter 7 section V.

Strong through your cause, but by your virtue weak.
B   -o-   B   -o-   B o   B

Line 10, although divided like all the others after the second beat, doesn't allow any of the final three beats to be weakened; the result is a more deliberate enunciation of a line about an unusual kind of enunciation:

You stop my tongue, and teach my heart to speak,
o   B   o B   o   B   o B   o   B

Each of the three quatrains has a different structural character, the first one consisting of four clearly separate lines grouped as two pairs, the second one of two pairs of lines each unified by a run-on in the middle, and the third one reverting to separate lines but now without a grouping in pairs. Spenser's unusual use of the Shakespearian form emphasizes the separateness of the quatrains by giving them completely different rhymes, and the closing couplet is marked off by its feminine endings.

IV

The framework of rules I have sketched thus allows us to produce a scansion of the poem showing the place of every syllable in realizing the iambic pentameter pattern. What, then, of the poem's content, which I have deliberately refrained from commenting on so far? The question I wish to ask, going back to Stanley Fish's challenge to stylistic analysis, is: are there grounds for saying that this scansion is objective, revealing what is actually there in the text quite apart from any interpretation or evaluation one might wish to give the poem?

The answer depends on what one means by 'objectivity' in this context. That the poem has fourteen lines is an objective fact only insofar as the meaning of the term 'line' is agreed by the community of readers engaged in the discussion. (If we were discussing Elizabethan fourteeners, often set out by Elizabethan printers as groups of eight and six syllables, the question could become a vexed one.) The same is true of any of the categories in our description, many of which would certainly have made no sense to Spenser, and some of which perhaps don't make much sense to the reader.[10]

---

[10] Some commentators make a great deal of the fact that modern attempts to develop a more accurate account of the working of rhythm and metre would not have made sense to the poets themselves, as if the writing of verse was an entirely conscious, mechanical application of a set of rules. By the same logic, one could discuss early uses of syntax only in the muddled terms of the grammars of the time, and would be barred from referring to the use of free indirect discourse in *Emma* or the relation between story and discourse in *Paradise Lost*.

Spenser's approval is neither here nor there, but if I can't convince my readers that these are real features of the poem, I shall have to go back to the drawing-board, since it's the community of readers who are the arbiters of what counts as 'objective'. My hope as an analyst of the poem, then, is not to produce an objective description in the strictest sense of the word, but a description for which I can command assent among the community I wish to address. One of the most effective ways in which I can secure agreement—especially from an audience whose interest is primarily literary—is to show that this way of describing the text actually works in the business of interpretation and evaluation.

There is a further reason why my account is not, and could not be, an objective description. Even if I were to confine myself to those categories upon which I know all those I am addressing would agree, I would come up against the question of selection. There are hundreds of objective facts about the poem's phonetic and graphic structure which I could mention, and which we would all agree are really there: I could count the phonemes in each word, I could classify them according to articulatory or acoustic categories, I could count the letters and tabulate them according to their position in the alphabet or with respect to the line, I could examine word beginnings and endings, the occurrence of diphthongs or consonant-clusters, the relation of parts of speech to phonological properties, etc., etc. My scansion, that is, makes the claim that the categories I have chosen to single out from all the possible categories, and the features of the poem to which these chosen categories refer (or more accurately, perhaps, which they bring into being), are the significant ones; and again, I need to persuade my audience that this is indeed the case, which I can only do by showing their importance in the task for which they are being used.

The particular task that I am concerned with is the enhancement of our understanding of the role of formal features—and metrical features in particular—in the reading, understanding, and enjoyment of poetry, in this case Renaissance poetry. There are many other tasks which a metrical theory might be called upon to perform, and in these cases a different metrical apparatus, singling out other categories of language, might be appropriate. Thus a scansion in terms of classical feet might give us something closer to Spenser's own sense of his metrical practice and possibly something closer to the analysis which readers trained in classical prosody would automatically apply as they read; such a scansion would not, however, reflect the rhythmic contours perceived most directly by native English speakers who have not had a training of this kind but who do have a reasonable knowledge of English verse. (As I've already remarked, this is not to argue that the way we read the poem today need bear no relation to the way Spenser read it; on the contrary, I take it that the existence of shared and delicate discriminations with regard to metrical effects—usually in the absence of an adequate theory—is allowable as evidence of a large degree of continuity between Spenser's time and our own in this aspect of spoken English and its rhythmic potential.)

It would appear, then, that there is no escaping the conclusion reached by Fish (and, of course, by many others): the description of a literary text, even an apparently neutral scansion, is inevitably predicated upon, and at every point involved with, the work of interpretation. What I have been attempting to show is that this doesn't invalidate the business of description, which can be carried out in a careful and empirically grounded manner. It does mean, though, that the metrical analyst, and any other stylistic commentator, needs to be aware of the context in which the analysis is made: the interpretative stance it serves, the critical assumptions it underwrites, the tasks which it is designed to further. These in turn relate to wider ideological assumptions about literature and the literary and educational institutions which constitute and promulgate it. The prosodist may appear to be calling the tune, but it is always worth asking who is paying the piper.

V

Our scansion claims to be useful in making certain kinds of statement about the poem, and, to the degree to which a single Spenserian sonnet can be regarded as representative of its time, about Renaissance poetry. One thing it shows clearly is that the full resources of accentual-syllabic metre were available to Spenser in the early 1590s, making it possible for him to write a poem that retains from start to finish its hold on a rhythmic base while allowing considerable variety in rhythmic forms. The same could, of course, be demonstrated for numerous Elizabethan poets, many of them distinctly less successful than Spenser. To possess these resources, then, was not to be a remarkable poet; just as many minor composers possessed the musical resources necessary to produce a reasonably polished song or consort-piece. Could one make a case that the potential of the metre—then not more than a few decades old (if we assume that Chaucerian practice was a closed book to the Elizabethans)—has been exploited with particular brilliance in this poem? Do the metrical features we have identified reinforce a particular interpretation? And what would be the theoretical consequences of making such claims on the basis of this metrical description?

Such a case might go like this. The poem sets out to counter the conventional notion (which clearly has real psychosexual correlates) that the eyes of a beautiful woman are responsible for the arousal of sexual desire in the male. The convention is that the woman's eyes send out beams which penetrate, via the man's eyes, to the heart, the seat of the affections and, by implication, the erotic instincts. In the Neoplatonic world of Spenser's fictional courtship, the lady's eyes do have a powerful effect, but it works on the mind and not the emotions, and it is a calming rather than an energizing effect, directing the lover to heavenly good and not earthly satisfaction. The poem's rhetoric of praise is therefore aimed at a quite different end from that of most Renaissance poems lauding a beloved's beauty, and its rhythmic characteristics are part of its strong counter-stand with respect to this tradition.

Before continuing, let me set out the poem with scansion symbols. (In doing so, of course, I am reflecting a particular way of reading the poem; this is one of the functions of scansion.)

> More than most fair, full of the living fire,
> B   -o-   B [o]B -o- Bo   B
> Kindled above unto the Maker near:
> B   -o- B o b o Bo   B
> No eyes but joys, in which all powers conspire,
> o B o B   -o-   BôB   o B
> That to the world nought else be counted dear.   4
> o b o B   o   B   o B o B
> Through your bright beams doth not the blinded guest
> o   B   O   B   o   B o Bo   B
> Shoot out his darts to base affections wound:
> O B o B   o B o Bo   B
> But angels come to lead frail minds to rest
> o Bo B   o B   O B   o B
> In chaste desires on heavenly beauty bound.   8
> o B   oB   o B   o Bo B
> You frame my thoughts and fashion me within;
> o B   o B   o Bo   b o B
> You stop my tongue, and teach my heart to speak;
> o B   oB   o   B   o B   o B
> You calm the storm that passion did begin,
> o B   o B   o Bo   b o B
> Strong through your cause, but by your virtue weak. 12
> B   -o-   B   o b o   Bo   B
> Dark is the world, where your light shined never;
> B -o-   B   o   B   O   Bo   Bo
> Well is he born, that may behold you ever.
> B -o-   B   o   b   oB   o Bo

The first and third quatrains and the final couplet are particularly firm in their metrical structure, a fact which contributes to their air of assurance and calm; this is due in part to the balance achieved, as already discussed, by the pause after the fourth syllable in many of these lines, a balance reinforced by patterns of alliteration (*fair–full, frame–fashion, stop–speak, tongue–teach, born–behold*). To the ear familiar with earlier alliterative Anglo-Saxon and English verse, these phonic repetitions on either side of a central division evoke echoes of an older poetic tradition. The balance is also, of course, semantic, whether between similar terms (*frame–fashion*) or contraries (*tongue–heart, strong–weak, dark–light*), and here the echoes we hear come from the Petrarchan tradition of carefully patterned love poetry, often proceeding by oppositions. We have already noted that the line-endings of the first quatrain reinforce the metrical hierarchy of line, pair of lines, and pair of pairs of lines, and the rhymes weld the whole unit into one. Lines 3 and 4 in fact follow the rhythmic structure of lines 1 and 2 very closely: a metrically complex line with a clear break after the fourth syllable followed by a much simpler line with a less marked break. Turning to the third quatrain, we may observe that lines 9–11, a catalogue of virtuous effects, are all very similar in phonetic structure; we might note in particular that 9 and 11 do not merely rhyme but echo at every point— the four stressed words are *frame/calm, thoughts/storm, fashion/passion,* and *within/begin*, and in both cases the fourth beat is achieved by promotion of an unstressed syllable. Line 12 comes as a secure culmination of this series, with its chiasmic structure producing a strong beginning and ending, and its metrical balance produced by the initial inversion and the promotion in the second half, yielding, as we have seen, something close to a four-beat line:

> Strong through your cause, but by your virtue weak.
> B   -o-   B   o   b o   B o   B

(The line means, presumably, 'You cause my passion to be strong, but at the same time your virtue weakens it'.)

In contrast to these two quatrains, the second quatrain has two run-on lines (the only two in the poem), two sequences where alternative scansions are possible, and only slight medial pauses which the reader is likely to ignore. The firm tread is re-achieved only in its fourth line, one of the most regular lines in the poem, and one in which the medial pause after the fourth syllable once more provides a stable balance. It is as if the poem's serenity is troubled by the conventional account in lines 5–7 of the arousing power of the mistress's eyes, and only recovers when the Neoplatonic alternative has been firmly stated in line 8, the run-on that precedes it functioning to lead the reader away from that disturbing notion to the calm pleasure of chaste desires on heavenly beauty bound. (We might note that the first run-on takes us immediately into an initial stress, creating a slight jolt whether we read it as an initial inversion or as an instance of demotion; whereas the second is followed by an offbeat, allowing a smoother transition between the lines.)

Another point of interest is the metrical positioning of the second person pronoun, which stands for the eyes, and by synecdoche for the beloved's beauty and the beloved herself. Each time it occurs, it is susceptible of a reading which gives it a strong emphasis or one which plays it down. In some cases this allows alternative scansions, as in lines 5, 12, and 13, or the gradations made possible by the phenomenon of indefinite stress, as in the openings of lines 9–11 and the penultimate word of 14. In other words the printed poem leaves open the degree to which an emphasis is put on the uniqueness of the woman being addressed—'it is you and you alone who have this effect, your beauty and your virtue which operate so powerfully'—or on the qualities themselves and their beneficent operation, thus allowing the particular woman to stand for all manifestations of heavenly beauty and heavenly good. The poem is, one might say, about this openness, about the possibility that a single poem can be both a love poem addressed to a particular woman and a poem in praise of the timeless and universal qualities of the divinity.

VI

Of the many possible responses to this analysis, I want to consider two. One response might be to find it persuasive in demonstrating that the expressive potential of the iambic pentameter has been fully exploited, that the rhythmic pattern supports and reinforces what the poem is doing, and leaves options open where this contributes to the overall effect. The analysis therefore either serves to confirm a previous admiration for the poem, or to instil a new admiration for it. The further implication of this response is that the same method of analysis when applied to a range of poems would be able to make distinctions between those that handle metre successfully and those that handle it clumsily or without any direct reinforcement or qualification of the meaning.

The second response is to argue that what has been demonstrated is that metrical analysis has available to it such massive resources that it makes it possible for a mildly interesting poem composed with average skill to be discussed as if it were a complex masterpiece. Once we have abandoned the notion that what we are doing is producing an objective description of the poem's metrical structure by means of an automatically applicable methodology, it is difficult to counter the suspicion that the metrical analysis is wholly after the fact, and that any interpretation and

evaluation (negative or positive) could be supported by the ingenious ma-
nipulation of the features identified by metrical description. My own pro-
cedures in this case don't offer much reassurance. Stylistic analysis usually
begins with the identification of a text which the analyst finds particularly
rewarding and for which he or she already has a clearly established reading
(whether that be a commonly accepted one, or one the commentator
wishes to argue for by means of the analysis). In the case of the poem
under discussion, it was chosen almost at random, and approached as an
exercise in metrical analysis, to see what kind of case could be made for it
(and I could have extended the analysis much further). If, like Stephen
Dedalus presenting his account of Hamlet, I were to be asked if I believe
my own analysis, I might have to answer, like him, in the negative. And
yet—and this is an interesting feature of detailed stylistic commentary—I
find that in carrying out the exercise, I have come close to persuading
myself of the validity of my case.

One way of putting this critique would be to argue that the technique
I have been using to relate metrical features to aspects of meaning is too
powerful to achieve valid results. Just as a linguist may be in search of the
weakest theory which will account for the empirical facts of language,[11] so
a theory of literary language should be just strong enough to explain what
is certainly the case in a literary text, but too weak to generate explana-
tions of what is only doubtfully the case. If all the metrical detail which
my apparatus captures is assumed to have semantic potential, and to be
capable of relating to meaning in a number of ways, I could probably
relate a given metrical texture to just about any semantic content what-
ever—after all, if sound and meaning can't be made to cohere I can always
claim that they operate in fruitful counterpoint or ironic interplay. We
need some way of specifying what metrical features really do have seman-
tic force in contributing to an interpretation, but our dilemma is this: if
what we identify as formally significant in the poem is only perceived to
be such by virtue of prior interpretative decisions, it cannot be regarded
as giving rise to a particular interpretation, nor can it be adduced as evi-
dence for a particular interpretation.

A possible way out of such circularity would be to ask whether readers
found that being exposed to this analysis changed their views as to the
meaning and worth of the poem; this would mean that the analysis had a
real purchase on the experience of reading, interpreting, and enjoying the
poem. Now stylistics, as an attempt at an objective, descriptive account of
the workings of language in literature, would be loath to make use of such

---

[11] See, for example, Noam Chomsky's comment, regarding syntactic theory, that 'we
should like to accept the least "powerful" theory that is empirically adequate' (*Aspects*, 62).

evidence; like structuralism, it claims to observe and explain how literature achieves its effects, and not to enter the arena in an attempt to change those effects. But if it is accepted that description and interpretation necessarily and continually interpenetrate, the project of detached observation is not feasible, and stylistics might as well accept with good grace its role in the critical debate. However, the implication of this is that the quality of individual stylistic accounts will depend on the quality of the critical context in which they are assessed, rejected, modified, or accepted. Progress in the field of stylistics will depend not on the achievement of greater objectivity and a set of universally applicable algorithms relating stylistic features to meanings, but on the development of more subtle and scrupulous modes of argument and more rigorous methods of assessing the claims that are made. It seems to me that literary criticism has some way to go in terms of establishing such a context for its operations. With a satisfactory context of argumentative procedures, the problem of objectivity becomes less acute, since the categories and relations that are identified will be objective in the only sense possible in the field of literary study: they will be the result of widely shared, and properly grounded, assumptions about the nature and function of poetry. And if no such widespread agreement can be found, at least the bases for certain positions would be more explicit, and the reasons for disagreement clearer.

In place of my hypothetical analysis of *Amoretti* viii (which I am not disclaiming, but merely setting aside until better tools for judging it are available than at present), let me end with some suggestions about the demands we should make, upon ourselves and upon others, in our discussions of the contribution made by the formal features of a poem such as this one to its success or failure. (There are other possible uses for the analytical tools I have described, of course: one example would be stylistic comparisons between authors and periods, and the use of such comparative evidence for purposes of identification and dating. But my concern here is strictly with the use of metrical commentary as part of a critical and interpretative account of poetry.)

(1) We should make use of the best information available about the material of the poem, phonetic and graphic, remembering that this material is not simply the physical substance of the words but a perceived reality, necessarily changing according to changes in the position and mode of perception. The rhythms of English poetry are derived from the rhythms of English speech, and we are gradually learning more about the latter (some of the evidence in fact coming from poetry). Spenser's poem is written in early Modern English, so we need to bear in mind what is known about the sounds of that stage of the language—we need to know,

for instance, whether 'wound' and 'bound' rhymed for Spenser, since the effect of an imperfect rhyme at a point of such resounding assertiveness would constitute a major flaw. At the same time, unless our goal is a purely archaeological one, we need to address the question of the poem's sound now—we may feel that an imperfect rhyme is less jarring to the ear than an archaic pronunciation would be. (I have quoted the text in modernized spelling to avoid the archaic look that Spenser's poetry so often has, but the original text should be scrutinized too.)

(2) We should make use of what we know of the poetic criteria in operation at the time of composition—not because these must be made to override our own, but because we may find our pleasure and understanding enhanced by the achievement of a degree of empathy with earlier expectations and conventions. Puttenham's *Arte of English Poesie*, for example, will give a good idea of the pleasure that many in the period found in elaborate artifice, and this might help us to concentrate more on the formal patterns of Spenser's sonnet for their own sake instead of assuming that their only justification is as expressive devices. For instance, we might think of the formal structure of this sonnet as a kind of proto-sonata form which might be a source of pleasure and satisfaction irrespective of the content: a firmly stated exposition, presenting the paradigmatic form of the quatrain, then a quatrain of development, varying that form, and a quatrain of recapitulation, restating the basic form but with a greater sense of closure (a 3:1 structure rather than a 2:2 structure), and finally a brief coda to sign off with.

(3) We should distinguish as clearly as possible among different kinds of claim about the relation of sound and meaning. It may be that mimetic or onomatopoeic devices are the least important—they have a habit of becoming self-parody as soon as we notice them, and if we don't notice them we can't be sure they work at all. Is the contrast between the abruptness of the first part of line 10 and the greater expansiveness of the second part imitative of the sense?:

> You stop my tongue—and teach my heart to speak

Once I have drawn attention to this contrast, it may be difficult to ignore; but was it working subliminally—and perhaps more powerfully—all the time? Another type of semantic effect produced by rhythm is its range of affective functions—the representation of the sounds and rhythms of the human voice; as with onomatopoeia the scope here for ingenuity in critical commentary is almost limitless, and we need to develop strong controls as well as a healthy vein of scepticism. However, it seems legitimate to say that the firm metrical regularity of most of this sonnet contributes to its effect of confident assertion. Metrical form can also work associatively, by calling up echoes of other verse: clearly this poem's use of the sonnet form and of dualistically patterned language invites the reader to consider it in the light of the tradition of Petrarchan love poetry. A further function of metre is as a device for emphasis (or de-emphasis): the word 'Shoot', for instance, may be said to carry added disruptive force from its position as an initial stressed syllable after a run-on line. Rhythmic parallels can also establish or reinforce connections between different parts of the poem, as I suggested earlier with regard to the first and the third quatrains. And all this is in addition to the more general (and still mysterious) functions of metrical patterning which pervade all regular verse and provide a pleasure, and a mnemonic power, which is shared by readers and hearers of all degrees of sophistication.

(4) We should work by constant comparisons: one of the greatest weaknesses of my analysis of the Spenser sonnet is that it is isolated. My observations about the regular pause after the fourth syllable, for instance, would carry more weight if I were to add that this is not the norm in the *Amoretti*; further comparison with other Elizabethan poems, and with other examples from the tradition of iambic pentameter verse, would enable us to place this poem even more accurately. One can find in Sidney's *Astrophil and Stella*, for example, sonnets written about ten years earlier that present a view of the Neoplatonic scheme (and the role of the beloved's eyes) exactly opposed to Spenser's in *Amoretti* viii; and among the questions to be asked is whether Sidney's greater freedom of metrical variation (within exactly the same set of rules and conditions) contributes directly to the sequence's anti-platonic drive, a drive that places less value on harmony and more on energetic action, dramatizing the unreality of the Neoplatonic stance when challenged by the base affections so serenely dismissed by Spenser.

(5) We should follow through the implications of our claims about the relationship of metrical features and content. For instance, one possible procedure is to rewrite a phrase or line about which a stylistic point is being made to find out what difference it makes. Thus I can test my assertion about the effects of the smooth run-on from line 7 to line 8 by trying out an alternative:

> But angels come to lead frail minds to rest
> Chastely in thoughts on heavenly beauty bound.

This does seem to me to lack the appropriate smoothness of the original, though it would always be possible to make a claim about the emphasis given to 'Chastely' and its significance as a key-word in the poem (and the sequence). Negative comparisons with other poems can also be useful; are similar metrical devices characteristic of Elizabethan poems which we would regard as inferior? If we find that this is the case, we will have to revise our claim that they contribute directly to the success or otherwise of a poem.

(6) We should maintain a judiciously sceptical approach to all claims regarding the expressiveness of this or that metrical or stylistic feature, reminding ourselves constantly of the ease with which we can believe our own fictions, and, with a little rhetorical skill, persuade others to believe them. But, and let this be my last prescription, we should remember that Sidney and Spenser, and Donne and Shakespeare, did develop a new mastery of the rhythms of English, and the effects of that mastery remain real today; there is something there to study and to account for, and above all to enjoy, even if it persistently slips from our grasp, which may, after all, be a necessary and not a contingent fact about lasting art.

7

An Enduring Form

The English Dolnik

I

The first poem in unmodernized English in the widely used *Norton Anthology of English Poetry*[1] is a moving four-line lyric, dating from the thirteenth century, on the Crucifixion:

> Nou goth sonne under wode—
> Me reweth, Marie, thi faire rode.
> Nou goth sonne under tre—
> Me reweth, Marie, thi sone and the. (15)

Reading this aloud, one has to make a few decisions about pronunciation: presumably final -*e* was pronounced (or sung), and 'Marie' probably had an accent on the second syllable rather than the first (though the points I am about to make would still hold, *mutatis mutandis*, for a modern pronunciation).

How far do traditional methods of scansion help us with this poem's versification—methods enshrined, for instance, in the *Norton Anthology*'s essay on 'Versification' contributed by Jon Stallworthy? We need, first, to decide what type of metre it employs. Stallworthy is entirely representative of conventional prosodic pedagogues in listing four types: *Accentual*, *Accentual-syllabic*, *Syllabic*, and *Quantitative*. Although the four lines bear some relation to the stress-based, or accentual, metre of Old English verse, they have a very different rhythmic feel: they move easily and regularly, they seem like a single unit to the ear, and they suggest not the unpredictable variety of speech but the rhythmicality of song—though they clearly do not *need* music to be experienced as musical. If this is not 'accentual' verse, which of Stallworthy's other three types of regular metre does it

---

[1] I am referring to the fifth edition of the *Norton Anthology* (2005), edited by Ferguson, Salter, and Stallworthy.

match? We can rule out both syllabic and quantitative types, so all that is left is accentual-syllabic. Standard introductions to metre assert that the basic unit of accentual-syllabic metre is the foot, described by Stallworthy as 'a combination of two or three stressed and/or unstressed syllables' (2030), of which several varieties, with their Greek labels, are named. Lines of verse are then understood to be made up of differing numbers of these feet, and given identifying designations accordingly. Let us examine our poem by the light of this account, asking what are the 'regular units' out of which its metre is constructed.

The first line divides nicely into four trochaic feet, if both final *-e*'s are pronounced (I use / to indicate a stressed syllable and x to indicate an unstressed syllable):

| / x | / x| / x | / x |
Nou goth sonne under wode—

The second line, however, does not follow this pattern. If we once more choose to divide the line into feet that begin with stressed syllables, we have to ignore the first syllable and allow two extra unstressed syllables in the line, turning two of the 'trochees' into 'dactyls':

x| / x x| /x x| / x| / x |
Me reweth, Marie, thi faire rode.

Alternatively, we could revisit line 1, and treat the opening syllable as anomalous and the ending as duple or 'feminine', which gives us a series of three iambs:

/ | x / |x /| x /|x
Nou goth sonne under wode—

Then we could treat line two as basically iambic, but with two anapaestic substitutions and a feminine ending:

|x /|x x /|x x / |x / |x
Me reweth, Marie, thi faire rode.

The third line could equally well be a series of trochees without a final syllable, or a series of iambs without an initial syllable:

| / x | / x|/ x | /
/ | x / |x / |x /|
Nou goth sonne under tre—

The final line, too, allows no straightforward decision between a trochaic and an iambic scansion. If we are preferring trochees, we would scan the final line as having an additional syllable at the beginning, three dactyls, and a missing final syllable—no trochees at all, in fact:

```
x|  /  x      x|  /x    x|  /  x x    |  /
Me  reweth,  Marie,  thi  sone  and  the.
```

An 'iambic' scansion of the poem is a little better: it does at least allow a single iamb:

```
|  x  /  |x      x /|x    x /|x  x      /|
Me  reweth,  Marie,  thi  sone  and  the.[2]
```

How, then, can the verse form of this lyric be described in the terms of foot-prosody? As freely varying iambic metre? As free trochaic metre? As shifting between iambic and trochaic? The fact that we have to pose this question at all, and the implication of all the difficulties of scansion that we have observed, is that, rhythmically, this lyric is highly complex and full of uncertainties. To the ear, however, even to the ear responding to the poem some eight centuries after it was composed, it has an immediately recognizable rhythmic form that goes with a distinctive swing.[3] Expectations are set up by the first line with its four clear beats, and these expectations are fulfilled in the lines that follow, each again with four beats, to finish conclusively on the final syllable (as in the previous chapter, I use upper-case B to signal beats):

Nou goth sonne under wode—
B   B   B   B

Me reweth, Marie, thi faire rode.
B   B   B   B

Nou goth sonne under tre—
B   B   B   B

Me reweth, Marie, thi sone and the.
B   B   B   B

I don't believe there is only one correct metrical description of any line of verse; different types of description are good for different purposes. For

---

[2] One could bring the lines closer to iambic or trochaic metres by pronouncing 'Marie' with two syllables, with stress on either the first or the second syllable. Bringing them even closer by not pronouncing the final *-e* of 'sone', on the grounds that it is followed by a vowel, might seem tempting, but it would create a problem for lines 1 and 3, where dropping the second syllable of 'sonne' would result in a foot of only one syllable—although it is possible to argue that the double consonant indicates syllabic final *-e*. With all these adjustments, however, the poem is still not unambiguously 'iambic' or 'trochaic'.

[3] One test of what I am calling the 'immediate recognizability' of a verse form—and what I also refer to later as its catchiness or graspability—is choral reading, as described in Chapter 5: ask a group of native speakers to read the poem in question in chorus, without a leader, and note how quickly everyone settles into an agreed rhythm, and whether or not there is unanimity in the reading.

my own part, I have always had pedagogical effectiveness in mind in discussing metre and rhythm, rather than the search for human universals or the annotation of minute phonetic details. In writing about rhythm, my central question has constantly been: how can we talk about these matters in a way that makes sense to those who are not specialists?—which means, for me, how can we best tap into the considerable rhythmic capability of the ordinary man or woman, girl or boy, who heard nursery rhymes as a child, enjoys the occasional dance, and listens from time to time to popular music? It is on this basis that I want to explore the metrical form represented by this early poem, which, as we shall see, has a history that stretches from the Middle Ages to the present.

II

Rhythm may be understood as a continuous movement in time, given forward impetus by a series of alternations, whether these be strong pulse/ weak pulse, call/answer, tension/relaxation, or statement/counter-statement. These alternations can be organized into groups in many ways; in language, groups can be created by word-divisions, punctuation, syntactic structures, or lineation on the page—but not by the rhythm itself, unless the poem is sung or chanted (as in rap), in which case the music (or the background beat) will have an independent rhythmic shape operating in an interplay with the natural rhythms of the language. Strict accentual-syllabic verse in the English tradition, invented by Chaucer and re-invented in the mid-sixteenth century after changes in the language rendered Chaucer's verse irregular, encourages the perception of small groups of syllables, the 'feet' of classical prosody, though using this terminology (and the accompanying scansion symbols) may create the false impression that these 'feet' are separate units divided by perceptible barriers. Let us examine our example to see if it is helpful to approach it in terms of such discrete units.

'Now Go'th Sun under Wood' (as the *Norton Anthology* titles it) is in the most straightforward rhythm of all, common not just in the English tradition but in many other languages as well, especially in popular and children's verse: the organization by means of syntax, rhyme, and—at least as usually printed—lineation into stretches of syllables that induce a performance based on groups of four beats. (We examined an example in Chapter 6.) There are four of these groups of syllables in the poem, producing a pattern that is a staple of popular verse from the thirteenth century to the present, and one that has frequently been employed in literary verse as well. Its simplicity is based on its generation by means of rhythmic doubling: a beat is added to a beat to form a two-beat group ('**nou** goth **sonne**'); to this is added another two-beat group to form a four-beat group ('**nou** goth **sonne** **under** **wode**'); to this is added another four-beat group, producing the first two lines of the poem; and to this eight-beat group is added another eight-beat group (itself of course generated by the same process of doubling) to realize the full sixteen-beat structure. This process of doubling provides places for rhymes, for potential emphases, and for rhythmic breaks; and it makes the conclusion feel strongly conclusive. (The *aabb* rhyme-scheme in our example assists in producing this sense of an ending, but not as much as in the *abab* pattern which later became common for this form.) These rhythmic features are built into the aural organization of the metrical structure, and lineation on the page is only a secondary matter—we would still be able to hear them, and feel them, if the poem were written out as prose, or as two long, or eight short, lines.

Much verse written in the four-line four-beat form observes the strict syllable-count of accentual-syllable metre. However, as we have already seen in the case of Milne's 'Disobedience', a strong, regular rhythm can be set up by varying the number of syllables per line while keeping the number of beats constant. It is nursery rhymes that show most clearly how certain variations can actually strengthen the regularity of the rhythm rather than diminishing it. Examples in which the number of beats per line remains four but the number of syllables varies extensively come to mind very easily (as in the previous chapters, o indicates a single offbeat, -o- a double offbeat, [o] a virtual offbeat, and ô an implied offbeat):

> Tom, Tom, the piper's son
> B [o]B   o   B o   B
>
> Stole a pig and away did run.
> B o B   -o-   B o   B
>
> Star light, star bright,
> BôB [o] Bô   B
>
> The first star I see tonight.
> o B ôBoB o B

Here, the absence of unstressed syllables between many of the beats encourages the emergence of a powerful, regular rhythm, propelling the reader away from the modulations of the spoken language and towards something more like a chant. The double offbeat in the second line of the first example ('and a-') slips easily into the governing movement. It is worth noting, too, that rhyme plays an important structural role.

Historically, these popular forms are all associated with song, and it may well be that the tendency to vary unstressed syllables with some freedom while observing the count of the stresses was encouraged by the independent musical rhythm, which took care of any potential irregularities or ambiguities; nevertheless, it is clear that this type of verse doesn't need a musical setting in order to be perceived as having a salient and consistent rhythm. It is equally clear that it doesn't lend itself to prosodic analysis in terms of traditional (which is to say Greek and Latin) 'feet'. At its heart is an important fact about spoken English, which we have noted in earlier chapters: there is a tendency for stressed syllables to be perceived as occurring at equal temporal intervals. This 'stress-timing' or 'isochrony' is only a tendency, and is not necessarily an objectively measurable duration, but it is a crucial factor in English metre—it is the reason, for instance, why purely syllabic verse in English is not rhythmically regular. We have already seen evidence for another feature of the insistent rhythms established by groups of four beats: beats can continue to be felt even when they are not realized in vocal utterance. Nursery rhymes again provide vivid examples (the felt but not spoken beat is indicated here by enclosing the B in square brackets, together with an o representing the necessary offbeat between the beats).

> Pease pudding hot,
> B ô B o   B   [o B]
>
> Pease pudding cold,
> B ô B o   B   [o B]
>
> Pease pudding in the pot,
> B ô B o   B   o B
>
> Nine days old.
> B ô B ô B   [o B]

The variety of four-by-four metre represented by 'Now Go'th Sun under Wood', and embodied in a large number of later poems and songs, has the following characteristics: (1) the number of syllables varies from line to line; the number of beats per line—four—is unchanging; (2) there is some freedom in the disposition of stressed and unstressed syllables, in contrast to stricter forms that control the number of syllables as well as beats; (3) the large majority of stressed syllables are felt as beats, and the large majority of unstressed syllables are felt as offbeats (or elements in offbeats); (4) if a syllable that normally does not carry a strong emphasis, like the first syllable of *under*, is treated as a beat, the forceful rhythm encourages the reader to give it some additional weight; (5) beats can be omitted and experienced silently under very particular conditions, while offbeats between beats can be omitted with slightly more freedom (neither of these occurs in this poem); (6) there are only rarely more than two syllables making up the offbeat between the beats—the norm is to vary between one and two, to produce single and double offbeats; (7) lines can begin and end on a beat or an offbeat; (8) the disposition of the different types of offbeat is such as to enhance the strength of the rhythm; (9) there are no feet.[4] Although this metrical form is highly familiar to any reader familiar with the tradition of English verse (and, indeed, many other verse traditions), it is not mentioned in Stallworthy's essay in the *Norton Anthology*, nor in most other introductions to English versification.[5] The student is left to struggle with the Procrustean task of mapping feet with Greek names onto resistant lines of verse, or manhandling sequences of elementary rhythms based on a simple principle of doubling into the complex abstract grids provided by traditional prosody.[6]

There have been many suggestions about naming this kind of verse; 'loose iambic' perhaps being the most popular[7] (though as we have seen,

---

[4] The allowable variation between one and two syllables in certain metrical forms has been discussed under such names as 'iambic-anapestic metre', 'resolution', and 'trisyllabic substitution', sometimes involving much complex phonological analysis. See, for example, Hanson, 'Resolution in Modern Meters', Hammond, 'Anapests and Anti-resolution', and, for a less technical discussion, Weismiller, 'Triple Threats to Duple Rhythm'. (Hammond, incidentally, cites some splendidly rhythmical examples of this form by the once-popular Robert Service, whose popularity no doubt derived in part from his successful exploitation of this metrical form's memorable rhythmic punch.)

[5] The handbook *Teaching with the Norton Anthology*, by Jeffreys and Fried, is more aware of the possibility of types of metrical verse that do not fall easily into the framework of accentual-syllabic verse. In discussing the 'Scansion of Variable and Indeterminate Meters' the authors note that 'many whole poems are not only metrically variable but indeterminate', and ask, 'At what point do we concede that a poem is not in any one meter?', admitting that 'there is no simple answer' (17–18). My answer is that there is a metrical form, not based on feet, and used by a great many poets, that produces these troublesome questions only if you approach it with the wrong assumptions.

[6] For introductory volumes that use a similar approach to the one advocated here, see Carper and Attridge, *Meter and Meaning*, and Furniss and Bath, *Reading Poetry*. In her introductory anthology of poems, Vendler begins the discussion of prosody promisingly with several examples of four-beat verse (*Poems, Poets, Poetry*, 70–1), but the appendix 'On Prosody' disappointingly confuses beats with feet (593–9). Rosenthal's comprehensive anthology, *Poetry in English*, contains an essay on versification by Sally M. Gall that supplements a conventional account of English metre with a summary of 'beat–offbeat' prosody based on *The Rhythms of English Poetry*, giving readers a better understanding of the forms of English poetry than the *Norton Anthology*.

[7] It may have been Robert Frost, in 'The Figure a Poem Makes', who popularized this term; for a recent version of the distinction between strict and loose iambic see Fabb and Halle, *Meter in Poetry*, 67–74. We shall encounter further uses of the term below.

it sometimes would not make a huge difference to call these lines 'loose trochaics'). But a name that distinguishes this verse form more clearly from accentual-syllabic verse is desirable, in order to signal plainly its identity as a recognizable metrical genre in its own right, and one that does not produce uncertainties about whether to divide up the line into iambic or trochaic feet. Although I hesitate to endorse the introduction of yet another foreign-sounding term into prosodic studies, I find the term promoted by scholars of Russian prosody, *dol'nik*, a useful one.[8] Its Anglicized variant, as 'dolnik', is short and memorable, and signals the translinguistic nature of the form in question, which is a staple in modern Russian prosody and common also in German, where, as in English, it has a venerable history.[9] (In Romance languages, where the syllable carries more of the rhythmic weight of the verse, such variations in the numbers of syllables tend to have the opposite effect, producing less, rather than more, regularity.) In the early 1990s Marina Tarlinskaja, in a pioneering study, used statistical methods to demonstrate the distinctiveness, across several centuries of English verse, of this form, which is characterized by its use of both single and double offbeats (to use my terminology), or both monosyllabic and disyllabic intervals, to use hers.[10] Tarlinskaja took iambic metre to be the norm from which dolnik verse deviated, and found that in a large sample of four-beat English verse there was a frequency gap between, on the one hand, verse with up to 10 per cent of its offbeats double and, on the other, verse that had 20 per cent or more of its offbeats double. In other words, there is a significant quantity of four-beat verse in which an extremely limited number of offbeats are double, verse which Tarlinskaja is willing to call 'loose iambic'; and there is also a large quantity of four-beat verse in which double offbeats occur frequently. She did not find a substantial amount of verse falling between these two groups, suggesting that poets gravitate towards one or other type of verse, instinctively regarding them as different, and as having different poetic capabilities.[11]

---

[8] Gasparov provides a valuable comparative perspective on the *dol'nik* in *A History of European Versification*; see 177–88, 275–8, and *passim*.

[9] Leech (*Language in Literature*, 70–85) discusses what I am here calling dolnik verse under the label 'sprung rhythm', although he acknowledges that he is extending Hopkins's application of the term. He observes the flourishing of this metrical form in English poetry of the second half of the nineteenth century. I discuss dolnik verse briefly—though without using the term—in *The Rhythms of English Poetry*, 96–100.

[10] Tarlinskaja, 'Metrical Typology' and *Strict Stress-Meter*.

[11] See Tarlinskaja, *Strict Stress-Meter*, 194–5. Tarlinskaja extends the category of dolnik metre (or 'strict stress-metre', as she terms it to distinguish it from purely accentual metres) to include pentameters with varying offbeats, such as occur in many of Frost's poems (among the examples cited by Tarlinskaja are 'Mowing' and 'Sceptic' (176–7)); if, however, one starts not with a

Identifying the metrical structure of a poem is, of course, only a small part of a full critical account of it, but doing so plays an important role in understanding how it functions; while an inadequate grasp of the rhythmic form is an impediment to full appreciation. Even worse, the imposition of a metrical scheme devised for a different kind of verse is likely to distort the poem—in our example, it would detract from the extraordinary poignancy produced by the combination of a very simple rhythm with a complexity and depth of meaning, enhanced by the poem's many puns. In its literal sense, the first line refers to the sunset over a wood, an idea repeated in the third line, with 'tree' replacing 'wood'. But the second line forces a reinterpretation of the first, as we realize that the 'sonne' is the sun of the world, Mary's son, and the wood the material of the cross.[12] Mary's 'faire rode' is her beautiful face, but also the rood, or cross, that is 'faire' only in its religious significance. We are now prepared for 'tre' in the next line to bring us back once more to the cross. Linguistic simplicity to match the poem's metrical simplicity is finally achieved in the last line.

III

The importance of the dolnik in the English tradition, including canonical verse, can be judged from the number of poems in the *Norton Anthology* from all periods that use the form, whether in the full stanza of four four-beat lines as represented by 'Now Go'th Sun under Wood' or in one of the familiar forms with virtual beats: the 4.3.4.3 ballad stanza or common measure, and the 3.3.4.3 stanza or short measure.[13] The majority of the thirteenth- to fifteenth-century lyrics printed in the *Norton Anthology* use

statistical definition but with a sensitivity to rhythmic qualities, one is likely to make a clear distinction between these four-beat and five-beat forms. (Other line-lengths than five-beat are usually felt to be versions of the basic four-beat rhythm.) Duffell, in *A New History*, employs the term 'dolnik' in his historical account of English metre, although he follows Tarlinskaja in extending it to five-beat verse, which means that it loses its capacity to distinguish the verse form I am discussing. He also excludes verse that has many 'zero intervals' between beats, whereas I see the unrealized offbeat as an important element in the dolnik's rhythmic capability.

[12] Although sonne (sun) and sone (son) were pronounced differently in Middle English, it seems likely that they were close enough to encourage the double meaning. See Dronke, *The Medieval Lyric*, 67.

[13] As in the previous chapters, I use a simple numerical indication of the number of beats per line; thus the four four-beat lines of 'Now Go'th Sun' are represented as 4.4.4.4. These stanza forms are also frequently used for strict accentual-syllabic metres; and their longer forms, fourteeners and poulter's measure, created by combining two lines into one, are almost always syllabically strict (lines of 14 syllables in the former case, and alternating 12 and 14 in the latter). In both dolnik and accentual-syllabic versions, the four-beat line is a basic element, even when only three beats are realized in the language: in such a case, the fourth beat is felt rather than spoken, hence the term 'virtual beat' (see Chapter 5 section I).

dolnik verse, including the famous 'I Sing of a Maiden' (79) (where the four-beat lines are written out as two two-beat lines) and the Corpus Christi Carol (83). A long poem not included in the anthology is the fourteenth-century *Pearl*, whose 101 stanzas, each made up of three quatrains, use a form of dolnik metre.[14] At the end of the fifteenth century, John Skelton introduced, and later gave his name to, a variety of this metre based on the two-beat line but sometimes extending it.

The ten-page selection of 'Early Modern Ballads' in the *Norton Anthology* (97–117) uses the dolnik form consistently, usually in the 4.3.4.3 version which is the staple for ballads. Here's a familiar example of a Scottish ballad, with the virtual beats and offbeats shown as usual in square brackets:

> The king sits in Dunfermline town
> o B ô B -o-   B   o   B
>
> Drinking the blude-red wine;
>   B   -o-   B   o   B   [o B]
>
> 'O whare will I get a skeely skipper
> o   B   -o- B o   B o   B o
>
> To sail this new ship o' mine?'
> o B   -o-   B o B   [o B]

Two of the 'Anonymous Elizabethan and Jacobean Poems' provide further variants ('To His Love' (119) and 'Tom o' Bedlam's Song' (124)). Strict accentual-syllabic metre, however, becomes the norm in literary four-beat verse during the course of the sixteenth century, from Wyatt to Marlowe. One form that has some of the characteristics of the dolnik and some of the characteristics of accentual-syllabic verse can be exemplified by Shakespeare's 'The Phoenix and the Turtle' (270):

> Let the bird of loudest lay,
> B   o B o B   o B
>
> On the sole Arabian tree,
> B   o B o B o   B
>
> Herald sad and trumpet be,
> B o   B o   B   o B
>
> To whose sound chaste wings obey.
> B   o B   o   B   o B

This form is often called 'trochaic' in handbooks on metre, though most lines are lacking the final offbeat one would expect in a fully trochaic line;

---

[14] Cable, arguing in 'Foreign Influence' against the notion that 'strong-stress metre' is foreign while 'accentual-syllabic' is native, has shown that the bulk of the medieval Harley lyrics are also in this verse form.

it might just as well be called 'iambic' without an initial syllable. (If we divide the lines into phrasal groups, the majority are either rising—'the bird', 'obey'—or a combination of rising and falling—'of loudest', 'Arabian', 'and trumpet'.) The final line contains examples of the common metrical features described earlier: *promotion* (unstressed 'To' takes a beat) and *demotion* (stressed 'chaste' functions as an offbeat). These terms do not imply an unnatural pronunciation, though in fully-fledged dolnik verse, promotion and demotion are often given vocal realization, as the language bends to the demands of the imperious rhythm. For this reason I haven't used a special symbol for demotion and promotion in this chapter, except in the metrical situation mentioned in n. 17.

Many of Shakespeare's songs use a variety of this dolnik-related metre, with lines that can begin and end on either a beat or an offbeat. This is also the metre used by Milton in 'L'Allegro' and 'Il Penseroso', perhaps in imitation of Shakespeare's songs. Since this metre observes the requirements for neither iambic nor trochaic verse, it has been a constant puzzle to prosodists, and, as with 'Now Go'th Sun under Wood', all attempts to analyse it in traditional terms end up making it sound extraordinarily complicated when, in fact, it is very easy on the ear—as Milton no doubt intended:

> Com, and trip it as ye go
> B   o   B o B   o   B
>
> On the light fantastick toe,
> B   o B   o B o   B
>
> And in thy right hand lead with thee,
> o   B   o B   o   B   o   B
>
> The Mountain Nymph, sweet Liberty.
> o   B   o   B   o   B o B
>
> ('L'Allegro', lines 33–6)

The dolnik in its canonical form does not, however, come back into fashion until the rise of Romantic aesthetic preferences at the end of the eighteenth century loosened the constraints that had been imposed in the sixteenth century. Blake's *Songs of Innocence and Experience,* for instance, contain many examples, and there are a few among Burns's and Moore's songs. Coleridge's *Rime of the Ancient Mariner* occasionally drops into dolnik-like rhythms, as in the following lines, which have the characteristic dolnik variation between single and double offbeats:

> For the sky and the sea, and the sea and the sky
>   -o-   B   -o-   B   -o-   B   -o-   B
>
> Lay like a load on my weary eye,
> B   -o- B   -o-   B o B

And the dead were at my feet.
-o-   B   o B   o B   [B]

The vast majority of the stanzas of *The Ancient Mariner* are, perhaps surpris-
ingly, in regular accentual-syllabic metre, as are Wordsworth's four-beat con-
tributions to *Lyrical Ballads*. There are flickers of dolnik freedom in 'We Are
Seven'—lines such as 'Two of us in the church-yard lie'; 'Twelve steps or
more from my mother's door'—but Wordsworth's versions of demotic poetry
almost always conform to a strict syllable-count (one of the reasons, perhaps,
why they sometimes betray a comic disparity between formality of utterance
and banality of content). For Coleridge's most important contribution to the
dolnik tradition, we need to turn to a poem written at the same time as the
poems in the first edition of *Lyrical Ballads* but not published until two dec-
ades later; we shall come to it in the next section of this chapter. Otherwise
he only rarely departs from accentual-syllabic norms.

   A poet of the period for whom dolnik became a favoured poetic re-
source was Scott. Here is the opening stanza of the first canto of *The Lay
of the Last Minstrel* (1805):

The feast was over in Branksome tower,
   o B   o B -o-   B   o   B
And the Ladye had gone to her secret bower;
   -o-   B -o-   B   -o-   B o B
Her bower that was guarded by word and by spell,
   o B   -o-   B   -o-   B   -o-   B
Deadly to hear, and deadly to tell—
   B   -o-   B   o   B   -o-   B
Jesu Maria, shield us well!
B -o- Bo B   o   B
No living wight, save the Ladye alone,
   o Bo   B   -o-   B   -o-B
Had dared to cross the threshold stone.[15]
   o   B   o B   o   B o   B

Although Scott doesn't group his lines into quatrains by rhyme here (some-
thing he does in many places in the poem), the characteristic dolnik lilt is
produced by the salient four stresses in each line, standing out from the
varied interval between them. The changing line-openings are typical of the
dolnik: whether the line starts with one unstressed syllable (lines 1, 3, 6,

---

[15] Scott, *Selections from the Poems*, 6. I scan 'tower' and 'bower' as single syllables because
in the third line 'bower' is pronounced most naturally as a monosyllable, to avoid a slightly
awkward triple offbeat.

and 7) or two unstressed syllables (line 2), or lacks an upbeat altogether (lines 4 and 5), it is the first occurring stress that sets the insistent rhythm of the line going. Most of the poem, however, is in regular four-beat accentual-syllabic metre, Scott's favoured form for his long poems. Two of the long poems that do make occasional use of dolnik rhythms are *The Bridal of Trem-ain* (1813) and *Harold the Dauntless* (1817), though it was in his ballads and lyrics that Scott most fully exploited the dolnik's potential. These included, among the ballads, 'The Eve of St John', 'The Gray Brother', and 'The Reive's Wedding', and among the songs, two of his most popular, 'Proud Maisie' and 'Pibroch of Donuil Dhu', both of which are in two-beat lines whose dolnik character becomes clearer if they are set out as four-beat units.[16]

Among the second generation of Romantic poets, only Shelley is re-membered for dolnik poems, the best known of which are 'The Sensitive Plant' and 'The Cloud'. The latter begins:

> I sift the snow on the mountains below,
> o B   o B   -o-   B   -o- B
>
> And their great pines groan aghast;
>   -o-   B O   B   B   [B]
>
> And all the night 'tis my pillow white
> o B o B   -o- B o   B
>
> While I sleep in the arms of the blast.[17]
>   -o- B   -o- B   -o-   B   [B]

The memorability of this poem is largely due to the almost incantatory swing of the dolnik rhythm, moving easily between single and double offbeats, the ballad metre, with its virtual beats at the end of the second and fourth lines, and the clinching rhyme at the end of each of the two eight-beat groups. Shelley's mastery of this form set a standard which poets who came after him were not slow to follow.

IV

One of the best-known lines in Victorian poetry has only three words—or, rather, only one word occurring three times: 'Break, break, break'. Given to a reader who doesn't know the poem (not an easy task among

---

[16] One immensely popular poem from this period, whose popularity is no doubt in part due to its use of the dolnik metre, is Charles Wolfe's 1816 'Burial of Sir John Moore after Corunna': 'Not a drum was heard, not a funeral note, | As his corse to the rampart we hurried', etc.

[17] Following the practice I introduced in the previous chapter, the upper case O under 'pines' in this scansion indicates that this word is stressed but functions in the rhythm as an offbeat; it is thus an example of demotion.

poetry-lovers), it presents a metrical puzzle. Is it perhaps the beginning of an iambic pentameter modelled on Milton's 'Rocks, Caves, Lakes, Fens, Bogs, Dens, and shades of death', in which case the first and third occurrences of 'break' are, nominally at least, in weaker positions than the second? Alternatively, has Tennyson ventured into free verse ahead of his time? But given with the rest of the stanza to a reader who is a native speaker of English, it poses no problems:

> Break, break, break,
>   On thy cold gray stones, O Sea!
> And I would that my tongue could utter
>   The thoughts that arise in me.
>
> (*Poems*, 602)

The rhythm emerges easily when the lines are read aloud, any uncertainty about the opening line being quickly resolved when the others are read. And it is the immediacy and strength of that rhythm, and in particular its manifestation in the opening three words, that has played a major part—perhaps *the* major part—in making the poem so well known and well loved. Yet this poem has provoked at least as much debate about its metrical form as any from the Victorian period. Yopie Prins notes that in 1892 the interest of its rhythms for composers was made manifest by its being singled out in a *Musical Times* article on settings of Tennyson's poems, and that at a 2008 conference on metre in Victorian poetry at Exeter University it was nominated as the 'adopted conference poem'.[18] Prosodists who favoured musical scansion repeatedly returned to the poem, as Prins shows, though with different suggestions as to how its rhythm might be represented by musical notes. Dana Gioia states the metrical conundrum clearly:

What is the metre of Tennyson's poem? A traditionalist might label it anapestic, but that scansion does not adequately account for the opening line, which can only be explained as stress metre. The lines range from three to nine syllables in length, and, if one divides them into accentual-syllabic feet, one discovers as many iambs as anapests (not to mention the recurring monosyllabic feet). To label this poem iambic or anapestic, therefore, is misleading since almost every line would then, to some degree, be irregular. Yet the poem is tangibly metrical— one hears a steady beat common to both the three syllable and nine syllable line.[19]

---

[18] Prins, '"Break, break, break" into Song', 107 and 109.
[19] Gioia, 'Meter-Making Arguments', 93. J. F. A. Pyre, in *The Formation of Tennyson's Style*, is equally bemused: 'Scarcely two verses have precisely the same movement. In the 16 lines there are twelve different combinations of iambs and anapaests' (107).

The poem's most significant forebear was a poem at least partly completed by 1798 and first published in 1816, with a preface explaining its unusual metre: Coleridge's 'Christabel'. 'The metre of Christabel', Coleridge famously wrote, 'is not, properly speaking, irregular, though it may seem so from its being founded on a new principle: namely, that of counting in each line the accents, not the syllables. Though the latter may vary from seven to twelve, yet in each line the accents will be found to be only four.' Coleridge's counting is mistaken: in fact, the lower limit on the number of syllables per line is well below seven. The opening five lines, for example, have syllable-counts of eleven, eleven, four, eight, and six:

> 'Tis the middle of night by the castle clock,
> *And the owls have awakened the crowing cock;*
> Tu---whit! -----Tu---whoo!
> And hark, again! the crowing cock,
> How drowsily it crew.[20]

Not only does the syllable-count contradict Coleridge's prefatory statement, but his comment on the number of accents seems wrong: even if we read the third line with four strong stresses, as the long dashes imply, a normal reading of the fifth line would unquestionably give it three accented syllables. Nevertheless, the general observation that the lines vary greatly in numbers of syllables but observe near consistency in the number of accents—the most frequent variation being an occasional line with two accents—and that the metre is not 'irregular' in that it produces a strong and regular rhythm holds true of the poem as a whole. Gioia's observation about 'Break, break, break' is equally true of 'Christabel': to label it with the traditional names of metrical feet would mislead, yet it is 'tangibly metrical'. It is an example of dolnik verse.

Why did Coleridge choose to introduce his new metre with lines of four accents, and not, for instance, five, which would have associated it with the noble tradition of the iambic pentameter? Whatever model he was consciously following, his ear would have told him that the 'new principle'— actually an old principle, which he would have encountered in ballad collections such as Percy's *Reliques* and in other popular verse—would only work if based on groups of four accents or, to use a more precise term (since 'accent' may be used of linguistic stress patterns irrespective of their role in the metre), and one very familiar to Victorian poets and prosodists, beats.[21] The standard ballad stanza relies on this rhythmic fact, the second and

---

[20] Coleridge, *Poetical Works*, 215.
[21] Another term with roughly the same meaning that appears in Victorian prosodic discussion is *ictus*; its use is complicated by its Latin inheritance, however.

Rhythm and Metre

fourth lines containing only three realized beats and a virtual beat; common measure in hymnody follows the same pattern, while short measure has four realized beats only in the third line (as is also the case in 'Pease pudding hot'). The virtual beat is made particularly evident in musical settings, in which the accompaniment continues while the voice remains silent (or a line-final syllable is extended over two beats). Some commentators on Victorian poetry would trace the form back to the four-stress mode of Anglo-Saxon verse, though the two forms are rhythmically distinct, in spite of the centrality of the four-beat group to both. The form known as 'accentual' or 'strong-stress' or 'stress' metre—such as Gioia attributes to the first line of Tennyson's poem—is a modern imitation of such verse, and doesn't induce the insistent rhythm of the dolnik. In popular verse, the dolnik remained a staple, and in the nineteenth century numerous examples are to be found, for instance, among collections of ballads and of Chartist verse.

Literary verse in the Victorian period, in contrast to the dominance of the five-beat line—and in particular the iambic pentameter—in the previous century, saw a flowering of both shorter and longer lines, most of them based on the four-beat rhythm. The taste for such poetry from earlier periods was enshrined in Palgrave's *Golden Treasury*, first published in 1861; Palgrave explains in his preface that 'blank verse and the ten-syllable couplet... have been rejected as alien from what is commonly understood by Song, and rarely conforming to Lyrical conditions in treatment' (n.p.). A later anthology that included a significant quantity of Victorian poetry in these song-like forms, the immensely popular 1900 *Oxford Book of English Verse* edited by Sir Arthur Quiller-Couch ('Q'), is testimony to this preference, and served to project it well into the twentieth century. It is no accident that all the seven 'well-known and representative' nineteenth-century poems named—and disparaged—by F. R. Leavis in the 1932 study that reshaped the poetic canon for a generation, *New Bearings in English Poetry*, are in four-beat forms (14).

When used in conjunction with end-stopping and rhyme, the four-beat metrical norm produces a verbal movement that evokes the regularity of song rather than the variety of speech; and the occurrence of virtual beats in the appropriate places enhances that rhythmic foregrounding. By the same token, judicious enjambment and avoidance of virtual beats can temper the song-like movement with something closer to speaking qualities; the pre-eminent nineteenth-century example of such poetry is Tennyson's *In Memoriam*. Triple rhythms, on the other hand, usually serve to increase rhythmic insistence, as does the introduction of a dipodic or quadruple quality to duple rhythm—that is, a tendency for beats to alternate in strength. Browning's 'How They Brought the Good News from Ghent to Aix'—'I sprang to the stirrup, and Joris, and he'—is a good ex-

ample of the former, while 'A Toccata of Galuppi's'—'Oh Galuppi, Bald-
assaro, this is very sad to find'—illustrates well his handling of the latter.
These strongly rhythmic forms are close to the dolnik (which often has an
underlying triple swing, and sometimes also evinces a quadruple alterna-
tion[22]), though each has its own distinctive character.

Let us return now to Tennyson and 'Break, break, break'. Here are the
first and last stanzas:

> Break, break, break,
> B [o] B [o] B [o B]
>
> On thy cold gray stones, O Sea!
> -o-   B   O   B   o   B   [o B]
>
> And I would that my tongue could utter
> -o- B   -o-   B   o   B o   [B]
>
> The thoughts that arise in me.
> o   B   -o-B o   B   [o B]

....

> Break, break, break,
> B [o] B [o] B [o B]
>
> At the foot of thy crags, O Sea!
> -o-   B   -o-   B   o B   [o B]
>
> But the tender grace of a day that is dead
> -o-   B   o   B   -o- B   -o- B
>
> Will never come back to me.
> o   B -o-   B   o   B   [o B]

In reading the poem aloud it is possible to ignore the virtual beats at the end
of most lines, but the result is unpleasantly hurried; whereas a pause allows the
implicit sadness in the contemplation of the scene to emerge more fully. The
various attempts at musical scansion of the poem clearly show rests in these
positions (see Prins, '"Break, Break, Break" into Song'). The penultimate line
is one of only two in the poem in which the final beat is sounded, making the
stanza a version of short measure, with lines of 3, 3, 4, and 3 realized beats.

Much has been written about the mimetic appropriateness of these
rhythms to the unstoppable crashing of the waves and the plangent tones
of the speaker's grief,[23] but less about the simplicity of the metrical scheme
underlying the apparent complexity of the lines, which vary in length
from three to eleven syllables (not nine, as Gioia claims). The memorabil-

---

[22] Four-beat forms involving virtual beats imply a quadruple or 'dipodic' rhythm, since the
stronger beats are all realized while some of the weaker beats are omitted. See Chapter 5.
[23] For a recent example, see Jason Rudy, *Electric Meters*, 71–2. Rudy interestingly relates
Tennyson's poem to Thomas Hood's popular parody, 'The Song of the Shirt'.

ity of the poem is largely due to this simple, strong rhythm, heightened
by the striking first line, with its syntactically and metrically induced
pauses making up for the lack of unstressed syllables.[24] It thus provides a
clear template for the rest of the poem, in which—apart from the repeat
of the first line—the beats are separated by one or two syllables. It is an
unambiguous example of dolnik verse's characteristic four-beat line (usu-
ally, as in this poem, in groups of four lines), varied offbeats, and strong,
easily grasped rhythm. Although most Victorian poets and prosodists still
thought in terms of classical feet, the age was one in which the dolnik—
for which classical prosody is inappropriate—was widely and inventively
used. One way of putting this is that, among the richly various explora-
tions of verse form that characterize the age, Victorian poets fully ex-
ploited the power of the rhythmic beat.[25]

V

There is, of course, no sharp division between dolnik verse on one hand
and accentual-syllabic verse with occasional variations in syllable-count
on the other, although, as I have noted, it has been shown that English
poetry tends to gravitate either towards the more syllabically regular forms
or towards the full-blown dolnik. There is also a gradation between un-
mistakable dolnik verse with its four-beat foundation and verse in which
the number of beats varies freely from line to line, disrupting the swing of
the rhythm, a freedom which reached an extreme in the so-called 'Spas-
modic' poets of the mid-nineteenth century. From the start of his career
as a poet Tennyson enjoyed varying both the numbers of beats in the line
and the number of syllables between the beats; the 1830 and 1832 vol-
umes of his verse contain many such examples. The following lines from
'Ode to Memory', for example, begin with what could be the opening of
a dolnik stanza but then move into a freer rhythmic mode:

Come not as thou camest of late,
o   B -o-   B -o- B [o B]

Flinging the gloom of yesternight
B   -o-   B   o B o B

[24] The role of these pauses can be judged by comparing this opening to 'Star bright star
light', where the reciter has to use a somewhat artificial pronunciation in order to stress the
words equally and allow the four beats to emerge.
[25] The *OED* credits Hopkins with the first use of the term 'beat' to refer to verse rhythm
(around 1873–4), but in fact Patmore used it in his 1857 essay on 'English Metrical Critics'
(136)—see section VI of this chapter.

On the white day; but robed in softened light
  -o-   B ô B   o B   o B o   B
      Of orient state.
      o B -o- B
                      (*Poems*, 211)

The potential dolnik rhythm produced by the variation between single and double offbeats and the different line-openings is dissipated by a number of features: the move from three to four realized beats (instead of four to three); the run-on after two lines, which in the dolnik is the major internal break; and the lines of five and two beats. It remains the case, however, that classical prosody cannot account for Tennyson's practice here, and merely imposes divisions on what is a freely varying rhythm.[26]

Tennyson was writing dolnik verse from an early age, however. If we go back to the 1827 *Poems by Two Brothers*, containing poems written by Alfred as a teenager together with poems by his brothers Charles and Frederick, we find imitations of traditional ballads in dolnik rhythms, including a poem that identifies clearly one of Tennyson's major sources for this metrical style. 'The Old Chieftain' has as its epigraph the opening line of the third canto of Scott's *Lay of the Last Minstrel*, whose use of the dolnik rhythm we have already noted. Tennyson's poem is in four-line stanzas rhyming *a b a b*, though they vary between stanzas with the usual ballad form of 4, 3, 4, and 3 realized beats, and stanzas with four realized beats in every line. Here is the third stanza:

For when I have chanted the bold song of death
  o   B -o-   B -o-   B   -o- B
    Not a page would have stayed in the hall,
      -o- B   -o-   B   -o-   B [o B]
Not a lance in the rest, not a sword in the sheath,
  -o- B   -o-   B   -o-   B   -o-   B
Not a shield on the dim grey wall.
    -o-   B   -o-   B   O B [o B]
                      (*Poems*, 127)

We may note the phrase 'dim grey wall', echoed by Tennyson many years later in 'cold gray stones': the strong rhythm of the dolnik allows a stressed syllable to appear in the position of the offbeat, and in so doing creates a distinctive movement in which all three syllables are stressed, but the outer two attract the beat. (We earlier encountered an instance in Shelley's 'great pines groan'.) This rhythmic figure became a distinctive feature of

---

[26] Ricks, surprisingly, states the that the poem is in iambics (Tennyson, *Poems*, 211).

much later dolnik verse, a notable example being the poetry of Swinburne, to whom we shall turn in due course. We may also note that the words 'song of' together constitute an offbeat, where the stressed word 'song' has to lose some of its normal emphasis to sustain the momentum of the line—a typical dolnik phenomenon. The link back to 'Christabel' is evident in Scott's line 'Jesu Maria, shield her well', which comes straight from Coleridge's poem.[27] It's not fanciful, therefore, to regard 'Break, break, break' as a direct descendant of Coleridge's pathbreaking metrical experiment.[28]

Tennyson continued to explore the possibilities of the dolnik, along with many other verse forms. The memorability of its rhythm contributed to the success of some of his most popular lyrics, including the haunting 'Poet's Song' (*Poems*, 736), 'Sweet and low' from *The Princess* (*Poems*, 772), and 'Come into the garden, Maud' from *Maud* (*Poems*, 1075–8). 'Sweet and low' begins with a superb manipulation of the dolnik's possibilities of rhythmic strength and variation:

> Sweet and low, sweet and low,
> B   o   B ô B   o   B
> Wind of the western sea
> B   -o-   B o   B   [o B]

Many of the songs in Tennyson's plays, as one might expect given the Shakespearian model, use dolnik verse. In his later life Tennyson developed a fondness for the six-beat dolnik, a form that breaks naturally in mid-line as well as at the end, though the reader can choose how much weight, if any, to give the mid-line break. Here is the opening of the final stanza of 'Rizpah', showing the possible virtual beat at the halfway mark:

> Madam, I beg your pardon! I think that you mean to be
> B   -o- B   o   B o [B]o B   -o-   B   -o-
> kind,
> B   [o B]

---

[27] Although 'Christabel' was published after Scott's poem, it was recited to Scott by John Stoddart in 1802, when the former was working on the *Lay*. Scott eventually acknowledged the indebtedness of his poem to Coleridge's. See Russett, *Fictions and Fakes*, 82–90.

[28] The importance to the young Tennyson of Scott's four-beat verse comes across in a notebook comment quoted by Hallam Tennyson in his memoir of his father: 'At about twelve and onward I wrote an epic of six thousand lines à la Walter Scott...with Scott's regularity of octo-syllables and his occasional varieties. Though the performance was very likely worth nothing I never felt myself more truly inspired. I wrote as much as seventy lines at one time, and used to go shouting them about the fields in the dark' (*Alfred, Lord Tennyson*, 12).

But I cannot hear what you say for my Willy's voice
  -o- B o B   -o-   B[oB]-o-   B o B

    in the wind—
      -o-   B [o B]

The snow and the sky so bright—he used but to call
  o B   -o-   B o B [oB] o B   -o-   B

    in the dark,
      -o-   B   [o B]

And he calls to me now from the church and not from the
  -o- B   -o-   B   -o-   B[oB]o   B   -o-

    gibbet—for hark!
    B   -o-   B   [o B]

                               (*Poems*, 1249)

This example has a predominantly triple rhythm, intermittently varied by the use of single-syllable offbeats ('**beg** your **pard**-', '**cannot hear**', '**Willy's voice**') and different line openings ('**Madam**', 'But I **cannot**', '**The snow**'). On the other hand, Tennyson's eight-beat lines, such as 'Locksley Hall', use regular accentual-syllabic verse, beginning and ending on the beat.

Another poet who knew well how to exploit the robust rhythms of the dolnik was Robert Browning. The first set of poems in his first volume of short poems, the 1842 collection *Dramatic Lyrics*, is entitled 'Cavalier Tunes'; the initial poem, 'Marching Along', begins:

    Kentish Sir Byng stood for his King,
    B   -o- B ô B   -o-   B

    Bidding the crop-headed Parliament swing:
    B   -o-   B   -o- B -o-   B

    And, pressing a troop unable to stoop
    o   B   -o- B   o B -o- B

    And see the rogues flourish and honest folk droop,
    o   B   -o-   B   -o-   B -o-   B

    Marched them along, fifty-score strong,
    B   -o- B [o] B -o-   B

    Great-hearted gentlemen, singing this song.
    B   -o- B -o-   B   -o-   B

                         (*Poems*, I, 347)

The first line—unsurprisingly, one of Browning's most catchy openings—announces its rhythmic lineage immediately: the predominantly triple rhythm is enhanced, not weakened, by the missing syllables at the midway point of the line, an effect repeated in line 5, where the anticipated four-line group is extended by a further two lines in marching mode. The placing of this implied offbeat is crucial: the rhythm would have been entirely different had it occurred elsewhere in the line ('Kentish Sir Philemon played King', for example, has none of the rhythmic immediacy of the original). The other two poems in this group are also examples of dolnik verse, the third with an opening line that serves as a refrain and demands an early virtual beat if the rhetorical emphasis on the first word, and the rhythm of four realized beats, is to be preserved:

> Boot, saddle, to horse, and away!
> B [o] B   -o- B   -o- B

Omitting the offbeat in this position doesn't produce the memorable rocking rhythm of 'Kentish Sir Bing', though the imagined musical setting—these are 'tunes', after all—would ensure the appropriate emphases.[29]

Many of Browning's most famous poems draw on dolnik rhythms, including 'Meeting at Night' and 'Parting at Morning', 'Evelyn Hope', 'Up at a Villa—Down at the City', 'The Patriot', 'The Statue and the Bust', and 'Prospice'. The first stanza of 'Home-Thoughts from Abroad' is in dolnik verse, and 'The Pied Piper of Hamelin' utilizes the dolnik's hyper-rhythmicality in many places. 'Abt Vogler' is in the same six-beat dolnik that Tennyson used for poems such as 'Rizpah'. Like Tennyson, Browning was an extraordinarily versatile handler of metre; he pushed the regularities of five-beat accentual-syllabic verse to the limit in representing emotional speech at the same time as he capitalized on the song-like properties of the dolnik and other four-beat forms. And like Tennyson, though less frequently, he wrote poems with varying line-lengths and offbeats that don't settle into an insistent rhythm and are correspondingly less likely to imprint themselves on the memory (examples are 'In a Gondola', 'The Flight of the Duchess').

A Victorian writer who capitalized on the same properties of the dolnik as Tennyson did in 'Break, break, break' was Charles Kingsley. 'Alton Locke's Song' begins:

> Weep, weep, weep and weep,
> B [o] B [o] B   o   B
>
> For pauper, dolt, and slave!
> o B o B o   B [o B]
>
> (*Andromeda and Other Poems*, 129)

And 'The Tide River', from *The Water-Babies*, remembers the opening of Tennyson's 'Sweet and low', but continues with a different rhythm:

---

[29] Browning, too, may have been influenced by Scott, since these 'Cavalier Tunes' appear to contain echoes of the latter's *Woodstock; or the Cavalier*: see Lowe, 'Scott, Browning, and Kipling'.

Clear and cool, clear and cool,
B   o   B [o] B   o   B

By laughing shallow, and dreaming pool
o B   o   B   -o-   B   o   B

(*The Water-Babies*, 42)

Other poems by Kingsley using dolnik rhythms include 'The Weird Lady', 'The Bad Squire', 'Scotch Song', 'A New Forest Ballad', 'The Outlaw', and 'The Three Fishers'.

Although Elizabeth Barrett Browning didn't favour dolnik for the most part, she used it for one of her most anthologized poems, 'A Musical Instrument', in which we hear the characteristic lilt right from the start, produced by the shift from double offbeats with two unstressed syllables to a single offbeat with a stressed syllable, and clinched by the familiar pattern of four realized beats followed by three:

What was he doing, the great god Pan,
B   -o- B   -o-   B   O   B

Down in the reeds by the river?
B   -o-   B   -o-   B o   [B]

Spreading ruin and scattering ban,
B   o   B -o-   B   -o-   B

Splashing and paddling with hoofs of a goat,
B   -o-   B   -o-   B   -o- B

And breaking the golden lilies afloat
o   B   -o-   B   o   B -o-   B

With the dragon-fly on the river.
-o-   B o   B   -o-   B o   [B]

(*Selected Poems*, 298)

Part of the effectiveness of Barrett Browning's use of the stanza here lies in the thwarting of the reader's expectation of a shorter fourth line, as in the ballad stanza: instead, we get two additional lines with four realized beats until reaching the concluding short line—two lines in which evidence of Pan's destructive violence continues to accumulate. She also used a variant of the dolnik for a long, and not at all light-hearted, poem: 'The Runaway Slave at Pilgrim's Point'.

'A Musical Instrument' was included by Q in his *Oxford Book of English Verse*, as were dolnik poems by James Clarence Mangan ('The Nameless One'), William Allingham ('The Fairies'), George Meredith ('Love in the Valley'), Wilfred Scawen Blunt ('The Desolate City'), and Robert Louis Stevenson ('Requiem'). As the titles of these poems alone reveal, the dolnik was used for a large variety of themes, with no sense that it was only suited to light verse. (It did, however, have a strong presence in comic verse, to which we shall turn later.) Also in Q's anthology were dolnik poems by poets seldom heard of today, such as John Todhunter ('Maureen'), William Watson ('Ode in May'), and Henry Charles Beeching ('Going Down Hill on a Bicycle'). James Thomson's 'Gifts' and 'The Vine' and John Davidson's 'Song' may be included in the list of dolnik verse by somewhat better-known poets.

To Q's own selection of dolnik poems by lesser-known Victorian authors many more could be added: Sir Alfred Lyall, Alfred Austin, Sir Henry New-bolt, Arthur Munby, and Lord Alfred Douglas all used the form.[30] William Morris's 'Judgement of God' starts as dolnik, but run-on lines soon disrupt the swing of the rhythm. Another longer work of the period that bears signs of the dolnik tradition is Matthew Arnold's 'Tristram and Iseult'. Many genuine ballads that have made it into anthologies of Victorian verse, as well as many literary ballads, use dolnik rhythms; among the latter are Barrett Browning's 'Lord Walter's Wife', Christina Rossetti's 'Noble Sister', and Newbolt's 'Gillespie'. The short lines of Rossetti's 'Goblin Market' fall at times into a dolnik rhythm, but the frequent variations in line-length and rhyme-pattern prevent it from sustaining that rhythm over any extended span. Across the Atlantic, Poe relished dolnik rhythms, too: well-known dolnik poems include 'The City in the Sea' and 'Annabel Lee'.

This is an appropriate place to mention Gerard Manley Hopkins, whose 'sprung rhythm' illustrates the fact that the dolnik rhythm is not entirely free in its disposition of stresses and intervening syllables. Hopkins goes beyond the limited variation and preferred patterns of dolnik verse to create a rhythmic style marked by torsion and overspill, requiring the reader to wrestle the language into the mould of the metre—a very different experience from the easy alternations of the dolnik. Before developing his characteristic rhythmic freedom, however, Hopkins showed his familiarity with the dolnik; an early poem entitled 'A Windy Day', enclosed in a letter of 1861, moves easily between different types of offbeat:

> The vex'd elm-heads are pale with the view
>   o B   O   B   o B   -o-   B
>
> Of a mastering heaven utterly blue[31]
>   -o- B -o-   B o B -o- B

---

[30] It is unfortunate that for the twentieth century the steady beating of the dolnik was often associated with militarism; see, for example, Meredith Martin's discussion of Newbolt (*The Rise and Fall of Meter*, 122–30). Newbolt's most famous poem, 'Drake's Drum', successfully combines quadruple ('dipodic') dolnik verse with strongly rhythmic five-beat lines.

[31] Hopkins, *The Major Works*, 11. An alternative stressing of 'elm-heads' would give the first syllable more weight, producing an implied offbeat, but my sense is that the poem's rhythm doesn't allow for this degree of variation.

A version of dolnik rhythm contributes to the effectiveness of what is perhaps Hopkins's first wholly successful poem, 'Heaven-Haven', and two of his most quoted poems, 'Spring and Fall' and 'Inversnaid' draw on dolnik rhythms (though Hopkins referred to the former as being in sprung rhythm). 'Inversnaid' is a particularly brilliant deployment of the dolnik lilt. The first stanza runs as follows:

> This darksome burn, horseback brown,
> o B o B [o] B o B
> His rollrock highroad roaring down,
> o B o B o B o B
> In coop and in comb the fleece of his foam
> o B -o- B o B -o- B
> Flutes and low to the lake falls home.
> B o B -o- B O B

> *(Major Works, 153)*

Where 'Spring and Fall' moves only between single and implied offbeats, 'Inversnaid' also introduces double offbeats that quicken and lighten the rhythm.

Although serious verse that uses a dolnik rhythm with a strong triple base is now hard to appreciate, its success as a medium for comic poetry remains undimmed. Edward Lear is the master, using dolnik variations to heighten rhythmicality in most of his classic poems, including 'The Jumblies', 'The Quangle Wangle's Hat', 'The Dong with a Luminous Nose', and 'The Pobble Who Has no Nose'.[32] 'The Jumblies', for example, exploits the dolnik's variations between single and double offbeat to heighten rhythmicality, and inserts an additional four-beat line into the 4.3.4.3 stanza:

> They went to sea in a Sieve, they did,
> o B o B -o- B   o B
> In a Sieve they went to sea:
> -o- B   o B o B [o B]
> In spite of all their friends could say,
> o B o B o B o B
> On a winter's morn, on a stormy day,
> -o- B o   B   -o- B o B
> In a Sieve they went to sea!
> -o- B   o B o B [o B]

> *(Complete Nonsense, 253)*

---

[32] Lewis Carroll, by contrast, prefers to observe the regularity of accentual-syllabic verse—as does Lear himself in his limericks.

Another writer of light verse who knew how to use the dolnik was Henry Sambrooke Leigh; here is the opening stanza of 'Weatherbound in the Suburbs', from *Carols of Cockayne*:

> The air is damp, the skies are leaden;
> oB o B   o B o B o
>
> The ominous lull of impending rain
> oB -o-   B -o- B o B
>
> Presses upon me, and seems to deaden
> B -o- B   -o-   B   o B o
>
> Every sense but a sense of pain.   (99)
> B -o- B   -o- B o B

Although the mood here seems to be one of Keatsian despair, the triple lilt that enters with the second line hints at a less grave condition, and the rest of the poem (picking up the temper of the title) confirms this. We could also include much of W. S. Gilbert's comic verse, written to be set by Arthur Sullivan, which often utilizes triple or quadruple rhythms, with metrical rests in places where the music can sustain the momentum.

Unsurprisingly, children's verse makes extensive use of dolnik rhythms: as we have seen, they are a staple of traditional nursery rhymes, and those who created verse in this vein naturally followed suit. One Victorian example was William Brighty Rands, whose 'The Pedlar's Caravan' starts as follows:

> I wish I lived in a caravan,
> o B o B -o- B o B
>
> With a horse to drive, like the pedlar-man!
> -o- B o B   -o- B o B
>
> Where he comes from nobody knows,
> B o B   o B -o- B
>
> Or where he goes to, but on he goes!
> o   B o B -o- B o B
>
> (*Lilliput Levee*, 164)

Another domain of Victorian verse which saw the dolnik flourish, in an odd coming-together of the learned and the popular, was the enterprise of imitating classical Greek metres. The dactylic hexameter, when translated into an English accentual hexameter, happens to produce a swinging dolnik rhythm (which has very little to do with the rhythm of the quantitative Greek original), thanks to its basically triple metre with allowable shifts into duple everywhere except before the last beat, and the tendency of the six-beat line to fall into two three-beat groups. The pre-eminent English poet in this mode is Arthur Hugh Clough. Here is the opening of part VII of *Amours de voyage* (I haven't marked the potential silent beats after every three realized beats, as Clough's verse rattles along without much in the way of pauses, so that virtual beats are registered only very faintly as articulations of the rhythm into lines and half-lines):

> So, I have seen a man killed! An experience that, among others!
> B   -o- B   -o- B   -o-   B -o-   B -o-   B o
>
> Yes, I suppose I have; although I can hardly be certain,
> B -o-   B o B   o B   -o-   B -o-   B o
>
> And in a court of justice could never declare I had seen it.
> B   -o- B   o B   -o-   B -o- B -o-   B   o

> (*Poems*, 181)

This metre is not very far removed from the six-beat dolnik used by Tennyson in 'Rizpah', a few lines of which I quoted earlier, or the many Victorian poems in a similar metre, though one important difference is that Clough, following classical precedent, doesn't use regular rhyme.

Another classical metrical form, carried, like the dactylic hexameter, from Ancient Greek into Latin, was the Sapphic; and here it was not the replacement of the Latin quantitative ictus by a stressed syllable but the original accentual pattern of the Latin that, fortuitously, produced a version of the dolnik rhythm, with three four-beat lines and a two-beat coda. The following is a characteristic stanza in Sapphic metre by Horace (*Odes*, 1.38), showing the beats that emerge in a reading attentive to Latin stressing. A characteristic feature of the Sapphic accentual rhythm is the triple offbeat before the final beat (indicated by -o-):

> Persicos odi, puer, apparatus,
> B -o- B o B   -o- B o
>
> desplicent nexae philyra coronae,
> B   -o-   B o B -o- B o
>
> mitte sectari, rosa quo locorum
> B -o- B o B   -o- B o
>
> sera moretur[33]
> B -o- B o

Henry Dearmer's translation of a hymn attributed to Gregory the Great, included in the former's *English Hymnal* of 1906, will give us an example of the English Sapphic:[34]

[33] John Conington's Victorian translation reads: 'No Persian cumber, boy, for me; | I hate your garlands linden-plaited; | Leave winter's rose where on the tree | It hangs belated' (39).

[34] I am terming it the 'English Sapphic' rather than the 'accentual Sapphic', the latter being a different metre, one which, on the model of the accentual hexameter, substitutes an accentual scheme for the quantitative one and does not produce a dolnik rhythm. Swinburne's 'Sapphics' is an example; it begins 'All the night sleep came not upon my eyelids, | Shed not dew, nor shook nor unclosed a feather'.

Father, we praise thee, now the night is over;
B   -o-   B   o   B   ⌢o⌢   B o

Active and watchful, stand we all before thee;
B   -o-   B   o   B   ⌢o⌢   B   o

Singing, we offer prayer and meditation;
B   -o-   B o   B   ⌢o⌢ B o

Thus we adore thee.[35]
    B   -o- B   o

The eleven-syllable lines have four main beats, and the first and second offbeats are, respectively, double and single (and the final five-syllable line follows the pattern of the openings of the earlier lines). It is between the third and fourth beats that the distinctive rhythm of the accentual Sapphic is created: three unstressed syllables, with the suggestion of a weaker beat on the middle one. Outside of the context of music, in fact, the longer lines come very close to iambic pentameter with an initial inversion, and a single line of this type would not be out of place in pentameter verse.[36] The consistent opening, so typical of the stronger dolnik rhythm, however, encourages a four-beat reading, and hence a speeding up of the second part of the line to accommodate it. A slow chant of these lines will reveal that a quadruple rhythm underlies them:

Fa-ther, we praise thee, now the night is o-ver
 B B   **B**   B **B**   B   **B** B

Emily Brontë's 'Remembrance' is probably most often read now as in somewhat free iambic pentameters, but if we hear it with a Victorian ear its rhythmic allegiance to the English Sapphic is clear, giving it a plangent musicality (I quote a stanza where this allegiance is especially clear):

Sweet Love of youth, forgive, if I forget thee,
  B   -o-   B   o B   ⌢o⌢   B   o

While the world's tide is bearing me along;
  B   -o-   B   o B   ⌢o⌢   B

Other desires and other hopes beset me,
  B   -o- B   o   B   ⌢o⌢   B   o

Hopes which obscure, but cannot do thee wrong!
  B   -o-   B   o   B   ⌢o⌢   B

(*Poems*, 130)

[35] Dearmer et al., *The English Hymnal*, 238. As an example of a musical setting that clearly brings out the four-beat rhythm of what might look like a five-beat line, see (and listen to) the hymn 'Lord of Our Life, and God of Our Salvation' set to Joseph Barnby's tune 'Cloisters': <http://newchurchmusic.org/drupal5/?q=system/files/858+Lord+of+Our +Life+and+God+of+Our+Salvation.png>.

[36] See Chapter 5 section III for a discussion of the common five-beat line with a break between the second and third beats, producing what I have called a 'sprung pentameter'.

Brontë removes the final unstressed syllable of the second line, and repeats this metre in place of the short final line; but the distinctive Sapphic form of the dolnik four-line stanza is still evident.[37]

VI

Since the practice of many Victorian poets indicates an acute awareness of the poetic potential of dolnik verse and its characteristic beat prosody, and since, presumably, their readers were able to appreciate their exploitation of that potential, we might expect that prosodic theory of the period would provide us with a clear account of its workings. Unfortunately, however, theorizations of the mechanics of versification in western poetry have, from the beginnings, been dogged by the difficulties of representing, either in linguistic or in graphic form, the experiences of the ear and body in responding to rhythmic arrangements in sound. Although the ear finds dolnik verse the easiest metrical form to grasp, we have seen that the prosodist working with the traditional tools finds it highly problematic. Nevertheless, there are some signs that the features of spoken English capitalized on by dolnik verse, and more generally by four-beat forms, were brought into consciousness more fully during Victoria's reign than in previous eras. Joshua Steele, in his *Essay towards Establishing the Melody and Measure of Speech* (1775)— later entitled *Prosodia Rationalis*—had led the way in using musical notation to represent the temporal relations of English speech, including pauses or silences. Edwin Guest's monumental *History of English Rhythms*, first published in 1838 and issued in a posthumous second edition in 1882, while approaching English metre as a matter of accent rather than time, registered in a few places the existence of dolnik verse and its dependence on temporal relations. Beats and offbeats felt by the reader but not manifested in the voice are termed 'sectional pauses', and Guest gives several examples, including the opening of Puck's song in *A Midsummer Night's Dream*:

> On the ground
> B   o B
>
> Sleep sound (281)
> B ó B

---

[37] For a fuller discussion of the Horatian Sapphic and English imitations, see Attridge, *Well-Weighed Syllables*, 211–16.

The dolnik's variation between single and double offbeats he discusses under the heading of 'tumbling-metre'; among his examples are the February eclogue in Spenser's *Shepheardes Calender*, which begins:

There grew an aged Tree on the greene
o   B   o B o   B   -o-   B

(Shorter Poems, 535)

The most important contribution to the Victorian understanding of the song-rhythms of the dolnik and other four-beat forms was made by Coventry Patmore, in a study that first appeared in the *North British Review* in 1857 as a review entitled 'English Metrical Critics' and was subsequently revised for further publication in editions of Patmore's poetical works, finally appearing as 'Essay on English Metrical Law' at the end of the second volume of his *Poems* (1886).[38] Patmore's basic premiss is that 'metre, in the primary degree of a series of isochronous intervals, marked by accents, is as natural to spoken language as an even pace is natural to walking' (10). On this basis, he is able to give Guest's 'sectional pauses' a fundamental role in metre, appreciating that the temporal movement set up by a regular alternating rhythm makes it possible for beats to be experienced even when they have no material embodiment, and recognizing, too, that 'the equality or proportion of metrical intervals between accent and accent is no more than general and approximate' (21). (By 'accent' Patmore means what I am calling 'stress', or more often 'stress functioning as a beat'.) He is thus able to say that there are 'two indispensable conditions of metre', first, 'that the sequence of vocal utterance, represented by written verse, shall be divided into equal or proportionate spaces', and second, '*that the fact of that division shall be made manifest* by an "ictus" or "beat", actual or mental' (15). These 'mental' beats, which I have been calling virtual beats, are a product of the isochronous tendency of the spoken language that Patmore has already emphasized; they exist, it is important to note, not in some abstract realm of mathematical relations but as realities in the mind as perceiver of rhythm.[39] When he goes on to say of this 'time-beater' that 'for the most part, *it has no material and ex-*

---

[38] For a modern edition see the dissertation by Roth, *Coventry Patmore's 'Essay on English Metrical Law'*. Quotations are from this edition.

[39] Rudy reveals clearly the problems that beset the prosodist who puts abstract metrical grids before the experience of the ear: he chides Patmore for placing 'a great deal of trust in the reader, who must intuit (physically? intellectually?) the poem's metrical structure' and asks, a propos of isochrony, 'what sort of regulation might come from a poem that most readers cannot scan?' (*Electric Meters*, 122). In fact, the regular beats of strongly isochronic English verse are felt by both the mind and the body, and any scanning difficulties are the product not of a complex metre but of inappropriate tools of analysis.

ternal existence at all', but is a result of the mind's delight in marking measure 'with an imaginary "beat"' (15), he is not arguing for a mechanical grid against which the realities of vocal rhythm are played, but for the immediacy in the reader's experience of rhythmic pulses, continuing beyond the sounding of the voice.

One example of Patmore's acute ear and careful analysis in applying his theory of isochrony to verse is his discussion of falling inversion in accentual-syllabic verse (see Chapter 6 section III): the occurrence of a virtual offbeat followed by a double offbeat. He cites the following line from *Paradise Lost* (I, 33; I have added scansion symbols):

> For one restraint, Lords of the world beside.
> o B   o B [o] B   -o-   B   o B

His comment is as follows:

In the proper delivery of this line, the same time, or very nearly, is allowed to elapse between the first and second, second and third, and third and fourth accents; but between the first and second there is *one* unaccented syllable; between the second and third, *none*; and between the third and fourth there are *two*; consequently, the trochee, '*Lords of*', and the iambus '*the world*', are both temporarily [i.e. temporally] deficient when considered as feet, the two unemphatic syllables, *of the*, being pronounced in the time of one of any of the other three unemphatic syllables in the line. (20)

That he appreciated the operation of what I am calling 'implied offbeats' is clear from his insistence that 'adjacent accents' should be read with a 'metrical pause' between them (24).

It is ironic that a prosodist who understood the significance of felt temporality in the mind's experience of regular verse should sometimes be hailed as the forefather of the prosodic theory of New Criticism, for which metre was exactly that abstract, mechanical grid.[40] So taken was Patmore by this insight into the experiential reality of beats that he over-generalized it, and claimed to find 'catalexis'—missing syllables 'substituted by an equivalent pause' (23)—in a wide variety of verse types. This argument was linked to a view that English verse is fundamentally dipodic or quadruple, so that any uneven number of beats in a line will always imply one more unsounded beat. Although, as we have seen, many Victorian poets found in dipodic verse a satisfying form, there are too many counter-examples (including most five-beat verse) to allow Patmore's argument to stand. Nevertheless, his account of rhythm and metre comes closest of

---

[40] The section in which Martin discusses Patmore is entitled 'Mistrusting the Ear' (67), and she later states that his 'new prosody' included the moving of metrical law into 'mental and metaphysical realms' (87).

any Victorian prosodic theory to explaining the workings of the dolnik metrical form so expertly exploited by many of his peers.[41] Had George Saintsbury not come to dominate early twentieth-century prosody through his monumental *History of English Prosody* (1906–10), with its suspicion of temporally based theories and its insistence on the existence of feet, Patmore's understanding of the physical and mental reality of beats might have persisted.[42]

VII

We may end this discussion of Victorian poetry by turning briefly to three poets at the end of the period who exploited the potential of the dolnik to the full, though in very different ways: Algernon Charles Swinburne, Rudyard Kipling, Thomas Hardy. Swinburne's most characteristic poems employ a variant of the dolnik that he developed early in his career and continued to exploit until its end. It is used in much of his best-known poetry, including 'The Triumph of Time', 'Hymn to Proserpine', 'The Garden of Proserpine', 'A Forsaken Garden', and the famous choruses from 'Atalanta in Calydon'. Here is the opening of 'The Garden of Proserpine':

> Here, where the world is quiet;
> B   -o-   B   o   B o   [B]
>
> Here, where all trouble seems
> B   -o-   B   o   B   [oB]
>
> Dead winds' and spent waves' riot
> O   B   o   B   O   Bo   [B]
>
> In doubtful dreams of dreams;
> o   B   o   B   o   B   [oB]
>
> I watch the green field growing
> o B   o   B   O   B o   [B]
>
> (*Selected Poems*, 75)

---

[41] In his own poetry, Patmore—though he made extensive use of four-beat verse, for instance in the lengthy *Angel in the House*—did not favour dolnik verse. His Odes are highly varied in line-length, but maintain a steady alternating beat.

[42] Patmore's account of English metre had an important follower in T. S. Omond, whose *English Metrists* (1907) advanced an anti-Saintsburian view of the centrality of temporal relations. Housman, in his own insightful study *The Name and Nature of Poetry*, states that 'a few pages of Coventry Patmore and a few of Frederic Myers contain all, so far as I know, or all of value, which has been written' on the laws of versification (4). Levin, in '"But the Law Itself"', argues convincingly that Omond was influenced by Swinburne's poetic practice.

As usual with verse that is consistently in lines of three beats, the fourth, virtual beat is only a slight presence, and Swinburne's enjambments contribute to its containment. One feature of his dolnik verse is the use of demotion in single offbeats, that is, the use of a stressed syllable between two other stressed syllables that take beats (recall Tennyson's 'dim grey wall' and 'cold gray stones'). This is a variation that may owe something to the classical example of the allowable substitution of a spondee for a dactyl in the dactylic hexameter. Demotion doesn't require a forced pronunciation, as the persistence of the four-beat rhythm in the mind—as Patmore understood—allows the alternation to be felt even if it is not objectively present. So 'waves' and 'field' in the lines above take their natural stress, but aren't experienced as beats. Initial stressed syllables—such as 'Dead'—can also be demoted in this way.

Where Swinburne cultivated a suave, melodic rhythm, Kipling explored the dolnik and other four-beat metrical forms in search of a jauntiness that contributed to his enormous popularity as a poet. Along with extensive use of quadruple and triple verse we find poems such as 'The Ballad of East and West', written in the seven-beat line realization of the 4.3.4.3 ballad stanza:

```
Oh, East is East, and West is West, and never the twain shall
o   B   o B   o   B   o B   o   B   -o-    B     o
   meet,
      B  [o B]
Till Earth and Sky stand presently at God's great Judgment
o B   o    B   o   Bo Bo B   O  B   o
   Seat;
      B  [o B]
But there is neither East nor West, Border, nor Breed, nor
o   B  o B  o B    o   B [o] B  -o-    B    0
   Birth,
      B  [o B]
When two strong men stand face to face, though they come from the
o   B   O   B   o   B  o B      -o-      B      -o-
   ends of the earth!
   B   -o-  B   [o B]
```

(Complete Verse, 190)

Whatever we may think of the sentiments expressed, there can be no doubt that this is a highly skilful deployment of dolnik verse, from the strong opening alternation of beats and single offbeats, through

the suggestion of syncopation when the offbeat is skipped between
'West' and 'Border', to the run of five stressed monosyllables in the
first part of the fourth line followed by the rapid sequence of beats
and double offbeats that finish the stanza. Among the other well-
known poems of Kipling in dolnik metres are 'The 'eathen', 'The
Light that Failed', 'When Earth's Last Picture is Painted', and several
of the poems in *The Jungle Book* and *Just So Stories*. A quadruple
metre poem that relies on the possibility of implied offbeats for its
distinctive march rhythm is 'Boots' ('We're foot—slog—slog—slog—
sloggin' over Africa').

Hardy, by contrast with Kipling, was able to encompass a much wider
range of rhythmic styles, and found a way of eliciting from the dolnik emo-
tional resonances of great depth and subtlety. His first collection, *Wessex
Poems and Other Verses* (1898), contains several dolnik poems, including
'Postponement' (light verse dating from 1866), 'Neutral Tones' (contrast-
ingly dark, from 1869), 'San Sebastian' (a plaintive spoken narrative), and
'Her Death and After' (a longer narrative poem, full of emotion). Examples
of dolnik verse in *Poems of the Past and the Present* (1901) include the potent
meditation on insect life 'An August Midnight', the seven-beat lines of
'In Tenebris II', and the unmistakably Hardeian lament at the irreversibility
of time, 'On the Departure Platform'. The last stanza of 'Neutral Tones' will
have to suffice as an example of Hardy's metrical brilliance:

> Since then, keen lessons that love deceives,
> o   B   O   B   -o-   B   o B
>
> And wrings with wrong, have shaped to me
> o   B   o   B   o   B   o B
>
> Your face, and the God-curst sun, and a tree,
> o   B   -o-   B   O   B   -o-   B
>
> And a pond edged with grayish leaves.
> -o- B   =o-   B o   B   [o B]
>
> (*Complete Poems*, 12)

The first two lines move steadily forward, all but one of the offbeats
being single, and the only moment of heightening is on 'keen', requir-
ing stress but serving as an offbeat. Then the run-on after 'shaped to
me' pushes against the four-beat expectation of a pause, while the fol-
lowing line piles on the elements in the scene with two double offbeats
and an emphasis on the powerful word 'curst' (in the second line of the
poem the sun was merely 'chidden' by God). Finally, the three-beat
closing line tenses the rhythm by including the strongly stressed word
'edged' as part of a double offbeat—there is a temptation to give it a
beat, allowing a pause after 'pond' to take a beat, and it is largely the

clearly three-beat lines of the three previous stanzas that determine the rhythm here.[43]

Victorian verse in metrical forms that rely on the popular rhythms of ballad, song, and nursery rhyme has been consistently underestimated since the poetic revaluation effected by Pound, Eliot, Leavis, and others in the first third of the twentieth century. A full appreciation of its achievements requires that we learn to appreciate once more the potential of a poetic form that, instead of tempering rhythm in the interests of dramatic speech, heightens its regular beating to create movements of language that are vivid, memorable, and often deeply affecting.

VIII

Notwithstanding the rise of free verse and the offensive against Victorian four-beat poetry that marked the early decades of the twentieth century, the dolnik survived, especially among more popular genres. A. A. Milne, discussed in Chapter 5, is one example; Walter de la Mare is another. I'm sure I am not the only grown-up poetry reader whose rhythmic nerve-ends were set tingling at a young age by de la Mare's 'The Listeners'. The brief story it told was part of its allure: the unnamed Traveller who knocks, for unknown reasons, at the door in the forest and receives no answer, unaware that he is being heard by a 'host of phantom listeners'. But de la Mare's brilliant exploitation of the dolnik rhythm surely played its part: catchy, musical, and with a rhythmic character not quite like that of any other poem. This is the opening:

> 'Is there anybody there?' said the Traveller,
>   -o-   B ~o~   B   -o-   B   o [B]
>
> Knocking on the moonlit door;
>   B   -o-   B   o B   [o B]
>
> And his horse in the silence champed the grasses
>   -o-   B   -o- B o   B   o B o
>
> Of the forest's ferny floor;
>   -o-   B o   B o B   [o B]

---

[43] All the dolnik verse in *Wessex Poems* involves a shorter last line or pair of lines, and it may well be, as Dennis Taylor has argued, that Hardy's fascination with the Sapphic and its final truncated line and mixture of dactyls and trochees is evident in these poems; see *Hardy's Metres and Victorian Prosody*, 258–62. Taylor lists 'Neutral Tones' as duple rising (230), with a 'mixture of iambs and dactyls'. He notes that E. B. Browning had used a similar form in 'The Deserted Garden' (261). Although Matthew Campbell, in *Rhythm and Will in Victorian Poetry*, analyses the poem in terms of classical feet, he observes of one of these shorter lines that 'it creates the very effect that Coleridge had envisaged in "Christabel"' (59).

And a bird flew up out of the turret,
   -o- B   -o- B   -o- B o[B]

Above the Traveller's head:
o B   o B o B   [o B]

And he smote upon the door again a second time;
   -o-   B   -o-   B   -o- B o   B

'Is there anybody there?' he said.
   -o-   B -o-   B   o B   [o B]

(Untermeyer, Modern British Poetry, 106)

I'm not sure if anyone has attempted to scan this poem by means of classical feet, but it would be a challenge. De la Mare uses the traditional 3.3.4.3 short measure, but deploys double and triple feet to brilliant effect to create a unique rhythmic world.

Another immensely popular poet is John Betjeman, who uses dolnik verse for equally disturbing topics, including 'Death in Leamington' and 'The Arrest of Oscar Wilde at the Cadogan Hotel'. In the first of these, published in 1932, the lilt of the dolnik is counterpoised against the grimness of the narrative, as the narrator tells of the discovery by a figure referred to simply as 'Nurse' of the dead body of the upstairs bedroom's lonely inhabitant. These are the final three stanzas:

Do you know that the stucco is peeling?
  -o-   B   -o-   B -o- B o   [B]

Do you know that the heart will stop?
  -o-   B   -o-   B   o B [o B]

From those yellow Italianate arches
   -o-   B -o-B -o- B   o [B]

Do you hear the plaster drop?
  -o-   B   o B o   B   [o B]

Nurse looked at the silent bedstead,
  O B   -o- Bo   B   o [B]

At the gray, decaying face,
  -o-   B   o B o   B   [o B]

As the calm of a Leamington evening
  -o-   B   -o- B   -o- B   o   [B]

Drifted into the place.
  B o B -o-   B   [o B]

She moved the table of bottles
  o B   o B -o- B o [B]

Away from the bed to the wall;
  o B   -o-   B -o-   B [o B]

And tiptoeing gently over the stairs
o   B -o-   B oB -o-   B
Turned down the gas in the hall.
B   -o- B -o- B [o B]

(*Collected Poems*, 2)

Again, there is the typical dolnik variation between single and double offbeats both within the line and at the start, enhancing the strong rhythm of the four-beat line. Line-endings are more regular: feminine and masculine alternate, a common feature of quatrains, except in cases where the fourth beat of the third line is realized, in which case the ending is masculine, as in the desolate final stanza. The sense of conclusion is enhanced by some departures from the most common patterns of the poem up to this point: the first stanza quoted is the only one in which every line begins with a double offbeat, leading into the three heartbreaking questions; the next stanza ends with the only beat-initial line in the poem, encouraging us to linger on the first word—'Drifted into the place'—and the penultimate line with its four realized beats takes its time over the Nurse's actions—'And tiptoeing gently over the stairs'—and leads into the plangent simplicity of the final line.

Contemporary poets with a wide readership who employ the dolnik for comic effect include Wendy Cope and Sophie Hannah. Here is the opening of what is probably Wendy Cope's most famous poem, 'Bloody Men':

Bloody men are like bloody buses –
B o B   -o-   B o Bo
You wait for about a year
o   B   -o- B o B [o B]
And as soon as one approaches your stop
  -o- B   o B   o   B   -o-   B
Two or three others appear.
B -o-   B   -o- B   [o B]

(*Two Cures for Love*, 19)

Rhythmic neatness strengthens the neatness of the comparison, and is a quality of much of Cope's dolnik verse. Hannah also frequently uses the dolnik form to describe lust or disappointment in love, and in the poem I am about to quote takes advantage of the difference between strict iambic tetrameter and the freer but still rhythmic dolnik. First the poem as it is printed:

I came this little seaside town
And went a pub they call The Crown
Where straight away I happened see
A man who seemed quite partial me.

> I proved susceptible his charms
> And fell right in his open arms.
> From time time, every now and then,
> I hope meet up with him again.
> (*Selected Poems*, 133)

The clue to the at first sight mystifying garbling of the sentences lies in the title, 'Wells-Next-the-Sea'. If we restore the missing 'to' in the same way that we would be tempted to restore it in the name of the town, we get the following more intelligible (though less interesting) poem:

> I came to this little seaside town
> And went to a pub they call The Crown
> Where straight away I happened to see
> A man who seemed quite partial to me.
> I proved susceptible to his charms
> And fell right into his open arms.
> From time to time, every now and then,
> I hope to meet up with him again.

It will be obvious that the introduction of the preposition in each line introduces also a double offbeat, thus loosening up the rhyme. Although this couldn't be called a full-blooded dolnik, it is made possible by the same principle of isochrony that underlies dolnik rhythmicality.

Dolnik verse in the twentieth century is not confined to poets characterized as 'popular', however. Yeats's 'Easter 1916' has dolnik features, as has Frost's 'Come In' and Langston Hughes's 'Song for a Dark Girl'.[44] A distinctively syncopated rhythmic quality is produced by Louis MacNeice's use of the dolnik in 'Bagpipe Music'. This is the last stanza of the poem, and I've indicated the rocking dipodic rhythm by using a bold font for the more emphatic beats that alternate with the weaker beats:

> Annie MacDougall went to milk, caught her foot in the heather,
> **B** -o-   **B** o **B** o B [o]**B**   o B -o-   **B** o
>
> Woke to hear a dance record playing of Old Vienna.
>   **B** o B o **B** [o]B o   **B** -o- B   oB o
>
> It's no go your maidenheads, it's no go your culture,
>   o **B**[o]**B** o   **B** o B   o **B**[o]**B** o   **B** o
>
> All we want is a Dunlop tyre and the devil mend the puncture.
> **B** o B -o- **B** o B   -o- **B** o B   o **B** o
> (Skelton, ed., *Poetry of the Thirties*, 72)

---

[44] For an analysis of the rhythmic features of 'Song for a Dark Girl', see Attridge, 'The Case for the English Dolnik'. Like the author of the first poem we considered, 'Now Go'th Sun under Wood', Hughes uses dolnik verse to express a woman's grief at the hanging of a man she loves.

Here we have the typical dolnik variations between beats—where we find no syllables, one syllable, and two syllables—and at the opening of the line—fifteen of the poem's thirty-four lines begin on an offbeat, the remainder on a beat. MacNeice avoids stressed syllables in the offbeats, keeping the rhythm light and ensuring that the infectious dipodic rhythm emerges clearly: another case in which the jauntiness of the rhythm contributes to the dark heart of the poem, in which a series of Scottish characters exhibit their cheerful improvidence while the social and political barometer keeps falling.

The master-metrist W. H. Auden used the dolnik in several poems, three of them—'As I Walked Out', 'Victor', and 'Miss Gee'—in ballad form. The latter two are blackly comic, exploiting the rhythmic drive of the dolnik to mimic heartlessness on the part of the narrator. 'As I Walked Out' is also a poem of dark emotions, turning the traditional ballad tale of young love into a bleak admonition. The following two stanzas carry the poem's climactic moment:

> 'O look, look in the mirror,
> o B [o]B -o- B o   [B]
>
>   O look in your distress;
>   o B o B o B   [o B]
>
> Life remains a blessing
> B o B o B o   [B]
>
>   Although you cannot bless.
>   o B   o B o B   [o B]
>
> 'O stand, stand at the window
> o B [o]B -o- B o   [B]
>
>   As the tears scald and start;
>   -o- B ô B o   B   [o B]
>
> You shall love your crooked neighbour
> -o- B o   B o B o   [B]
>
>   With your crooked heart.'
>   B o B o B   [o B]

(*Collected Shorter Poems*, 86)

Both stanzas begin with a repetition made all the more insistent by the virtual offbeat between the repeated words, inducing a pause or a lengthening of the first word. Auden has taken the traditional form of the ballad, and although his version is not intended to be sung, has retained the type of freedom between beats that characterized the sung ballad; the result is a poem with a strong narrative drive that can produce moments of powerful poetic resonance.

One of Auden's best-liked poems has a predominantly falling rhythm which makes use of the dolnik freedom at the start of the line, though it remains very regular thereafter: the well-known 'Lullaby'. I've scanned the second stanza (the lower case b indicates a promoted syllable—in other words, an unstressed syllable which, because of its position between two other unstressed syllables, can function metrically as a beat while remaining without stress):

Soul and body have no bounds:
B   o   B o B   o B

To lovers as they lie upon
  o B o   b   o B o B

Her tolerant enchanted slope
  o B o b o   B o   B

In their ordinary swoon,
b   o B o b o   B

Grave the vision Venus sends
B   o Bo   B o B

Of supernatural sympathy,
o   B o B-o- B   o   b

Universal love and hope;
B o B o B   o   B

While an abstract insight wakes
B o B   o B o   B

Among the glaciers and the rocks
o B   o B o b   o B

The hermit's sensual ecstasy.
  o B o B o B ob

(*Collected Shorter Poems*, 108)

Approached in terms of foot-prosody, this stanza is a puzzle: half the lines begin with an iamb and half with a trochee. In the rest of the poem, trochees dominate, so that may settle the question for our foot-prosodist—though we still have the problem that occurs with most so-called 'trochaic' tetrameter, that the 'trochaic' lines, as well as the 'iambic' lines, end on a beat, and therefore their last foot is defective. (Unless, of course, they are actually headless iambic lines.) If we forget all about iambs and trochees, we can say that this is duple verse with four realized beats per line which displays the dolnik's freedom at line-beginnings but eschews it thereafter. The effect is of great simplicity of rhythm, tending towards a chant but kept from it by the varying line-openings, the extensive use of promotion, the ten-line stanza with its intricate rhyme-scheme, and the frequent enjambments.

To end, a recent example that, to my mind, finds a new use for the dolnik. James Fenton included several dolnik poems in his 1993 collection *Out of Danger*, using the form not for light verse but for poetry on huge themes—the killings in Cambodia and Tiananmen square, for instance, or a rewriting of the story of Christ and Judas. In some of the poems—a few of which are several pages long—the swing of the dolnik contributes to the apocalyptic tone, making it more like a comic-book apocalypse but not the less serious for all that. Kipling's military uses of the dolnik are somewhere in the background too. 'I Saw a Child' has stanzas with five four-beat lines, one of which is divided, and characteristic dolnik freedom in the offbeats. It ends as follows:

> Far from the wisdom of the blood
> I saw a child reach from the mud.
> Clutch my hand.
> Clutch my heart.
> The fields are mined and the moon is dark.
> The Blue Vein River is in full flood.
>
> Far from the wisdom of the heart
> I saw a child being torn apart.
> Is this you?
> Is this me?
> The fields are mined and the night is long.
> Stick with me when the shooting starts.
>
> *(Selected Poems*, 75)

Fenton's poems show that the dolnik has plenty of life in it yet, for purposes entirely relevant to our current condition. To use it is to look back to an 800-year-old tradition, as well as to a flowering in the first part of the twentieth century, and to look forward to new explorations and exploitations of its poetic resources.

8

Lexical Inventiveness and Metrical Patterns

Beats and Keats

BEATS

The term *beat*, as we use it in poetic analysis, rests on an analogy between verse and music—not because the metrical foot is seen as a parallel with the musical bar, as is sometimes claimed,[1] but because the metrical foot does not correspond to the felt rhythmic divisions of music. (Musical bars or measures always begin on the beat; metrical feet seldom do.) The term 'beat' comes from the action of the conductor moving the baton up and down to signal to an orchestra the rhythmic shape of the music. Beats are not, however, imposed on the music; they are part of its fabric, part of what we hear when we hear its sounds moving through time. They are the moments when any one of us might be tempted to perform a physical action—to move the hand like a conductor, to nod, to tap the foot. And what this indicates is that the rhythmical beat is closely tied to the physical body.

When I set out a theory of English metre in *The Rhythms of English Poetry* in 1982, I found that the concept of the beat helped me understand how the spoken rhythms of English, when organized in a certain way, produced a similar effect. When I read simple metrical verse aloud, there is no question about the points at which I might move my hand to signal that I am sensing a beat. For instance, here is the first stanza of Robert Herrick's 'To Daffadills':

---

[1] See, for example, the entry for *beat* in the 1974 *Princeton Encyclopedia of Poetry and Poetics*, ed. Alex Preminger: 'The term is often used instead of "stress" by prosodists who are pressing the analogies between verse and music and who are thinking of the metrical foot as an almost exact parallel with the musical bar' (73). For my attempt at a brief account of the term, see the fourth edition, ed. Roland Greene et al.

> Faire Daffadills, we weep to see
> You haste away so soone:
> As yet the early-rising Sun
> Has not attain'd his Noone.
>
> (*The Complete Poetry*, 171)

If we accompany certain syllables with a muscular movement, these are almost certainly 'Daff-', '-dills', 'weep', 'see', 'haste', '-way', 'soone', and so on.

But what produces this physical response? As we have already noted, regular metrical verse in English harnesses the rhythmic features of the language in a distinctive way. Spoken English, like many other languages, is characterized by two simultaneous rhythmic principles, to some extent in tension with one another: syllabic rhythm and stress rhythm. Putting it crudely, each of these rhythms tends towards perceptual regularity, the syllables trying to space themselves out at even intervals, the stresses doing the same. In normal spoken English, the stress rhythm nearly always wins the contest, and the syllables have to compress or elongate themselves to suit the dominant principle.

What happens in regular verse is that words are chosen in such a way that the two principles coincide: by alternating stressed and unstressed syllables (or stressed syllables and pairs of unstressed syllables), the stresses can fall at perceptually even intervals, and so can the unstressed syllables. And when *this* happens, we find ourselves responding with the characteristic muscular movement I have described; in other words, we experience beats. It's important to note, however, that a beat is not an isolated phenomenon: it is a phase in a sequence, a pulse or little explosion coming after a phase of build-up and preceding a phase of relaxation. Beats occur only in conjunction with offbeats, the phase between beats, just as offbeats occur only in conjunction with beats.

My attempt to describe much more complex verse than this little example builds on this simple foundation: there are many ways in which beats can be strengthened or weakened, delayed or hurried, and there are many ways in which the offbeats can be varied too. The units into which the verse falls are also a matter of beats; in the Herrick example, the lines have four and three beats in alternation, but if we pay attention to the physical experience of the lines we are likely to feel the presence in those shorter lines of a fourth beat in the pause between lines. It is therefore an example of what we have seen is one of the most common forms of English regular verse, four-beat verse, and the commonest grouping of four-beat verse, into four lines.[2] (Four-beat verse can occur in many different line-lengths,

---

[2] It is not dolnik verse as discussed in the previous chapter, however; Herrick observes the strict rules of accentual-syllabic metre.

since divisions on the page don't always coincide with the fundamental units of rhythm. But you can always *hear*, or rather *feel*, the distinctive four-beat rhythm underlying the movement of the language.) The other major rhythmic unit is the five-beat unit discussed in Chapter 6, a unit which nearly always appears on the page in lines of that length, and is much stricter in its control of syllables. In the second part of this essay, when we turn to Keats, we shall see how subtle that control can be.

One of the most basic errors in discussing English verse is to confuse beats with stresses (see, for example, the sentence I quoted from the first edition of the *Princeton Encyclopedia* in n. 1). Although in our simple example beats coincide with stresses, and offbeats with unstressed syllables, this is far from a universal rule.[3] Much of the life of English poetry in regular metres comes from the possibility of unstressed syllables functioning as beats and stressed syllables as offbeats. This is not an uncontrolled possibility, of course: promotion and demotion, as we have seen in the two previous chapters, can happen only under certain conditions, conditions which prevent the experience of beats disappearing altogether. A couple of the places in which they do happen are exemplified in the opening of another Herrick poem:

> Gather ye Rose-buds while ye may,
>   Old Time is still a flying:
> And this same flower that smiles today,
>   To morrow will be dying.

('To the Virgins, to Make Much of Time', *Complete Poetry*, 117)

We may well want to stress 'Old' in 'Old Time' and 'same' in 'this same flower'—and of course we can, although the words will not carry beats. If we imagine a melody for the lines, we don't have any doubt where the beats come—and it's not on these words. When reading the lines, however, it is possible to sustain the sense of rhythm without over-emphasizing the syllables on which the beats fall; the experience can be thought of as a *blurring* of the beat–offbeat rhythm, a momentary suspension which contributes to the rhythmic vitality of the poetry.

These lines have one other very common deviation from the strict alternation that characterizes regular verse: the first line begins not with an offbeat, as do the rest of the lines (and in fact the rest of the poem), but with a beat, underlining the force of the imperative with which the poems opens: 'Gather ye Rose-buds while ye may'. Traditionally called 'initial inversion', this rhythmic figure switches the expected sequence 'unstress–stress' to

---

[3] The opening of the Herrick example is the most complex part of the stanza, since 'Faire' demands some emphasis even though it is an offbeat, and the last syllable of 'Daffadills' carries only secondary stress but takes a beat.

'stress–unstress', producing what I've called a 'double offbeat' between the first two beats. Inversion can happen within the line as well as at the beginning, and can happen between an unstressed syllable and a following stressed syllable, and vice versa.

Regular metrical verse in English, then, is a matter of beats. This is to say that it is a matter of the physical experience of pronouncing the language as an engagement with deeply seated rhythmic habits in the musculature of the body, especially in the respiratory system of diaphragm and lungs. The rhythm of Herrick's poems is not fundamentally different from the rhythm produced when we sing a song, dance to music, or just walk along the road.

But what about prose, then, and free verse that utilizes the rhythms of prose? This obviously has rhythmic qualities, too. Sometimes, we can feel beats of the same kind as regular verse. Here is a sentence by Dickens, a natural description from *Martin Chuzzlewit*:

The wet grass sparkled in the light; the scanty patches of verdure in the hedges—where a few green twigs yet stood together bravely, resisting to the last the tyranny of nipping winds and early frosts—took heart and brightened up; the stream which had been dull and sullen all day long, broke out into a cheerful smile; the birds began to chirp and twitter on the naked boughs, as though the hopeful creatures half believed that winter had gone by, and spring had come already. (57)

If we notate the stressed and unstressed syllables by / and x respectively, the pattern that emerges looks like this:

x / / / x x x / x / x / x x /x x x / x x x / / / x / x / x / x x / x x x / x / x x x / x / x /
x / x / x / x / x / x / x / x / x / / / x / x x x / x / x / x / x / x / x x x / x / x / x / x /
x /x / x / x x x / x / x / x / x

What you see here is many sequences of simple alternation of stressed and unstressed syllables, characteristic of the most straightforward metres; they are interspersed with runs of three stressed or three unstressed syllables, which happen to be the sequences in which promotion or demotion happen most often—'the wet grass sparkled', ' a few green twigs', 'sparkled in the light', 'resisting to the last'. (We might compare the first two with the phrases 'dim grey wall' and 'cold gray stones' in the previous chapter, and with 'this same flower' in Herrick's 'To the Virgins'.)

We can mark the beats in the passages as follows (as usual, B for beat on a stressed syllable, b for beat on an unstressed syllable, i.e. promotion):

The wet grass sparkled in the light; the scanty patches of verdure in the hedges—
  B   B   b   B   B   B   B   b   B

where a few green twigs yet stood together bravely, resisting to the last the
  B   B   B   B   B   B   b   B

tyranny of nipping winds and early frosts—took heart and brightened up; the
B b B   B   B   B   B   B   B

stream which had been dull and sullen all day long, broke out into a cheerful
B   B   B   B   B   B   B   b   B

smile; the birds began to chirp and twitter on the naked boughs, as though the
B   B   B   B   B   b   B   B   B

hopeful creatures half believed that winter had gone by, and spring had come
B   B   B   B   B   b   B   B   B

already.
B

In this sentence, as often in Dickens's more lyrical passages, it is not diffi-
cult, with a little exaggeration perhaps, to tap in time with a fairly regular
rhythm; the author is harnessing some of the resources of metrical poetry to
convey a sense of ease and cheerfulness.[4] But writing in prose seldom ex-
ploits beats in this way; on the contrary, most skilful uses of rhythm in prose
avoid the emergence of beats by varying the arrangement of stressed and
unstressed syllables. Here is another sentence from *Martin Chuzzlewit*:

First, there was Mr Spottletoe, who was so bald and had such big whiskers, that
he seemed to have stopped his hair, by the sudden application of some powerful
remedy, in the very act of falling off his head, and to have fastened it irrevocably
on his face. (107)

Here's the pattern of stresses and unstressed syllables:

/ x x / x / x x x x / / x x / / / x x x / x x / x / x x / x / x / x x x / x x / x x x x / x / x /
x / x / x x x / x x x / x x x x x /

This is very different from the pattern of the other sentence—only short
sequences of stress/unstress alternation, quickly brought to a halt by a
longer string of unstressed syllables. The rhythmic quality of this sentence
lies in the variety of its pace: the emphatic beginning on a stress, 'First';
the dactylic name, like so many comic names ('Chuzzlewit' being another
example); the slowing of the rhythm on the successive stresses of 'so bald'
and 'such big whiskers'; the dramatic emphasis imparted by the alternat-
ing rhythm of 'the very act of falling off his head'; the comic effect of the
many unstressed syllables in 'and to have fastened it irrevocably on his

---

[4] Dickens was not unaware of this tendency; on 25 April 1844 he replied to Charles
Watson, who had written to him on the subject, 'I am perfectly aware that there are several
passages in my books which, with very little alteration—sometimes with none at all—will
fall into blank verse, divided off into Lines. It is not an affectation in me, nor have I the
least desire to write them in that metre; but I run into it, involuntarily and unconsciously,
when I am very much in earnest' (*Letters*, IV, 112–13).

face'. Dickens's rhythmic genius, I would argue, emerges more from the passages that, in their constant shifts and swerves, resist beats than from those that draw on the resources of regular verse to create a kind of metrical prose.

KEATS

To illustrate the usefulness of a beat-based approach to prosody, and to highlight the detailed attention to the movement of language that characterizes the writing of a superb poetic technician, I want now to examine a particular feature of Keats's use of rhythm. Here are a few lines that I believe anyone familiar with the history of English poetry would unhesitatingly call 'Keatsian':

> 'Mid hush'd, cool-rooted flowers, fragrant-eyed
>
> Singest of summer in full-throated ease
>
> My head cool-bedded in the flowery grass
>
> That fosters the droop-headed flowers all
>
> Thy hair soft-lifted by the winnowing wind

These lines, as many readers will have recognized, come from five of the six Odes.[5] The sensuousness of tone and image, the lacework of repeated sounds, and the experience of absorption into the physical world, are all recognizable Keatsian trademarks; but the feature of these lines I want to focus on is their distinctive rhythm. I take rhythm to be a matter not of pure sound, but of *meaningful* sound: perceived lexical and syntactic relationships working inseparably from the movement of syllables and stresses to produce a sequence of tension and relaxation, of regularity and irregularity, operating at several levels simultaneously.

Part of the distinctive rhythm of each of the lines I've quoted is generated by the inclusion of a compound adjective formed from two words, the first in all cases but one an adjective, the second a verb in the past tense: 'cool-rooted', 'full-throated', 'cool-bedded', 'droop-headed', 'soft-lifted'. This formation, which I'm going to call the 'nonce-compound', is one of Keats's favourite methods of verbal creation and intensification. Three of the examples I have given do in fact occur in the *Oxford English Dictionary*—'cool-rooted', 'full-throated', and 'droop-headed'[6]—but in

---

[5] All citations are from Keats, *Poems*, ed. Stillinger.
[6] Oddly, the *OED* lists two examples from the 'Ode to Psyche'—'soft-conched' and 'soft-handed'—but not 'soft-lifted'.

each case the only citation given is the Keatsian example itself. (Why these three alone should be chosen by the dictionary's lexicographers is not obvious.) In some of his nonce-compounds, Keats followed established lexical precedent, as with the use of 'full' and 'soft'; in others, his choice of the first unit in the compound is an unusual one. For instance, the *OED* lists only one use of 'droop' followed by a verb in a compound adjective: a horse might be said, in the eighteenth century, to be 'droop-arsed'. It's an intriguing thought that the delicacy of 'droop-headed' might derive from a somewhat earthier forebear.

Such compounds can have a number of rhythmic profiles, depending on the disposition of stresses in each of the units, but my interest is in one particular profile, to which all of these examples conform: a monosyllabic first unit followed by a disyllabic second unit stressed on the first syllable. My reason for focusing on this type is that it does not slot into the iambic metre in any straightforward way: its pattern of two stressed syllables followed by one unstressed syllable clashes with the alternation of beat and offbeat that produces duple metre.[7] Here are all the examples in the Odes:[8]

'Psyche' has six: *soft-conchéd, cool-rooted, calm-breathing, soft-handed, dark-clustered, wild-ridgéd*
'Nightingale' has three: *light-wingéd, full-throated, deep-delvéd*
'Melancholy' has two: *tight-rooted, droop-headed*[9]
'Indolence' has one: *cool-bedded*
'Autumn' has two: *soft-lifted, soft-dying*

Only the 'Ode on a Grecian Urn' has no examples (though it has a very similar adjective-plus-adjective compound: 'high-sorrowful').[10] Similar metrical issues arise with noun compounds that have the same rhythmic shape—such as 'yew-berries' and 'hedge-crickets'—but these are much rarer and tend to be lexically orthodox, so I shall leave them aside and concentrate on the adjectival compounds.

It seems clear that this is a peculiarly Keatsian construction. To take one important predecessor, there is only a single example of it in Wordsworth's

[7] Compounds formed of two monosyllables—such as 'half-reaped', 'chain-swung', and 'leaf-fring'd'—may also seem to clash with the duple metre, but in these cases it is easy to follow the two stresses with a third, permitting a simple demotion of the already slightly weaker second stress to occur (an option not available with the type of compound I am discussing).

[8] For purposes of clarity, I use an accent where the final syllable of the past participle could be elided but is prevented from doing so by the metre.

[9] The cancelled first stanza includes one example, though like much of that stanza, it lacks originality: 'blood-stainéd'.

[10] Compounds of this type might sometimes appear without the hyphen, as was frequently the case in sixteenth- and seventeenth-century printing, but in Keats's poetry the hyphen appears to be consistently used in compound adjectives.

verse in duple metres in the 1798 *Lyrical Ballads* (line 47 of 'The Female Vagrant' has 'sore-traversed', where for metrical reasons one must assume an accent on the first syllable of 'traversed'). The picture is not very different if we turn to Wordsworth at his most creative in extended iambic pentameter verse: in the first six books of the 1850 *Prelude*—around 6,500 lines—I found fewer examples than in the 321 lines of Keats's Odes (thirteen as opposed to fourteen). What's more, Wordsworth's examples are al most all familiar compounds, like 'wide-spreading', 'slow-moving', 'short-sighted', and 'good-natured', or at any rate make use of a first unit that is very common in such compounds, like 'ill-' or 'far-'. The only example with Keatsian richness about it is an evocative adjective in Book 4, describing the mountains at sunrise as 'grain-tinctured' (line 328), a word we can be sure Keats would have admired had the poem been published in his lifetime.

The obvious model for this lexical creativity is Shakespeare. It's interesting to note that among the phrases underlined by Keats in his copy of *King Lear* are '*ear-bussing* arguments', 'Alack, *bare-headed*', '*Milk-liver'd* man!', and 'A most *toad-spotted* traitor', while in *Antony and Cleopatra* he marked '*Broad-fronted* Caesar' (my emphases).[11] Another source may be gleaned from a well-known anecdote recorded by Charles Cowden Clarke in *Recollections of Writers*: reading Spenser's *Faerie Queene*, Keats 'singled out epithets, for that felicity and power in which Spenser is so eminent. He *hoisted* himself up, and looked burly and dominant as he said, "*What an image that is—sea-shouldering whales!*"' (126). These Shakespearian and Spenserian examples all use the *stressed–stressed–unstressed* pattern that was so fruitful in Keats's hands. He may also have received encouragement from another work he admired greatly: Chapman's translation of Homer makes free use of compound adjectives, though relatively few follow the monosyllable plus disyllable format, and these for the most part lack any Keatsian creativity.[12]

Semantically, what is particularly fruitful in these compounds is the unconstrained nature of the relationship between the two terms. Keats is particularly fond of an adjective yoked to a verb—parts of speech which don't normally come into direct semantic contact, since only adverbs can directly modify verbs. The relationship therefore has something of a metaphoric character: it's the reader who makes the necessary connections. The least marked type involves a verb that indicates no more than the possession of an object or quality—'strong-minded', 'hard-headed',

---

[11] See White, *Keats as a Reader of Shakespeare*, 184–6; and Kucich, 'Keats and English Poetry', 193.

[12] I found thirteen examples in the first four books of Chapman's *Iliad* translation, the most inventive of which are 'White-wristed *Iuno*' (I.597), 'Strength-breathing *Abants*' (II.478), and 'starre-bearing hill' (IV.70).

'broad-shouldered', and so on. But Keats's use of the combination is almost always more innovative than this, involving a complex relation between adjective and verb.

Thus, for example, the *adjective* 'soft' can't qualify the *verb* 'lift'; we may treat it as an adverb, and understand the compound 'soft-lifted' as meaning 'softly lifted', emphasizing the lightness of the wind; or we may treat it as an adjective and look for an implied noun—presumably the hair, whose softness and fineness make it particularly easy for the wind to lift. Of course in reality we don't make the choice: what Keats valued about the compound (beside its internal assonance) was precisely the open-endedness of the connection, making the action of lifting the hair itself almost an entity that could be described as soft. Similarly, 'calm-breathing' is not the same as 'calmly breathing'—it could, for instance, if we take 'calm' as a noun, mean 'breathing calm', where calm is what is being breathed. 'Full-throated' would require a lengthy discussion to elucidate the relation between adjective and verb (and the noun from which the verb is derived); and 'tight-rooted' suggests both that the plant is rooted tightly in the earth and that the roots themselves form a tight cluster (with the added possibility that it is in the twisting—to produce poison—that they become tight). It's perhaps not too much of an exaggeration to say that Keats's compound words point the way to Joyce's portmanteaus in *Finnegans Wake*—Keats himself, in fact, coined a portmanteau worthy of Joyce in referring in a letter to the 'rogueglyphics in Moor's Almanack'.[13]

It's easy to find instances of this particular lexico-rhythmic compound in other poems by Keats;[14] here are some more from a few of his best-known works:

The Eve of St Agnes: *deep-damask'd, sole-thoughted, smooth-sculptured*
Hyperion, Book I: *branch-charméd, lawn-shading, calm-throated*
Lamia, Part I: *lute-finger'd, self-folding, tress-lifting*
'Bright star': *soft-fallen*

Compounds of this type are rare in the early verse, and it's perhaps significant that John Croker, in his notorious *Quarterly* review of *Endymion*, objected

---

[13] See Stewart, 'Keats and Language', 137.
[14] One such compound was nipped in the bud, presumably because as he was writing it Keats realized that it went beyond the limits of decency: in a *Hyperion* draft we find the following:

> Into a hue more roseate than sweet pain
> Gives to a Nymph new-r

He changed the sentence to the only slightly less offensive:

> Gives to a ravish'd Nymph when her warm tears
> Gush luscious with no sob

(Ridley, *Keats's Craftsmanship*, 93)

to these nonce-compounds but to the placing of adverbs at the beginnings of verbs when they normally go at the ends—'out-sparkled', 'up-followed', and 'down-sunken' are among his examples (O'Neill, *Critics on Keats*, 11). These compounds do not present the rhythmic challenge of the type I am considering, since the adverb takes very little stress, even though they distort word-order in what Keats no doubt meant to be an antique style.

It seems reasonable to suggest that the lexico-rhythmic figure I am identifying plays a particularly significant role in the Odes, not just in its greater numerical frequency but also in the inventiveness and semantic density with which it is deployed. I'd like to look now at the way in which Keats handles them, rhythmically speaking, and to examine thereby how far an approach to English metre based on an acknowledgement of the importance of beats can illuminate his craft.

The first question to ask is: how would these compounds be stressed in prose? The answer isn't simple. If we take compounds of this type that have become common enough to appear in dictionaries, we find a general preference for a stronger stress on the *second* item: hard-**heart**ed, soft-**cent**red, limp-**wrist**ed. We can take this to be the unmarked pronunciation, the one that would be used in isolation. But put these compounds into sentences, and it turns out that it's quite normal for the *first* item to take the main stress: 'the **hard**-hearted ladies' maid' (contrast this with 'You're horribly hard-**heart**ed').[15] Clearly, even in prose, rhythm plays a determining role in the pronunciation of these compounds. Moreover, the Keatsian compounds we're dealing with are unusual, consisting of two words which both resist the kind of reduction in stress that is appropriate for a familiar collocation like 'hard-hearted'. Yet giving both stresses equal weight goes against the grain of the language as well, since the creation of a compound out of two separate words is signalled by the establishment of a stress-hierarchy: there is only one main lexical stress in a compound.

How does Keats deal with this anomaly—or, rather, how does he turn this lexico-rhythmic problem to his advantage?

One way of slotting the stressed–stressed–unstressed sequence into iambic verse is to use a very common variation: stress demotion. Demotion, as we have seen, occurs when a stressed syllable is both followed and preceded by another stressed syllable, allowing the outer syllables to carry the beats and the middle one to function as if it were an offbeat. All Keats

---

[15] Thus *Everyman's English Pronouncing Dictionary*, after showing the main stress on the second syllable for 'hard-headed' and 'hard-hearted', notes that an initial stress is also possible 'according to sentence-stress'; similarly 'cool-headed' and 'tight-fisted' are given with main stress on their second syllables, but on the first 'when attributive'—i.e. before a noun.

has to do is to place a stressed syllable before the compound, as follows
(I underline the words in question, and scan the first two examples):

In 'Psyche':

> 'Mid <u>hush'd, cool-rooted</u> flowers, fragrant-eyed
>   B   O   B   o

and

> They <u>lay calm-breathing</u> on the bedded grass
>   B O   B   o

We should also include the following line, in which the sense makes it necessary
to stress 'own':

> Even into thine <u>own soft-conchéd</u> ear

In 'Nightingale':

> That <u>thou, light-wingéd</u> Dryad of the trees

In 'Indolence':

> My <u>head cool-bedded</u> in the flowery grass

In 'Autumn':

> Thy <u>hair soft-lifted by</u> the winnowing wind

And in 'Grecian Urn', that slight variant I mentioned earlier:

> That leaves a <u>heart high-sorrowful</u> and cloy'd

What is the effect of this placing of the compound? Although a demoted
stress need not be pronounced with any less emphasis than the syllables on
either side for the duple rhythm to be sustained, we tend to hear, or, better,
feel, the syllable as less strongly stressed than its neighbours. This means that
we can either accept a slight diminution of attention to the first word of the
compound, or we can give it full weight and sense its pull against the alterna-
tions of the metre. My preference in these examples is for the latter, as I find
I want to bring out the rich implications of words like *cool*, *calm*, and *soft*.
(Demotion also commonly occurs on the first syllable of the line, but in the
Odes Keats doesn't place any of his nonce-compounds in this position; the
nearest we get is the line-opening on a familiar compound noun in 'Hedge-
crickets sing'—though we're more likely to put the emphasis on the first
unit, as is usual with compound nouns, to produce an initial inversion.)

If, however, Keats wants to encourage the reader to give each of his
terms equal emphasis—approximating, that is, the stress pattern of two
separate words, each with lexical stress—he uses not demotion but inver-
sion. In doing so, he employs the most disruptive of the accepted devia-
tions in iambic metre, giving the two words in the compound unusual

salience in the line and causing the rhythm to lose some of its regular alternating swing. There are two kinds of inversion, which I've called 'falling inversion' and 'rising inversion',[16] although traditional prosody often disguises the existence of the latter as it occurs in two separate 'feet' and gets called something like 'pyrrhic followed by spondee'. The first type occurs (without any compounds) in the 'Ode on Melancholy' in the line, where the successive stresses of 'green hill' create an implied offbeat:

> And hides the <u>green hill in an</u> April shroud;
>   B ô B -o-

'Green' and 'hill' are both strongly stressed, and each takes a beat; this excess of beats is compensated for by a deficiency of beats in 'in an'. One might expect Keats to use this figure for his nonce-compounds, but in fact he doesn't. Let's imagine him doing it:

> *Singest of love in <u>full-throated de</u>light
>   B ô B   -o-

If in reading this made-up example we give both 'full' and 'throat' sufficient emphasis to take beats (and if we didn't do this we would get an anomalous four-beat line), the result is very awkward. The reason for this is that the inversion's second beat and the first part of the double offbeat are in the same word ('throated'), a phenomenon I've called *linkage* and one that most poets avoid in both kinds of inversion.[17] For inversion to run smoothly there needs to be a word-boundary between the two stressed and the two unstressed syllables. So Keats can't situate his nonce-compounds of this type in falling inversions.

Rising inversion, however, is another matter. The compounds we're looking at all begin with a monosyllabic word—usually, as we've seen, an adjective; there is therefore always going to be a word-boundary between the two unstressed syllables that make up the double offbeat and the two stressed syllables—now *following* them—that realize the two beats. And Keats makes full use of this possibility (the scansion I give in the first example applies to all):

In 'Psyche':

> As if disjoin<u>éd by soft-hand</u>ed slumber
>   -o- B ô B o

In 'Nightingale':

> Singest of summ<u>er in full-throat</u>ed ease

---

[16] See Chapter 6 section III on inversion.

[17] The avoidance of linkage explains why generative metrists have noted that compounds of this type always begin in a 'weak' or 'odd' position: the only way they can begin in a 'strong' or 'even' position is in falling inversion with linkage. See Attridge, *The Rhythms of English Poetry*, 265–75.

Cool'd a long age <u>in the deep-delv</u>éd earth

And in 'Melancholy':

That fost<u>ers the droop-head</u>ed flowers all

Another line from the 'Psyche' ode perhaps belongs here:

Far, far around <u>shall those dark-cluster'd</u> trees

I admit, however, that there is a temptation to make the rhythm easier by emphasizing 'those' (which the sense allows); this produces the smoother beat–demoted beat–beat sequence:

Far, far around shall **those** dark-**cluster'd** trees
      o   B   O   B o

In these lines, we are encouraged to linger on both elements of the compound: both take beats, and there is no intervening syllable to smooth out the rhythm into the expected alternations. If you try reading with the second word weakened, you find the line turns into an unwanted rollicking four-beat line:

That **fosters** the **droop**-headed **flowers all**
    o B -o-   B   -o-   B o B

On the other hand, if you let the first word lose its emphasis, you get an uncomfortable run of unstressed syllables within which it's hard to locate a beat:

That fost<u>ers the droop-</u>**head**ed **flowers all**

So we have to give equal emphasis to both words in these compounds: both 'full' with its many resonances and 'throat', with its self-reflexive attention to the very means by which we speak the word; both 'deep', with its suggestion of caves of remarkable profundity, and 'delve', with its evocation of the labour required to dig them; both the evocative 'droop' and the defamiliarized 'head'. It's as if the compound is made to look back at its constituent words and give their meanings full weight.

A third situation in which we find two stressed syllables together in iambic verse, but one which injects significant tension into the rhythm of the line, is when we have an additional stress within an inversion—where, in other words, we would expect an unstressed syllable. There are two occurrences of this unusual figure in the Odes:

In 'Psyche':

<u>Fledge the wild-ridg</u>éd mountains steep by steep

In 'Autumn':

While barréd clouds <u>bloom the soft-dying</u> day

One way to treat the first example is to take it as an instance of the very common figure of initial inversion, complicated by a stressed syllable where an unstressed one should be. Here's the normal pattern:

*Fledging the ridgéd mountains steep by steep
B   -o- B o

But 'wild' will not allow itself to be treated as an unstressed syllable: it kicks back, and in its wildness momentarily perturbs the rhythm. If we try a different tack, and treat the line as starting with a rising inversion, we have to suppress 'Fledge', and that is just as difficult. Perhaps the least disruptive way of reading the line, though it transgresses the rules followed by most iambic poets, is to let 'wild' have the beat, and start the line as if it were trochaic.

Fledge the wild-ridgéd mountains steep by steep
B   o B -o- B o B o B

In this case, it is the second item of the compound which is suppressed, to form part of the double offbeat whereby the trochaic rhythm is corrected to an iambic one.[18] A final possibility is that we give all stressed syllables their due, and regard the line as having, in a temporary departure from the five-beat norm, six beats. In any event, the visual violence of the scene—which is located, it will be recalled, in some untrodden region of the speaker's mind—is inseparable from the violence done to the regular metre.

The example from 'Autumn'—'While barréd clouds <u>bloom the soft-dying</u> day'—offers the same four alternatives: we can demote 'soft', producing a falling inversion; we can demote 'bloom', producing a rising inversion; we can demote the 'dy-' of 'dying', producing a postponed compensation for the missing syllable between 'clouds' and 'bloom'; or we can read the line with six beats. In all these alternatives, or in a reading which alludes to more than one of them, we sense a suspension of the normal rhythmic drive, a suspension that is also present in the day's slow death.

Conventional foot-prosody, by contrast, tends to lump all these very different ways of dealing with the *stressed–stressed–unstressed* compound under the general heading of 'spondees'. Thus Walter Jackson Bate tells us that in the Odes 'abundant use is made of the spondee', and gives us percentages of 'spondaic feet' for each of the odes, without noticing that his examples include the very different rhythmic figures of demotion and

---

[18] In *The Rhythms of English Poetry* I called this variation 'postponed compensation' (191); a famous example—in one way of reading the line, at least—is Shakespeare's '**Let me not** to the marriage of true minds'.

inversion (137–8). He also notes the increased use of '-*ed* ending epithets' without connecting this increase to the 'abundant spondees'.

Only one compound of our type in the Odes remains to be discussed: the one that occurs in the extraordinary opening of the 'Ode on Melancholy':

> No, no, go not to Lethe, neither twist
> Wolf's-bane, tight-rooted, for its poisonous wine.

Had Keats used a more conventional word-order he would have achieved a more conventional rhythm as well:

> *Tight-**rooted** **wolf**'s-bane for its poisonous wine
>   O   B   o   B   o

This would have allowed both 'tight-rooted' and 'wolf's-bane' their un-marked pronunciation and sustained an easy iambic rhythm. Even with the word-order Keats chose, it's tempting to give the compounds this ac-centuation, and to read the second line as beginning with an inversion:

> **Wolf**'s-bane, tight-**rooted**...
>   B   -o-   B   o

However, this performance requires the suppression of 'tight', whose complex of meanings we've already noted, as well as the significant word 'bane'. I prefer to give each of these first four stresses equal weight, allow-ing demotion to occur both before the line's first beat and between it and the next beat:

> Wolf's-**bane**, tight-**rooted**...
>   O   B   O   B   o

In this performance, the colourful alternative name for aconite becomes more than just a quaint label, and the complexity of 'tight-rooted' is fully brought out in another of Keats's rhythmic triumphs.

There is no reason to assume that Keats was conscious of the way in which the rhythmic expressiveness he achieved derived from the delicate manipulation of beats and offbeats. In trying out various combinations of words and syllables, he trusted his ear to tell him what worked and what didn't. And numerous readers have responded to that expressiveness with-out being aware of how it was achieved (though some, of more scholarly bent, have misattributed it). Does our analysis in the terms of beat pros-ody unweave the rainbow, as Keats's Lamia melted at the touch of cold philosophy? My sense is that it doesn't, that, on the contrary, deeper un-derstanding increases the reader's pleasure in, and admiration of, Keats's remarkable rhythmic skill.

9

Poetry Unbound?

Observations on Free Verse

I

Very few have doubted that traditional metres in English are a matter of rules, even if those rules are resistant to straightforward formulation. For this reason, prosody has always constituted a semi-scientific domain within the body of literary criticism; but for the same reason, poetic forms that do not appear to result from the application of rules to language have tended to receive short shrift from those who study rhythmic form from the perspective of linguistics. Free verse in English has usually been treated either as a deviation from the norms of metrical poetry, a kind of wilful transgression of the rules which nevertheless still takes its bearings from those rules, or as a domain in which the traditional rigorous methods of analysis do not apply, and have to be replaced by a more impressionistic and idiosyncratic approach.[1] The striking difference between the number of essays on metrical and on free verse listed in Brogan's mammoth bibliography—1,440 as against 153—is not entirely to be accounted for by historical periodization: the majority of these books and essays were written when free verse was already an established form. It became established more through the efforts of poets than of critics, however. When Graham Hough delivered the 1957 British Academy Warton Lecture on the subject 'Free Verse', he was careful to play down the importance of his chosen

---

[1] A notable exception is the treatment of free verse in John Hollander's *Vision and Resonance*; see especially chapter 5, ' "Sense Variously Drawn Out": On English Enjambment', chapter 11, 'Observations on the Experimental', and chapter 12, 'The Poem in the Eye'. See also Hollander's exemplification of various kinds of free verse in *Rhyme's Reason*, 26–30. In 'Free Verse', Ramsey highlights the resistance of free verse to definition by listing nine possible definitions, and adding a tenth which embraces all the previous ones. Berry, in 'The Free Verse Spectrum', also approaches the question of definition by identifying a spectrum. A valuable account of the emergence of free verse in English poetry is given by Duffell, *A New History*, 187–212. See also Kirby-Smith's discussion of the prehistory of this rhythmic form in *The Origins of Free Verse*.

topic: 'It would seem that we have in free verse materials for a yet unwritten chapter of English poetical history. Only a chapter, and probably not a very long one; for we find comparatively little written in free verse before this century, and we find little now' (157). Now we are able to look back, the picture looks very different: we can say with confidence that free verse was the most characteristic poetic form of the twentieth century.

The task of redressing this critical imbalance is a daunting one, and all I shall venture here are some suggestions that point towards a possible reconceptualization of the notion of free verse, in the hope that this will remove one or two of the barriers that at present stand in the way of a full understanding of what it is that poets (and readers) are doing around us every day. An example of such a barrier is the conceptual opposition between 'free verse' and 'regular' or 'metrical' verse, with its implied historical opposition between the 'modern' and the 'traditional'. Although this dichotomy has an obvious validity, there is something to be said for considering other ways in which the rhythmic variety of poetry in English might be categorized. This may mean treating with some scepticism the claims made by poets about their own formal revolutions, but it will, I believe, allow us to see their achievements as more continuous with the rich history of English poetic practice.[2]

A minimal definition of verse might be that it is a form of language which heightens the reader's awareness of its own working—its movement, its sounds, its capacity to represent and convey sensations and feelings. And it would be widely agreed that the minimal device whereby verse achieves this heightened awareness is the division of the continuous flow of language into segments, even though no sharp distinction can be made between verse and prose on this basis alone.[3] (A more familiar term than 'segments' is 'lines', but for reasons that will become evident I am avoiding it here.) What I wish to concentrate on is the method by which a text's division into segments, constituting it as verse, is signalled.

There are two ways in which this signal can be given. The first involves a sense of structural units arising directly from the way in which the properties of the spoken language have been organized. Here is an example:

> There was a young poet of Kew,
> Who failed to emerge into view;
> So he said: 'I'll dispense
> With rhyme, metre, and sense.'
> And he did, and he's now in *Who's Who*.[4]

---

[2] See Hollander's brilliant chapter on metrical experimentation in *Vision and Resonance* (chapter 11).

[3] This position is argued by Perloff in 'The Linear Fallacy' and 'Between Verse and Prose'. A study which takes an opposing position is Hartman's *Free Verse*.

[4] Parrott, ed., *The Penguin Book of Limericks*, 116.

Anyone hearing this stretch of language without seeing it on the page would have no difficulty in perceiving it as a structure of separate units, and could easily write it out as five lines. Unmistakable signals—for a hearer conversant with the English popular verse tradition—are given by the closely controlled interrelation between a metrical pattern of alternating beats and double offbeats on the one hand and a system of rhymes and syntactically or informationally determined breaks on the other; the result is the familiar limerick structure. (Of course that structure is announced in the conventional opening, 'There was a young...', so that the listener's ears are attuned to hear it from the beginning.)

The verse form requires no *additional* signal beyond its own verbal components to make its segments perceptible: the listener has no visual layout to serve as a guide, and the reciter does not need to employ a trick of the voice to indicate the ends of the segments. In a sense, the issue of individual segments disappears, since the limerick structure is so familiar, and so firmly grounded in more general rhythmic principles involving the hierarchical doubling of beat-offbeat units, that it is perceived as a structural whole: it would make little difference if, by convention, limericks were printed as four instead of five lines, with an internal rhyme in the third line. In the regular forms of rhymed English verse the relation between metre, segmentation, rhyme, and end-stopping is predominantly one of mutual reinforcement: and once rhyme and end-stopping divide an alternating metre into units of a length that conforms to one of the standard patterns, that familiar pattern takes on a power of its own to structure the material to come and to further emphasize the segmental divisions.

Here is another example. Imagine hearing this poem—it's by William Carlos Williams and is entitled 'Poem'—recited without having the text in front of you:

> The rose fades
> and is renewed again
> by its seed, naturally
> but where
>
> save in the poem
> shall it go
> to suffer no diminution
> of its splendour

(Pictures from Brueghel, 39)

Only if the speaker inserted vocal signals of some kind would you be able to guess at its divisions into segments and larger units. Unlike the limerick, there is nothing in its metrical structure, its sound repetitions, its informational groups, or its syntactic units to indicate how it is divided up. Printed without the visual divisions, it yields no clue as to where these fall:

The rose fades and is renewed again by its seed, naturally, but where save in the poem shall it go to suffer no diminution of its splendor.

Read on the page, of course, the poem poses no problems of segmentation: it appears as two four-line paragraphs, each line consisting of two to four words. It thereby evokes a long tradition in English lyric verse which uses four-line stanzas (an allusion which operates rather like the imitation of wooden structures carved in stone in Greek temples, preserving in a different medium a memory of earlier modes of construction). The line- and stanza-divisions are presented unambiguously to the eye, and their resistance to the onward drive of the sentence is felt irrespective of the degree of aural realization they are given in the reading. Unlike the limerick, however, this poem loses its structure entirely when printed without any graphic indication of lines and paragraphs.

These two examples mark extremes between which we could place any poem in English. However, the spectrum of verse-types that would result would not be one that would divide easily between regular verse and free verse. The axis which runs between what we might call *intrinsically segmented* and *extrinsically segmented* verse (which is not strictly a division, since much verse has elements of both) is quite distinct from that which runs from metrical to non-metrical verse. The former type signals structurally significant segments by means of the properties of language and rhythm (primarily syntax, metre, and/or rhyme); the latter type by means of aural or visual presentation.

To illustrate this point, let me offer two more examples. Here is a section of Milton's *Samson Agonistes*, laid out on the page without any external indications of lines:

Or do my eyes misrepresent? Can this be hee, that Heroic, that Renownd, irresistible *Samson*? Whom unarmd no strength of man, or fiercest wild beast could withstand; who tore the Lion, as the Lion tears the Kid, ran on embatteld Armies clad in Iron, and weaponless himself, made Arms ridiculous, useless the forgery of brazen shield and spear, the hammerd Cuirass, *Chalybean* temperd steel, and frock of mail Adamantean Proof. (lines 124–34; *Poems*, 350)

Like the limerick, this is regular metrical verse, but without any visual assistance it is impossible to detect the division into lines. The blind Milton doubtless saw the patterns of lines on his mind's page, and perhaps envisaged a formal delivery that would signal the changing lengths by oral means, thereby mimicking the sung choral odes of Greek drama.

Here is the passage as he had it set out; one can imagine it being read or recited with a distinct pause at the end of each line:

> Or do my eyes misrepresent? Can this be hee,
> That Heroic, that renownd,
> Irresistible *Samson*? Whom unarmd
> No strength of man, or fiercest wild beast could withstand;
> Who tore the Lion, as the Lion tears the Kid,
> Ran on embatteld Armies clad in Iron,
> And weaponless himself,
> Made Arms ridiculous, useless the forgery
> Of brazen shield and spear, the hammerd Cuirass,
> *Chalybean* temperd steel, and frock of mail
> Adamantean Proof.

The reason why it is impossible to detect the line-divisions if they are not signalled visually or orally is that choral passages like this in *Samson Agonistes* not only employ unrhymed run-on lines with many metrical variations (including the freedom to drop the initial iambic syllable), but lines with differing, and unpredictable, numbers of beats.[5] Milton has chosen a verse form that depends absolutely on the eye for a full apprehension of its segmentation. Johnson's notorious comment in his *Life of Milton* that 'blank verse seems to be verse only to the eye' (said to be the opinion of an 'ingenious critick')[6] may be a debatable proposition about *Paradise Lost* but it is certainly true of *Samson*. On the spectrum from intrinsic to extrinsic segmentation it is very close to the non-metrical example by Williams; and the experience of reading it on the page, allowing the visual image to structure the text, impede the onward drive of sense and syntax, and draw attention to the materiality of the language, is similar to that of reading much modern free verse.

Let us turn now to our other example, a poem in free verse by Sylvia Plath entitled 'Crossing the Water'. Would a reading of this poem without any special vocal signalling of line-ends be perceived by listeners as falling into the lines we can see on the page?

> Black lake, black boat, two black, cut-paper people.
> Where do the black trees go that drink here?
> Their shadows must cover Canada.

---

[5] See Edward Weismiller's illuminating discussion of the prosody of *Samson* in 'The "Dry" and "Rugged" Verse'. *Samson* has often been treated as a forerunner of free verse; Kirby-Smith, in *The Origins of Free Verse*, treats it as free verse itself, claiming that many of the choruses 'decidedly cannot be' scanned as iambics (17–18)—a dubious claim he does not substantiate. The most one can say is that a few lines are metrically ambiguous, depending on how one treats a missing initial syllable (see Adams, *Poetic Designs*, 150–1).

[6] *The Lives of the Poets*, 113.

A little light is filtering from the water flowers.
Their leaves do not wish us to hurry:
They are round and flat and full of dark advice.

Cold worlds shake from the oar.
The spirit of blackness is in us, it is in the fishes.
A snag is lifting a valedictory, pale hand;

Stars open among the lilies.
Are you not blinded by such expressionless sirens?
This is the silence of astounded souls.

                                                    (*Collected Poems*, 190)

Even without vocal signals, the poem would probably be heard as twelve separate units, each with a certain degree of syntactic and informational completeness; and listeners may sense each group of three lines as having some internal cohesion, especially the first two groups. What this means is that, like the limerick, this poem's structure is implicit in the language out of which it is made, and unlike either the Williams poem or the passage from *Samson Agonistes*, no special signalling is necessary to create a sense of its constituent units. Thus, although it is free verse, it belongs to the intrinsically segmented category. It works primarily as an *aural* entity, an accretion of segments each with its own cohesion, and each continuing and complicating what has gone before. In this example, the lack of any counterpoint between segmentation and syntax has the effect of leeching out some of the potential emotional force and tension; the blackness, coldness, silence, expressionlessness of the scene is reinforced by the formal structure. Imagine, for instance, how much more dramatic would be a visual break in the third line:

                    Their shadows must cover
                    Canada.

At present our ability to talk about effects of segmentation is limited by our imperfect understanding of the way language is perceived as a series of units. It is widely assumed that this is simply a matter of syntax, and that run-on effects, for instance, can be discussed as a relationship between the line-break and the syntactic structure it cuts through. But the work of Richard Cureton, discussed in Chapter 2, addresses the way in which we tend to organize the language we read or hear into *hierarchical* structures, with distinctive patterns of rise and fall, departure and arrival, at the various levels of the hierarchy.[7] At every level, from syllables and words, through phrases of various kinds, to sentences and blocks of sentences, we

---

[7] See Cureton's *Rhythmic Phrasing in English Verse* and his long review of Stephen Cushman's *William Carlos Williams and the Meanings of Measure*.

habitually perceive English utterances as sequences of *groups* (not necessarily coinciding with syntactic units), each of which has a peak and may have a rise before it, a fall after it, or both. Groups at one level cohere into larger groups at the next level, obeying perceptual rules that also operate well beyond the domain of language. In metrical verse, these groups operate with, and are to some extent influenced by, the patterns of beat and offbeat that constitute the metre, but in free verse they function more independently to create the rhythmic character of the poem as they interact with its segmental divisions.

One way of explaining the curious immobility of Plath's poem, for example, would be to show how unusual it is in its lack of a clear grouping structure and of the onward drive that goes with the identification of strong peaks of energy. Consider this line, for instance:

> The spirit of blackness is in us, it is in the fishes.

This sentence is obviously a single group with two constituents, but which is the strong one? Does the line fall from a statement about 'us' to a statement about the 'fishes', or does it rise? At the next level down, the first group divides again into two constituents, 'The spirit of blackness' and 'is in us', but on which one does the major emphasis fall? The same ambiguities occur at higher levels when we try to relate one line or one verse paragraph to its neighbours. Moreover, the poem's segmentation into lines and paragraphs corresponds very closely to its group organization, so there is no generation of tension through counterpoint. By contrast, the Williams poem we considered earlier is a strongly organized structure of rising and falling groups: the sentence forms a two-constituent rising group, and each of these constituents would also form simple rising groups, were it not for the single word 'naturally', which is balanced against all that has gone before, and thus strongly emphasized. At lower levels there are both rising and falling groups, providing a complex onward momentum. But the visual division into lines and paragraphs only partially coincides with the major grouping divisions, to create a tension that is not finally resolved until the last word.

II

What I am suggesting, then, is that we can come closer to an adequate understanding of the way segmentation operates as a crucial feature in both regular and free verse, and at the same time make more subtle (and I would hope useful) distinctions among the formal choices open to poets, by thinking in terms of two broad categories of verse, with a considerable

area of overlap in the middle. In one type—what I have called 'intrinsi-
cally segmented verse'—very little is lost if the poem is read aloud without
any particular attention to the visually indicated line-divisions; the major
units of the verse are determined independently of its appearance on the
page or the vocal choices made by the reader. The mode of existence of
such verse is primarily aural (or, to be more accurate, aural and muscular,
since rhythm is as much felt as heard), and its written or printed form
functions largely as a transcription; it's possible to imagine it being passed
on purely in spoken form. Most rhymed verse is of this kind, rhyme being
an ancient aural signal of segmental division. (It remains somewhat puz-
zling that the most strongly regular metrical structures, with full end-
stopping, seem to demand rhyme, even though in such verse there may be
no need for a further device to mark segmentation. It's perhaps a matter
of cultural conditioning: our expectation for rhyme at terminal points in
such structures is extremely strong—so much so that its absence can be
used for comic effect, as in this well-known limerick, or anti-limerick:

> There was a young man from St Bees
> Who was stung on the arm by a wasp;
> When asked, 'Does it hurt?'
> He replied, 'No it doesn't—
> It's a good thing it wasn't a hornet.')

That free verse with prominent rhymes is a type of intrinsically segmented
poetry is made very clear by Ogden Nash: his verse could be written out
as prose, or read without pauses at the ends of run-on lines, without the
reader or listener being in any doubt as to the line-breaks. Admittedly,
most of Nash's verse uses Whitmanian long lines corresponding to major
syntactic units, but there are some exceptions; this example is the opening
of 'Hearts of Gold, or A Good Excuse is Worse than None':

> There are some people who are very resourceful
> At being remorseful,
> And who apparently feel that the best way to make friends
> Is to do something terrible and then make amends.

> (*The Face is Familiar*, 75)

Other than rhyme, the most common way of achieving intrinsic segmen-
tation is a combination of end-stopping and some principle of coherence
binding the segment itself into a unity. One example is medieval allitera-
tive verse, where the pattern of alliteration coupled with four strong beats
produces coherence and end-stopping marks segmental divisions:

> I fond there of freris alle the foure ordres,
> Prechying the peple for profyt of the wombe,

And glosede the gospel as hem good likede;
For coveytise of copis contraryed somme doctours.

William Langland, Piers Plowman (I, 56–9)

When Surrey introduced blank verse to the English language in his trans-
lation of Books II and IV of Vergil's *Aeneid* (published in 1554, after his
execution), he made sure the hearer would seldom be in any doubt as to
segmentation, thanks to a regular and easily recognized metre and, for the
most part, clear end-stopping:

> It was the time when, graunted from the godds,
> The first slepe crepes most swete in wery folk.
> Loe, in my dreame before mine eies, me thought,
> With rufull chere I sawe where Hector stood:
> Out of whoes eies there gushed streames of teares,
> Drawn at a cart as he of late had be,
> Distained with bloody dust, whoes feet were bowlne
> With the streight cordes wherwith they haled him.

(Book II, lines 340–7)

Shakespeare's early plays, too, use frequent end-stopping (and a sprin-
kling of rhyme) to signal the five-beat units in an unmistakeable manner.
Here is Gloucester praising Henry the Fifth in the first scene of *Henry VI
Part One*:

> England ne'er had a king until his time.
> Virtue he had, deserving to command:
> His brandish'd sword did blind men with his beams:
> His arms spread wider than a dragon's wings:
> His sparkling eyes, replete with wrathful fire,
> More dazzled and drove back his enemies
> Than mid-day sun fierce bent against their faces.

(I.i.8–14)

The single run-on line here is a weak enjambment where a pause would
be natural.[8]

Much blank verse uses a mixture of end-stopped and run-on lines, and
whether a given example can be considered intrinsically or extrinsically
segmented will depend on the number and the strength of the latter. Here
are two samples from Tennyson's 'The Princess' set out as prose:

Men hated learned women: but we three sat muffled like the Fates; and often
came Melissa hitting all we saw with shafts of gentle satire, kin to charity, that

---

[8] See Chapter 2 section II, on the varying strength of enjambments.

harmed not: then day droopt; the chapel bells called us: we left the walks; we mixt with those six hundred maidens clad in purest white, before two streams of light from wall to wall. (II, 442–9; *Poems*, 772)

Morn in the white wake of the morning star came furrowing all the orient into gold. We rose, and each by other drest with care descended to the court that lay three parts in shadow, but the Muses' heads were touched above the darkness from their native East. (III, 1–6; *Poems*, 773)

The second passage yields more readily to a metrical reading, inviting pauses at the ends of pentameter segments; the first, thanks to its strong run-ons and caesurae, is much harder to appreciate as a sequence of five-beat units. Here are the passages as they were printed:

> Men hated learned women: but we three
> Sat muffled like the Fates; and often came
> Melissa hitting all we saw with shafts
> Of gentle satire, kin to charity,
> That harmed not: then day droopt; the chapel bells
> Called us: we left the walks; we mixt with those
> Six hundred maidens clad in purest white,
> Before two streams of light from wall to wall.

> Morn in the white wake of the morning star
> Came furrowing all the orient into gold.
> We rose, and each by other drest with care
> Descended to the court that lay three parts
> In shadow, but the Muses' heads were touched
> Above the darkness from their native East.

Instead of being combined with a *metrical* pattern, end-stopping can be combined with syntactic or semantic *parallelism* to create coherent and intrinsically demarcated segments. By parallelism I mean the sense that two or more different linguistic units have a relation to one another of similarity or contrast, whether in terms of form or content, or both. Roman Jakobson has argued that parallelism (he takes the word from Hopkins) is the fundamental property of poetic language, operating at all levels to create a system of equivalences that enrich and reinforce the poem's meaning.[9] I am much less hopeful that it is possible to find an essence of poetic language, but the notion of parallelism is a useful one in relation to lineation, and has of course has been important for a long time in the study of biblical verse.[10]

---

[9] See Jakobson, *Language in Literature*, 5–6.
[10] The notion of parallelism owes its prominence in biblical studies to the work of Robert Lowth in the third quarter of the eighteenth century. Berlin discusses biblical parallelism in the light of Jakobson's theory of the 'poetic function' in 'The Dynamics of Biblical Parallelism'. Kirby-Smith devotes a useful chapter of *The Origins of Free Verse* to parallelism (135–78).

Parallelism of various kinds has been a distinctive component within the English verse tradition, whether in the strong form used by Christopher Smart, William Blake, Walt Whitman, or D. H. Lawrence— what John Hollander calls the 'oracular' tradition[11]—or in more muted forms, such as the Plath poem I quoted earlier. Here's the opening of Lawrence's 'Bare Almond-trees'; the listener who doesn't have sight of the printed poem may not be able to tell with absolute certainty where every printed line-break falls, but it matters very little, since the rhythmic structure is dominated by patterns of grouping and repetition:

> Wet almond-trees, in the rain,
> Like iron sticking grimly out of earth;
> Black almond trunks, in the rain,
> Like iron implements twisted, hideous, out of the earth,
> Out of the deep, soft fledge of Sicilian winter-green,
> Earth-grass uneatable,
> Almond trunks curving blackly, iron-dark, climbing the slopes.

> (*Complete Poems*, 300)

III

The other broad category of poetry—extrinsically segmented verse—consists mainly of poems that have their being simultaneously in the aural and the visual medium, and cannot be experienced fully in only one of these.[12] (It's possible to imagine a verse-tradition in which external signalling—by special pronunciation or musical accompaniment at line-ends—is transmitted without the poem's ever being committed to the page, but this is unlikely in a print-dominated culture.) Within this category there are poems which can be quite successfully rendered orally by using line-end pauses (most run-on blank verse is of this sort), and others in which a great deal is lost if the poem is not seen as well as heard. The voice cannot, for instance, distinguish easily between sentence-breaks in

---

[11] See Hollander's illuminating discussion of Whitman's poetic line in *Vision and Resonance*, 231–2. A few poems using the biblical line developed by Whitman have been identified; see Kirby-Smith, *The Origins of Free Verse*, 154–8.

[12] The poet whose work has been most effective in enforcing critical awareness of this duality is, not surprisingly, Williams (in spite of the auditory emphasis of his own metrical theorizing). See, for instance, Berry, 'Williams' Development of a New Prosodic Form'; Cushman, *William Carlos Williams and the Meanings of Measure*, especially chapters 1 and 2; and Perloff, '"To Give a Design": Williams and the Visualization of Poetry', chapter 4 of *The Dance of the Intellect*. A forerunner of Williams is Stephen Crane, whose short lines often rely on their visual representation to be perceived.

mid-line and at the end of the line, or between different lengths of white space. (There is, of course, verse that exists purely in the visual medium—concrete poetry—but that has tended to remain a peripheral genre.) The origins of visual–aural verse lie perhaps in the attempts by a large number of poets during the Renaissance to write quantitative verse in English in imitation of Latin poetry; this verse often existed on the page rather than in the ear (quantities, for instance, were often determined more by the way a word was spelled than the way it was pronounced).[13] And the classical model remained important in this tradition of English verse, since the reading of Latin and Greek poetry was for a long time a page-oriented phenomenon. On the page, the unrhymed, frequently run-on verse of the classical poets had a clear structure, which could be scanned by marking vowel lengths and counting consonants, but as pronounced in the various European countries until the pronunciation reform movements early in the last century, it had very little segmental coherence unless this was imposed by an artificial pronunciation.[14]

The tradition of extrinsically segmented verse is a long one. Classically trained poets found a twin model in Greek literature for visual–aural poetry written without rhyme in varying line-lengths: Pindar's Odes and the choruses from the tragedies. Milton drew on both (and on Cowley's *Pindarique Odes*) for the choruses in *Samson Agonistes*, and we know from diary entries that at least two of the poems Matthew Arnold wrote using a similar form in the mid-nineteenth century were conscious attempts at pindarics, while two others are obviously imitations of Greek choruses.[15] A different source for a strongly run-on style of unrhymed verse is Jacobean drama, though this has more to do with a suitable style for the stage than the influence of the page. Later admirers of Shakespeare, however, would often have come to know his plays in printed form, and this experience undoubtedly encouraged freer blank verse in non-dramatic poetry—not only Milton's but that of many nineteenth-century writers. Browning, perhaps, goes furthest to baffle the ear of its desire to identify the beginnings and ends of iambic pentameters, and Browning is acknowledged as an influence by the twentieth century's most influential proponent of the visual–aural mode, Ezra Pound.

A few Victorians wrote poems—not particularly distinguished poems, it must be said—with freely varying line-lengths and without rhyme, making

---

[13] This is one of the arguments of my *Well-Weighed Syllables*, 118–19 and *passim*.

[14] Hollander observes that 'free verse' in English in the twentieth century is often 'modeled on line-for-line prose translations of the classics' (*Vision and Resonance*, 205–6).

[15] See headnotes to 'The Youth of Nature', 'The Youth of Man', 'Fragment of an "Antigone"', and 'Fragment of Chorus of a "Dejaneira"', in *The Complete Poems*. The best known of Arnold's poems in this verse form are 'The Strayed Reveller' and 'Rugby Chapel'.

it essential to see them on the page (or hear them read with line-end pauses) to appreciate their structure.[16] It is this mode that dominates the writing of poetry today, as almost any little magazine or current anthology will testify. Even some rhymed verse relies on the page more than on the ear, since—notwithstanding the example of Ogden Nash cited earlier—without regular metre and a fixed line-length or stanza form, chiming syllables may not be enough to signal segmentation.[17] There are also regular metres that, based not on the salient rhythmic features of English but on other features, do not establish an aural rhythm strong enough to be perceived without extrinsic signalling: the most common example is syllabic verse, such as most of Marianne Moore's poetry and a little of Dylan Thomas's and Thom Gunn's.

There has always been resistance to verse that relies on the page for its full effect, a resistance that takes the form either of a dismissal of the poetry itself or of an unwillingness to accept the contribution made by the eye in a full response to it. Blank verse—even in Surrey's end-stopped style—caused bafflement in the sixteenth century, and we have already noted Johnson's endorsement of the dismissive view that blank verse such as Milton's is 'verse only to the eye'.[18] In the twentieth century, the fierce arguments about the legitimacy of free verse provide a great deal of evidence for a similar hostility.[19] Poems arranged on the page to make visual images—pattern poems or concrete poems—may have a long history, but have never been treated as major contributions to the literary tradition. Even Hough, in his 1957 Warton Lecture, resists the notion of a poetry that works partly by visual means: in the face of a mass of evidence to the contrary, he asserts that the free verse line is only a line because it is 'a unit of sense, a unit of syntax' (174). Such responses are part of a deep cultural distrust of the written word, with its capacity to elude the individual will and the guarantee of personal commitment; most readers remain deeply attached to the phonocentric myth of the speaking voice as the unmediated channel of human truth, and prefer to think of their favourite poems as utterances rather than as texts to be performed.

---

[16] Kirby-Smith gives examples by George Meredith, W. H. Henley, and John Davidson (*The Origins of Free Verse*, 126–30).

[17] This is demonstrated by an exercise reported by Hartman in *Free Verse*, 75–7: he gave his students a copy of Auden's 'Museé des Beaux Arts' typed out as prose and asked them to guess at the line-breaks. In doing so, they ignored the poem's rhymes. Much of Hopkins's verse, though rhyming and founded on a metrical base, stretches the forms of English verse to such an extent that we need the page to be sure of line-divisions.

[18] For a discussion of this debate in the seventeenth and eighteenth centuries, see Bradford, ' "Verse only to the Eye" '. (Bradford exaggerates the degree to which the lines of *Paradise Lost* are solely typographical entities, however.)

[19] See Steele, *Missing Measures*, for a late twentieth-century example of this hostility.

IV

These two kinds of verse (whether used exclusively in a single poem, or, as is often the case, combined) exploit the rhythmic potential of language in different ways to heighten attention, create a sense of order, modulate emotion, control emphasis, and complicate verbal meaning. To appreciate their difference is, I believe, to gain a fuller appreciation of the range and expressiveness of English verse. In order to suggest some of the ways we might talk about what I have called the visual–aural mode, I shall comment briefly on one free verse poem. In doing so, I'm conscious that many of the discussions I have encountered of the formal operation of free verse seem to fall far short of the actual experience of reading such poetry. What discussions of this kind often demonstrate is that it is not at all difficult to identify in free verse patterns of stressed and unstressed syllables, repetitions of sounds, momentary exemplifications of traditional metres, marked run-ons, and the emphatic placing of words: the problem is that this can be done with the weakest as well as with the most powerful of poems. There often seems no connection between our responses to a range of poetry and our analytical machinery—though this frequently goes unnoticed, since we use the machinery only on poems we admire. One technique that could be used more often is the testing of any claim that this or that feature produces this or that effect by rewriting the poem to alter the feature in question, and asking exactly what difference has been made. We have a great deal to learn about how poetry works—and our endeavours are always haunted by a paradox: if we *could* explain all the effects in a poem we enjoy, the poem would, by that fact, become trite and valueless.

The poem I am going to discuss is Geoffrey Hill's 'September Song'.[20] But first here is what Hill *might* have written: a free verse poem in the aural mode, where the segmentation is largely determined intrinsically by the syntactic breaks and the parallel structures of the language itself. Or, to put it differently, this is a visual representation of the poem as it might be heard by someone without any clues to the poem's actual layout on the page:[21]

---

[20] Jon Silkin and Christopher Ricks have both published valuable readings of this poem; Ricks includes Silkin's account in his own discussion, in *The Force of Poetry*, 295–304. Both critics comment valuably on the lineation of the sentence in parentheses, and Ricks stresses some of the features of the poem which can only be appreciated on the page—not only the lineation, but also the italics and numerals in the subheading, and the parentheses themselves.

[21] Hartman's exercise with 'Museé des Beaux Arts' referred to in n. 17 suggests the degree to which readers without other clues assume a coincidence between syntactic breaks and line-divisions.

SEPTEMBER SONG
born 19.6.32—deported 24.9.42

Undesirable you may have been,
untouchable you were not.
Not forgotten or passed over at the proper time.
As estimated, you died.
Things marched, sufficient, to that end.
Just so much Zyklon and leather, patented terror,
so many routine cries.
(I have made an elegy for myself it is true)
September fattens on vines.
Roses flake from the wall.
The smoke of harmless fires drifts to my eyes.
This is plenty.
This is more than enough.

The poem in this form begins strongly with a set of angrily ironic state-
ments, mirroring in their rigid assertiveness the horrifying system
against which they protest. Then there is a line in parentheses which
seems to mute the anger in a moment of slightly embarrassed self-reflec-
tion, after which the poem's energy evaporates: a series of descriptive
statements gives way to the banality of the last two lines. Syntactic par-
allelism is used throughout to provide a formal structure, and to suggest
something of the oral tradition (the tradition of repetitive lament, per-
haps), which is no doubt one reason why the clichés of the final lines
seem so feeble.

Now here is the poem as it actually appears in Hill's *King Log*. To read
it aloud from the page is to experience it in its dual existence as words to
be seen and to be heard.

SEPTEMBER SONG
born 19.6.32—deported 24.9.42

Undesirable you may have been, untouchable
you were not. Not forgotten
or passed over at the proper time.

As estimated, you died. Things marched,
sufficient, to that end.
Just so much Zyklon and leather, patented
terror, so many routine cries.

(I have made
an elegy for myself it
is true)

September fattens on vines. Roses
flake from the wall. The smoke

of harmless fires drifts to my eyes.
This is plenty. This is more than enough. (19)

Rather than poetry which creates a speaking voice, this is poetry that re-
sists the voice, since the visual dimension defies the vocal continuities of
the sentences, and there's no metrical pattern to help produce a sense of
closure at line-end. It's only on the page that the words occur in lines, and
the result is a movement of language more complex than that of a single
speaking voice, whose rhythms are determined by sense and syntax. In-
stead of the rather obvious irony of the first two lines heard as parallels in
my aural version, we have a line that begins with 'undesirable' and ends
with 'untouchable', retaining the emphasis on the two words, with their
associations of class and caste prejudice, but hinting for a moment that
the subject of the poem was regarded both as undesirable *and* untoucha-
ble. It is only after the visually inserted break that the pathos of the irony
emerges: how much better if this child *had* been regarded as untouchable,
but the Nazi murderers know no such scruples. The rearrangement of the
lines allows for an immediate repetition of 'not' in the second line that
produces a different irony—the child was 'taken good care of' by the Nazi
authorities—but instead of the flat statement of the single line, all too like
the voice of authority that is being ironized, the broken sentence hesitates
before moving on to the multiple tonalities of 'passed over', with its allu-
sion to Jewish history and ritual, and the complex bitterness of 'proper'.
The first two lines could also be described in purely rhetorical terms, as
structured round a form of epanalepsis—the line ending with a word
which almost repeats the word it had begun with—followed by its mirror
image, a central epizeuxis, the repetition of 'not' across a syntactic break.
This formal organization replaces the straightforward parallelism of my
rewritten version with a more complicated, but equally satisfying,
balance.

These three lines are followed by a space; a visual simulation of the divi-
sion between stanzas, as in Williams's 'Poem'. (Real stanzas in metrical
verse have their own internal organization, of course, and usually do not
need to be graphically signalled—in lengthy poems they often include a
specific stanza-end signal, like a final couplet or a longer line.[22]) At first
glance, the reader takes in the structure of the poem as five paragraphs,
the last a paragraph of only one line, and this visual organization contrib-

---

[22] *Terza rima* is an interesting instance: the continuous interlocking rhyme-scheme (*a b
a b c b c d c d e d e f e...*) would not be heard as divided into threes without fairly frequent
strong end-stopping at the end of the tercets, such as Dante employs in the *Commedia*. In
Shelley's 'Ode to the West Wind', by contrast, it is only the visual form on the page that
produces the division into three-line units.

utes to the interpretation, each paragraph constituting a single semantic block. (That the poem is in fourteen lines, and thus could be seen as a distant relative of the sonnet tradition, is an insight that is likely only as a result of conscious study.)

Again in the second paragraph the somewhat wooden parallelism of the purely aural version I presented becomes a more precisely articulated irony in the poem as lineated by Hill. The word 'sufficient', instead of just qualifying 'Things marched', is also part of the separate segment 'sufficient, to that end', implying the terrible efficiency both of the machinery of death and the pseudo-philosophical attitudes that produced it. (The isolation of 'Things marched' may give that phrase, too, a simultaneous physical and abstract meaning.) The following line also forms a whole, with 'patented' looking back to the name 'Zyklon' (we are dealing with a society in which poison gas is developed and authorized in the same way as a commercial product with a marketable trade-name) and to the word 'leather', producing a momentary image of an artificial glossy surface; then it runs over the visual gap to the unexpectedly unironic noun 'terror', and the return of the angry irony of 'routine'.

As a single line, '(I have made an elegy for myself it is true)' sounds like an admission—'I have to accept that in lamenting the death of this child I am actually selfishly preoccupied with my own mortality.' But divided on the page it becomes multi-layered, since this apologetic tonal inflection is contradicted by the assertiveness of 'I have made' as a single segment, and by the strongly felt insistence on the truth of the poet's art that emerges from the division of 'it' and 'is true'. There is no way a single voice could manifest these conflicting tones, which raise the irresolvable question: how can poetry capture the 'truth' of such an event?

When the imagery shifts in the next paragraph, the run-ons prevent the three sentences from settling into a comfortable parallel arrangement of noun-verb-preposition-noun, and also from the movement of regular accentual-syllabic verse that is much clearer in my rewritten version (in that version the final line of this trio is a regular iambic pentameter). They thus help to keep the connection with what has gone before: these benign autumnal images cannot be isolated from the death-camps. And then in the poem's close a line-by-line parallelism is once more resisted, the last two apparently trite phrases transformed by being yoked together for the eye (there is no way the voice can signal this union, since we will always hear a break between sentences). I find it impossible to ascribe a specific tone to this line, and its complexity could not emerge from a single utterance of it: there is one voice that is dismissive, using 'plenty' in the sense of 'enough', then correcting that to '*more* than enough' (this is the voice of the Nazi authorities we have already heard in the opening seven lines),

another that is bitterly sarcastic, for which these words mean just the op-
posite of what they say, and another that is gravely calm, for which 'plenty'
means 'fertile richness', and 'enough' contrasts weightily with 'sufficient'
and 'Just so much'. Finding ourselves safe in such a world—and to be
writing, the poet (like the poetry-reader) must in some sense be safe—we
have no option but to combine, in an impossible fusion, rage at what is
done by human beings to human beings and both guilt and a profound
thankfulness that it is not done to us. The poem ends hovering between
page and voice, eye and ear, a song of plenitude, as the ironic title hints,
that is also a vision of dearth.[23]

V

The choice facing the poet today should not be characterized, then, as
primarily and overridingly one between regular or free verse, traditional
or modern forms, but a choice among a wide range of possibilities and
combinations. The propaganda of the free verse poets earlier in this cen-
tury can now be seen for what it was: poetry did not leap gratefully out of
its bonds, but discovered new ways to bind the protean substance of lan-
guage, exploiting more fully than had been done in previous centuries its
dual existence as speech and writing. Free verse is not more 'natural' than
metrical verse, nor does it permit of a specially 'organic' relation between
rhythm and sense; these are cultural myths descending from the tradition
of Romanticism. They have been valuable in extending the range of Eng-
lish verse forms, but have now served their purpose and can only limit our
appreciation of the achievements of twentieth- and twenty-first-century
poetry.

I would like to end by quoting what might be regarded as the forerun-
ner of all our modern free verse visual–aural poems. In 1602, Thomas
Campion published an extraordinary pamphlet called *Observations in the
Art of English Poesie* (to 'observe', let us remember, is both to say and to
see), in which he fused the native aural tradition of accentual verse with
what was for the Renaissance the visual tradition of classical quantitative
verse. One of the examples he wrote to demonstrate the potential of his
proposed metrical blend was the well-known 'Rose-cheeked Laura'. We
do not have to be aware of its carefully crafted quantitative structure in

---

[23] Something similar can be achieved in metrical verse, where the regular metre may
have the effect of multiplying the possible readings and emotional colourings and moving
the poem away from the representation of a single voice. See my discussion in *The Rhythms
of English Poetry*, 311–14, 350–1.

order to appreciate the skill and effectiveness with which it counterpoints the visual and the aural dimensions of language, culminating in a mid-word, speech-defying run-on that a twentieth-century free verse experimenter would be proud of. The first stanza announces that the counterpoint of the visual and the aural is not just the poem's method, but also its subject (I reproduce the modernized version in Levao, ed., *Selected Poems*):

> Rose-cheeked Laura, come
> Sing thou smoothly with thy beauty's
> Silent music, either other
>   Sweetly gracing.
>
> Lovely forms do flow
> From concent divinely framed;
> Heav'n is music, and thy beauty's
>   Birth is heavenly.
>
> These dull notes we sing
> Discords need for helps to grace them;
> Only beauty purely loving
>   Knows no discord,
>
> But still moves delight,
> Like clear springs renewed by flowing,
> Ever perfect, ever in them-
>   selves eternal.

Campion's exquisite orchestration of sight and sound, accent and quantity, in praise of 'lovely forms' that last beyond the present moment seems an appropriate way to end this study, as a final example of the capacity of rhythmically modulated language to move and delight readers and audiences (or, as Campion says, insisting on the inseparability of the two experiences, to 'move delight') across the centuries.

APPENDIX

Scansion Symbols

B	beat
o	offbeat
-o-	double offbeat
-o= =o-	double offbeat with demotion
⁓o⁓	triple offbeat
[B]	virtual beat
[o]	virtual offbeat
ô	implied offbeat
b	beat by promotion
O	offbeat by demotion
B/B	stronger and weaker beats in quadruple (dipodic) verse

Bibliography

Adams, Robert M. *Proteus, his Lies, his Truth: Discussions of Literary Translation*. New York: Norton, 1973.

Adams, Stephen J. *Poetic Designs: An Introduction to Meters, Verse Forms and Figures of Speech*. Peterborough, Ontario: Broadview Press, 1997.

Agamben, Giorgio. *The End of the Poem: Studies in Poetics*, trans. Daniel Heller-Roazen. Stanford, Calif.: Stanford University Press, 1999.

—— *Stanzas: Word and Phantasm in Western Culture*, trans. Ronald L. Martinez. Minneapolis: University of Minnesota Press, 1993.

Aitchison, Jean. ' "Say, Say It Again Sam": The Treatment of Repetition in Linguistics'. In Andreas Fischer, ed., *Repetition*, Swiss Papers in English Language and Literature 7. Tübingen: Gunter Narr Verlag, 1994. 15–34.

Allen, W. Sidney. *Accent and Rhythm: Prosodic Features in Latin and Greek: A Study in Theory and Reconstruction*. Cambridge: Cambridge University Press, 1973.

Alssid, Michael W. *Dryden's Rhymed Heroic Tragedies: A Critical Study of the Plays and of their Place in Dryden's Poetry*. 2 vols. Salzburg: University of Salzburg, 1974.

Arleo, Andy. 'Counting-out and the Search for Universals'. *Journal of American Folklore* 110 (1997): 391–407.

Armstrong, Isobel. *The Radical Aesthetic*. Oxford: Blackwell, 2000.

Arnold, Matthew. *The Complete Poems*, ed. Kenneth Allott, rev. Miriam Allott. London: Longman, 1979.

Aroui, Jean-Louis, and Andy Arleo, eds. *Towards a Typology of Poetic Forms: From Language to Metrics and Beyond*. Amsterdam: John Benjamins, 2009.

Arvaniti, Amalia. 'Rhythm, Timing and the Timing of Rhythm'. *Phonetica* 66 (2009): 46–63.

Ashbery, John. *Houseboat Days*. New York: Viking, 1977.

—— *Selected Poems*. New York: Viking, 1985.

Atkinson, A. D. 'Keats and Compound Epithets'. *Notes and Queries* 197 (1952): 186–9, 301–4, 306.

Attridge, Derek. 'Beyond Metrics'. *Poetics Today*. Special Issue, 'Metrics Today II', ed. Christoph Küper, 17.1 (1996): 9–27.

—— 'The Case for the English Dolnik, or, How Not to Introduce Prosody'. *Poetics Today* 33.1 (Spring 2012): 1–26.

—— ' "Damn with Faint Praise": Double Offbeat Demotion'. *Eidos* 4 (1987): 3–6.

—— *Peculiar Language: Literature as Difference from the Renaissance to James Joyce*. Ithaca, NY: Cornell University Press and London: Methuen, 1988; reissued London: Routledge, 2004.

—— *Poetic Rhythm: An Introduction*. Cambridge: Cambridge University Press, 1995.

—— *The Rhythms of English Poetry*. London: Longman, 1982.

—— *Well-Weighed Syllables: Elizabethan Verse in Classical Metres*. Cambridge: Cambridge University Press, 1974.

Auden, W. H. *Collected Shorter Poems*. London: Faber and Faber, 1966.

Bate, Walter Jackson. *The Stylistic Development of Keats*. London: Routledge, 1945.

Berlin, Adele. *The Dynamics of Biblical Parallelism*. Bloomington, Ind.: Indiana University Press, 1985.

Berry, Eleanor. 'The Free Verse Spectrum'. *College English* 59 (1997): 873–97.

—— 'Williams' Development of a New Prosodic Form—Not the "Variable Foot", but the "Sight-Stanza"'. *William Carlos Williams Review* 7.2 (1981): 21–30.

Betjeman, John. *Collected Poems*, ed. Lord Birkenhead. London: John Murray, 1970.

Blake, William. *The Complete Poems*, ed. W. H. Stevenson and David V. Erdman. London: Longman, 1971.

Boulton, Marjorie. *The Anatomy of Poetry*. London: Routledge, 1953.

Boyle, Roger, Earl of Orrery. *Dramatic Works*, ed. William Smith Clark. 2 vols. Cambridge, Mass.: Harvard University Press, 1937.

Bradford, Richard. '"Verse only to the Eye"? Line Endings in *Paradise Lost*'. *Essays in Criticism* 33 (1983): 187–204.

Brinton, Ian, ed. *A Manner of Utterance: The Poetry of J. H. Prynne*. Exeter: Shearsman Books, 2009.

Brogan, T. V. F. *English Versification 1570–1980: A Reference Guide with a Global Appendix*. Baltimore: Johns Hopkins University Press, 1981.

Brontë, Emily. *Poems*, ed. Barbara Lloyd Evans. London: Batsford, 1992.

Brooks, H. F. 'Dryden's *Aureng-Zebe*: Debts to Corneille and Racine'. *Revue de littérature comparée* 46 (1972): 1–34.

Browning, Elizabeth Barrett. *Selected Poems*, ed. Marjorie Stone and Beverly Taylor. Peterborough, Ontario: Broadview, 2009.

Browning, Robert. *The Poems*, ed. John Pettigrew. 2 vols. New Haven: Yale University Press, 1981.

Bruns, Gerald L. *The Material of Poetry: Sketches for a Philosophical Poetics*. Athens, Ga.: University of Georgia Press, 2005.

Burling, Robbins. 'The Metrics of Children's Verse: A Cross-linguistic Study'. *American Anthropologist* 68 (1966): 1418–41.

Burt, Stephen, and David Mikics. *The Art of the Sonnet*. Cambridge, Mass.: Harvard University Press, 2010.

Cable, Thomas. 'Foreign Influence, Native Continuation, and Metrical Typology'. In Judith Jefferson and Ad Putter, eds., *Approaches to the Metres of Alliterative Verse*. Leeds: Leeds Texts and Monographs, 2009. 219–34.

—— 'Kaluza's Law and the Progress of Old English Metrics'. In Paula Fikkert and Haike Jacobs, eds., *Development in Prosodic Systems*. Berlin: Mouton de Gruyter, 2003. 145–58.

Campbell, Matthew. *Rhythm and Will in Victorian Poetry*. Cambridge: Cambridge University Press, 1999.

Campion, Thomas. *Works*, ed. Walter R. Davis. London: Faber and Faber, 1969.

Canfield, Dorothea Frances. *Corneille and Racine in England*. New York: Columbia University Press, 1904.

Caplan, David. *Poetic Form: An Introduction*. New York: Pearson Longman, 2007.

Carper, Thomas, and Derek Attridge. *Meter and Meaning: An Introduction to Rhythm in Poetry*. London: Routledge, 2003.

Carruth, Hayden. 'Lear'. *Georgia Review* 46 (1992): 516–21.

Chapman, George, trans. *The Whole Works of Homer in his Iliads and Odyssey* [1616]. Literature Online. Chadwyck-Healey. <http://lion.chadwyck.co.uk/>.

Chomsky, Noam. *Aspects of the Theory of Syntax*. Cambridge, Mass.: MIT Press, 1965.

Clarke, Charles Cowden, and Mary Cowden Clarke. *Recollections of Writers*. New York: Charles Scribner's Sons, 1878.

Clough, Arthur Hugh. *Poems*. London: Macmillan, 1862.

Coleridge, Samuel Taylor. *Poetical Works*, ed. Ernest Hartley Coleridge. Oxford: Oxford University Press, 1969.

——*Shakespearean Criticism*, ed. T. M. Raysor. 2 vols. London: Dent, 1960.

Cooper, G. Burns. *Mysterious Music: Rhythm and Free Verse*. Stanford, Calif.: Stanford University Press, 1998.

Cope, Wendy. *Two Cures for Love*. London: Faber and Faber, 2008.

Corn, Alfred. *The Poem's Heartbeat: A Manual of Prosody*. Ashland: Story Line Press, 1997.

Corneille, Pierre. *Tite et Bérénice*. Théâtre Tome 3. Paris: Flammarion, 1999.

Creaser, John. 'Rhymes, Rhyme, and Rhyming'. *Essays in Criticism* 62 (2012): 438–60.

—— ' "Service Is Perfect Freedom": Paradox and Prosodic Style in Paradise Lost'. *Review of English Studies* 58 (2007): 268–315.

Cureton, Richard. Review of Stephen Cushman, *William Carlos Williams and the Meanings of Measure*. *William Carlos Williams Review* 12.2 (Fall 1986): 34–52.

——*Rhythmic Phrasing in English Verse*. London: Longman, 1992.

Curl, Traci S., John Local, and Gareth Walker. 'Repetition and the Prosody–Pragmatics Interface'. *Journal of Pragmatics* 38 (2006): 1721–51.

Cushman, Stephen. *William Carlos Williams and the Meanings of Measure*. New Haven: Yale University Press, 1985.

Dacey, Philip, and David Jauss, eds. *Strong Measures: Contemporary American Poetry in Traditional Forms*. New York: Harper and Row, 1986.

Davenant, William. *The Siege of Rhodes, Part I*, ed. Ann-Mari Hedbäck. Uppsala: University of Uppsala Press, 1973.

Davie, Donald. *Articulate Energy: An Inquiry into the Syntax of English Poetry*. London: Routledge & Kegan Paul, 1955.

Deane, Cecil V. *Dramatic Theory and the Rhymed Heroic Play*. London: Oxford University Press, 1931.

Dearmer, Henry, et al., eds. *The English Hymnal*. London: Oxford University Press, 1906.

de Bolla, Peter. *Art Matters*. Cambridge, Mass.: Harvard University Press, 2001.

Dent, Edward J. *Foundations of English Opera*. Cambridge: Cambridge University Press, 1928.

Derrida, Jacques. *Glas*, trans. John P. Leavey, Jr and Richard Rand. Lincoln, Nebr.: University of Nebraska Press, 1986.

Dickens, Charles. *Letters 1820–1870* (2nd Release). Electronic Edition. 12 vols. Charlottesville, Va.: InteLex Corporation, 2001.

—— *The Life and Adventures of Martin Chuzzlewit*, ed. P. N. Furbank. Harmondsworth: Penguin, 1968.

Drabble, Margaret, ed. *The Oxford Companion to English Literature*. Oxford: Oxford University Press, 1985.

Dronke, Peter. *The Medieval Lyric*. Woodbridge: Boydell and Brewer, 1996

Dryden, John. *Of Dramatick Poesie*, ed. James T. Boulton. London: Oxford University Press, 1964.

—— *'Of Dramatic Poesy' and Other Critical Essays*, ed. George Watson. 2 vols. London: Dent, 1962.

—— *Four Tragedies*, ed. L. A. Beaurline and Fredson Bowers. Chicago: University of Chicago Press, 1967.

—— *Prose 1668–1691*, ed. Samuel H. Monk and A. L. W. Maurer. Vol. XVII of *Works*. Berkeley and Los Angeles: University of California Press, 1971.

Duffell, Martin J. *A New History of English Metre*. London: Legenda, 2008.

Dufter, Andreas, and Patrizia Nel Aziz Hanna. 'Natural Versification in French and German Counting-out Rhymes'. In Aroui and Arleo, eds., *Towards a Typology*, 101–21.

Durant, Alan. 'The Concept of Secondary Orality'. *Dalhousie Review* 64 (1984): 332–53.

Eagleton, Terry. *Criticism and Ideology*. London: New Left Books, 1976.

—— *How to Read a Poem*. Malden, Mass.: Blackwell, 2007.

—— *Literary Criticism: An Introduction*. Oxford: Blackwell, 1983.

Eccles, F. Y. *Racine in England*. Oxford: Clarendon Press, 1922.

Eliot, T. S. *John Dryden: The Poet, the Dramatist, the Critic*. New York: Terence & Elsa Holliday, 1932.

Elliott, Jane, and Derek Attridge, eds. *Theory after 'Theory'*. Abingdon: Routledge, 2011.

Elwert, W. Theodor. *Traité de versification française des origines à nos jours*. Paris: Klincksiek, 1965.

Empson, William. *Collected Poems*. London: Chatto and Windus, 1955.

Fabb, Nigel, and Morris Halle. *Meter in Poetry: A New Theory*. Cambridge: Cambridge University Press, 2008.

Fekete, John. *The Critical Twilight*. London: Routledge & Kegan Paul, 1978.

Fenton, James. *An Introduction to English Poetry*. London: Viking, 2002.

—— *Selected Poems.* London: Penguin, 2006.

Ferguson, Margaret, Mary Jo Salter, and Jon Stallworthy, eds. *The Norton Anthology of Poetry.* 5th edition. New York: W. W. Norton, 2005.

Fish, Stanley. *Is There a Text in This Class? The Authority of Interpretive Communities.* Cambridge, Mass.: Harvard University Press, 1980.

France, Peter. *Racine's Rhetoric.* Oxford: Clarendon Press, 1965.

Frédéric, Madeleine. *La Répétition: Étude linguistique et rhétorique.* Tübingen: Max Niemeyer, 1985.

Freud, Sigmund. *Beyond the Pleasure Principle,* trans. James Strachey. New York: Norton, 1961.

Fried, Debra. 'Rhyme Puns'. In Jonathan Culler, ed., *On Puns: The Foundation of Letters.* Oxford: Blackwell, 1988. 83–99.

Friedberg, Nila. 'The Russian Auden and the Russianness of Auden: Meaning and Form in a Translation by Brodsky'. In Aroui and Arleo, eds., *Towards a Typology,* 229–46.

Frost, Robert. *The Complete Poems.* London: Cape, 1951.

—— 'The Figure a Poem Makes' [1939]. In *Selected Prose of Robert Frost,* ed. H. Cox and E. C. Lathens. New York: Holt, Rinehart and Winston, 1966. 33–46.

Fry, Stephen. *The Ode Less Travelled: Unlocking the Poet Within.* London: Hutchinson, 2005.

Furniss, Tom, and Michael Bath. *Reading Poetry: An Introduction.* 2nd edition. Harlow: Pearson Education, 2007.

Gall, Sally M. 'Metrical Supplement'. In M. L. Rosenthal, ed., *Poetry in English: An Anthology.* New York: Oxford University Press, 1988. 1161–79.

Gasparov, M. L. *A History of European Versification.* Oxford: Clarendon Press, 1996.

Gaut, Berys, and Dominic McIver Lopes, eds. *The Routledge Companion to Aesthetics.* London: Routledge, 2001.

Gervais, David. 'Racine Englished'. *Cambridge Quarterly* 28 (1999): 181–9.

Gioia, Dana. 'Meter-Making Arguments'. In David Baker, ed., *Meter in English: A Critical Engagement.* Fayetteville, Ark.: University of Arkansas, 1986. 75–96.

Grammont, Maurice. *Petit traité de versification française.* Paris: Armand Colin, 1965.

Greene, Roland, et al., eds. *The Princeton Encyclopedia of Poetry and Poetics: Fourth Edition.* Princeton: Princeton University Press, 2012.

Guest, Edwin. *A History of English Rhythms, 2nd Edition,* ed. W. W. Skeat. London: George Bell and Sons, 1882.

Guiraud, Pierre. *Langage et versification d'après l'œuvre de Paul Valéry.* Paris: Klincksiek, 1953.

Hall, Jason, ed. *Meter Matters: Verse Culture of the Long Nineteenth Century.* Athens, Oh.: Ohio University Press, 2012.

Halle, Morris, and Samuel Jay Keyser. 'Chaucer and the Study of Prosody'. *College English* 28 (1966): 187–219.

Hammond, Michael. 'Anapests and Anti-resolution'. In B. Elan Dresher and Nila Friedberg, eds., *Formal Approaches to Poetry: Recent Developments in Metrics*. Berlin: Mouton de Gruyter, 2006. 93–110.

Hannah, Sophie. *Selected Poems*. London: Penguin, 2006.

Hanson, Kristin. 'Resolution in Modern Meters'. Ph.D. Dissertation, Stanford University. 1992.

—— and Paul Kiparsky. 'A Parametric Theory of Poetic Meter'. *Language* 72 (1996): 287–335.

Hardy, Thomas. *The Complete Poems*, ed. James Gibson. London: Macmillan, 1976.

Harrison, Tony. *Phaedra Britannica*. London: Rex Collings, 1975.

Hartman, Charles O. *Free Verse: An Essay on Prosody*. Princeton: Princeton University Press, 1980.

Hayes, Bruce. *Metrical Stress Theory*. Chicago: University of Chicago Press, 1995.

Heaney, Seamus. *North*. London: Faber and Faber, 1975.

Herrick, Robert. *Complete Poetry*, ed. J. Max Patrick. New York: Doubleday, 1963.

Hill, Geoffrey. *King Log*. London: André Deutsch, 1968.

Hill, Leslie. *Radical Indecision: Barthes, Blanchot, Derrida, and the Future of Criticism*. Notre Dame, Ind.: University of Notre Dame Press, 2010.

Hogg, Richard M., and C. B. McCully. *Metrical Phonology: A Coursebook*. Cambridge: Cambridge University Press, 1987.

Hollander, John. *Rhyme's Reason: A Guide to English Verse*. New Haven: Yale University Press, 1981.

—— *Vision and Resonance: Two Senses of Poetic Form*. New Haven: Yale University Press, 2nd edition, 1985.

Hopkins, Gerard Manley. *The Major Works*, ed. Catherine Phillips. Oxford: Oxford University Press, 2002.

Horace. *The Odes and Carmen Saeculare*, trans. John Conington. London: George Bell and Sons, 1882.

Hough, Graham. 'Free Verse'. *Proceedings of the British Academy* 43 (1957): 157–77; reprinted in *Image and Experience: Studies in a Literary Revolution*. London: Duckworth, 1960.

Housman, A. E. *The Name and Nature of Poetry*. Cambridge: Cambridge University Press, 1933.

Howard, Robert. *Four New Plays*. London: Henry Herringman, 1665.

Hughes, Langston. *Selected Poems*. New York: Random House, 1959.

Hunter, J. Paul. 'Seven Reasons for Rhyme'. In Lorna Clymer, ed., *Ritual, Routine, and Regime: Repetition in Early Modern British and European Cultures*. Toronto: University of Toronto Press, 2006. 172–98.

Hurley, Michael D., and Michael O'Neill. *The Cambridge Introduction to Poetic Form*. Cambridge: Cambridge University Press, 2012.

Jakobson, Roman. *Language in Literature*, ed. Krystyna Pomorska and Stephen Rudy. Cambridge, Mass.: Harvard University Press, 1987.

Jakobson, Roman. *Selected Writings*, III: *Poetry of Grammar and Grammar of Poetry*, ed. Stephen Rudy. The Hague: Mouton, 1981.

—— and Linda R. Waugh. *The Sound Shape of Language*. Brighton: Harvester, 1979.

Jarvis, Simon. 'Why Rhyme Matters'. *Thinking Verse* 1 (2011): 17–43. <http://thinkingverse. com/issue01/Simon%20Jarvis,%20Why%20rhyme%20pleases. pdf>.

Jeffreys, Mark, and Debra Fried. *Teaching with the Norton Anthology: A Guide for Instructors*. New York: Norton, 1997.

Johnson, Samuel. *The Lives of the Poets: A Selection*, ed. Roger Lonsdale and John Mullan. Oxford: Oxford University Press, 2009.

Jones, Daniel. *Everyman's English Pronouncing Dictionary*, rev. A. C. Gimson. London: J. M. Dent, 1977.

Kastner, L. E. *A History of French Versification*. Oxford: Clarendon Press, 1903.

Kawin, Bruce F. *Telling It Again and Again: Repetition in Literature and Film*. Ithaca, NY: Cornell University Press, 1972.

Keats, John. *Poems*, ed. Jack Stillinger. Cambridge, Mass.: Harvard University Press, 1978.

Kingsley, Charles. *Andromeda and Other Poems*. London: John W. Parker and Son, 1858.

—— *The Water-Babies*. Boston: Burnham, 1864.

Kinzie, Mary. *A Poet's Guide to Poetry*. Chicago: University of Chicago Press, 1999.

Kipling, Rudyard. *The Complete Verse*. London: Kyle Cathie, 1996.

Kirby-Smith, H. T. *The Origins of Free Verse*. Ann Arbor: University of Michigan Press, 1996.

Kirsch, Arthur C. *Dryden's Heroic Drama*. Princeton: Princeton University Press, 1965.

Knight, R. C. 'On Translating Racine'. In L. J. Austin, Garnet Rees, and Eugène Vinaver, eds., *Studies in Modern French Literature Presented to P. Mansell Jones*. Manchester: Manchester University Press, 1961. 181–95.

Kucich, Greg. 'Keats and English Poetry'. In Susan J. Wolfson, ed., *The Cambridge Companion to Keats*. Cambridge: Cambridge University Press, 2001. 186–202.

Küper, Christoph, ed. *Current Trends in Metrical Analysis*. Frankfurt: Peter Lang, 2011.

Langland, William. *Piers Plowman*, ed. Elizabeth Salter and Derek Pearsall. London: Edward Arnold, 1967.

Lanier, Sidney. *The Science of English Verse*. New York: Scribner, 1880.

Lawrence, D. H. *Complete Poems*, ed. Vivian de Sola Pinto and F. Warren Roberts. New York: The Viking Press, 1971.

Lear, Edward. *The Complete Nonsense and Other Verse*, ed. Vivien Noakes. London: Penguin, 2006.

Leavis, F. R. *New Bearings in English Poetry* [1932]. Harmondsworth: Pelican, 1972.

Leech, Geoffrey. *Language in Literature: Style and Foregrounding.* Harlow: Longman, 2008.

Leigh, Henry Sambrooke. *Carols of Cockayne.* London: John Camden Hotten, 1869.

Leighton, Angela. *On Form: Poetry, Aestheticism, and the Legacy of a Word.* Oxford: Oxford University Press, 2007.

Lennard, John. *The Poetry Handbook: A Guide to Reading Poetry for Pleasure and Practical Criticism.* 2nd edition. Oxford: Oxford University Press, 2005.

Lentricchia, Frank. *After the New Criticism.* Chicago: University of Chicago Press, 1980.

Lerdahl, Fred, and Ray Jackendoff. *A Generative Theory of Tonal Music.* Cambridge, Mass.: MIT Press, 1983.

Levao, Ronald, ed. *Selected Poems of Thomas Campion, Samuel Daniel and Sir Walter Ralegh.* London: Penguin, 2001.

Levin, Yisrael. ' "But the Law Itself Must Be Poetic": Swinburne, Omond, and the New Prosody'. In Hall, ed., *Meter Matters,* 178–95.

Levine, George, ed. *Aesthetics and Ideology.* New Brunswick, NJ: Rutgers University Press, 1994.

Levinson, Marjorie. 'What Is New Formalism?' *PMLA* 122 (2007): 558–69.

Lewis, Roy. *On Reading French Verse.* Oxford: Clarendon Press, 1982.

Loesberg, Jonathan. *A Return to Aesthetics: Autonomy, Indifference, and Postmodernism.* Stanford, Calif.: Stanford University Press, 2005.

Longenbach, James. *The Resistance to Poetry.* Chicago: University of Chicago Press, 2004.

Lowe, R. L. 'Scott, Browning, and Kipling'. *Notes and Queries* 197.5 (1952): 103–4.

McKie, Michael. 'Semantic Rhyme: A Reappraisal'. *Essays in Criticism* 46 (1996): 340–58.

Martin, Meredith. *The Rise and Fall of Meter: Poetry and English National Culture, 1860–1930.* Princeton: Princeton University Press, 2012.

Matthews, Pamela R., and David McWhirter, eds. *Aesthetic Subjects.* Minneapolis: University of Minnesota Press, 2003.

Mengham, Rod, and John Kinsella. 'An Introduction to the Poetry of J. H. Prynne'. *Jacket* #7, <http://jacketmagazine.com/07/prynne-jk-rm.html>.

Meschonnic, Henri. *Critique du rythme: Anthropologie historique du langage.* Paris: Verdier, 1982.

—— and Gabriella Bedetti. Interview. *Diacritics* 18.3 (1988): 93–111.

Milne, A. A. *When We Were Very Young.* London: Methuen, 1924; reprinted 1987.

Milton, John. *Poems,* ed. Helen Darbishire. London: Oxford University Press, 1958.

Molière, *The Misanthrope,* trans. Richard Wilbur. New York: Harcourt, Brace, 1955.

—— *The Misanthrope,* trans. Tony Harrison. London: Bellew, 1973.

—— *Tartuffe,* trans. Richard Wilbur. New York: Mariner, 1968.

Nash, Ogden. *The Face is Familiar.* London: Dent, 1954.

Nicoll, Allardyce. *A History of English Drama 1660–1900*. 4th edition. Cambridge: Cambridge University Press, 1952.

O'Donnell, Brennan. *The Passion of Meter: A Study of Wordsworth's Metrical Art*. Kent, Oh.: Kent State University Press, 1995.

Oliver, H. J. *Sir Robert Howard (1629–1698): A Critical Biography*. Durham, NC: Duke University Press, 1963.

O'Neill, Judith, ed. *Critics on Keats*. London: George Allen and Unwin, 1967.

Opie, Iona, and Peter Opie. *Children's Verse*. Oxford: Oxford University Press, 1973.

Osborne, Peter, ed. *From an Aesthetic Point of View: Philosophy, Art and the Senses*. London: Serpent's Tail, 2000.

Oswald, Alice. *Memorial*. London: Faber and Faber, 2011.

Otway, Thomas. *Works*, ed. J. C. Ghosh. 2 vols. Oxford: Clarendon Press, 1932.

Padel, Ruth. *52 Ways of Looking at a Poem*. London: Chatto and Windus, 2002.

Palgrave, F. T., ed. *The Golden Treasury of the Best Songs and Lyrical Poems in the English Language*. London: Macmillan, 1861.

Parrott, E. O., ed. *The Penguin Book of Limericks*. Harmondsworth: Penguin, 1984.

Paterson, Don. 'The Domain of the Poem'. *Poetry Review* 100.4 (Winter 2010): 81–100 and 101.1 (Spring 2011): 72–95.

—— *God's Gift to Women*. London: Faber and Faber, 1997.

—— *Landing Light*. London: Faber and Faber, 2003.

—— 'The Lyric Principle'. *Poetry Review* 97.2 (Summer 2007): 56–72 and 97.3 (Autumn 2007): 54–70.

—— *Orpheus*. London: Faber and Faber, 2006.

—— *Rain*. London: Faber and Faber, 2009.

—— *Reading Shakespeare's Sonnets: A New Commentary*. London: Faber and Faber, 2010.

—— 'Rhyme and Reason'. *Guardian*, 6 November 2004.

—— and Charles Simic, eds. *New British Poetry*. St Paul, Minn.: Graywolf, 2004.

Patmore, Coventry. 'English Metrical Critics'. *North British Review* 27.53 (August 1857): 127–61.

—— *Poems: Second Collective Edition*. 2 vols. London: George Bell and Son, 1886.

Paulin, Tom. *The Secret Life of Poems: A Poetry Primer*. London: Faber and Faber, 2008.

Pepys, Samuel. *The Diary of Samuel Pepys*, ed. Robert Latham and William Matthews. 11 vols. London: G. Bell and Sons, 1970–83.

Perloff, Marjorie. 'Between Verse and Prose: Beckett and the New Poetry'. *Critical Inquiry* 9 (1982): 415–33; reprinted as chapter 6 of *The Dance of the Intellect: Studies in the Poetry of the Pound Tradition*. Cambridge: Cambridge University Press, 1985. 135–54.

—— 'The Linear Fallacy'. *Georgia Review* 3 (1981): 855–69.

—— 'Presidential Address 2006: It Must Change'. *PMLA* 122 (2007): 652–62.

Persson, Gunnar. *Repetition in English: Part I—Sequential Repetition*. Acta Universitatis Upsaliensis: Studia Anglistica Upsaliensa 21. Uppsala, 1974.

Phelan, Joseph. *The Music of Verse: Metrical Experiment in Nineteenth-Century Poetry*. London: Palgrave, 2012.

Pike, Kenneth L. *The Intonation of American English*. University of Michigan Publications in Linguistics, vol. I. Ann Arbor, 1945.

Plath, Sylvia. *Collected Poems*, ed. Ted Hughes. London: Faber and Faber, 1981.

Pope, Alexander. *Poetical Works*, ed. William Warburton. London: J. and P. Knapton, 1751.

Preminger, Alex, ed. *The Princeton Encyclopedia of Poetry and Poetics*. Princeton: Princeton University Press, 1974.

Prince, Alan, and Paul Smolensky. *Optimality Theory: Constraint Interaction in Generative Grammar*. Malden, Mass.: Blackwell, 2004.

Prins, Yopie. '"Break, break, break" into Song'. In Hall, ed., *Meter Matters*, 105–34.

——'Historical Poetics, Dysprosody, and The Science of English Verse'. *PMLA* 123 (2008): 229–34.

Prior, Moody E. *The Language of Tragedy*. New York: Columbia University Press, 1947.

Prynne, J. H. *Field Notes: 'The Solitary Reaper' and Others*. Cambridge: privately printed, 2007.

——'Mental Ears and Poetic Work'. *Chicago Review* 51.1 (2009): 126–57.

——*Poems*. Fremantle: Fremantle Arts Centre Press and Newcastle: Bloodaxe, 2005.

——'Poetic Thought'. *Textual Practice* 24 (2010): 595–606.

——*Stars, Tigers and the Shape of Words*. The William Matthews Lectures 1992. London: Birkbeck College, 1993.

——'Tintern Abbey, Once Again'. *Glossator*, 1 (Fall 2009). <http://solutioperfecta.files.wordpress.com/2011/10/prynne-tintern-abbey-once-again-8x10.pdf>.

Pyre, J. F. A. *The Formation of Tennyson's Style*. New York: Phaeton, 1968.

Q (Quiller-Couch, Sir Arthur). *The Oxford Book of English Verse 1250–1900*. Oxford: Oxford University Press, 1900.

Racine, Jean. *Andromache, Britannicus, Berenice*, trans. John Cairncross. Harmondsworth: Penguin, 1967.

——*Andromache*, trans. Douglas Dunn. London: Faber and Faber, 1990.

——*Andromache*, trans. Erik Korn. New York: Applause Theatre Book Publishers, 1988.

——*Berenice*, trans. John Masefield. London: Heinemann, 1922.

——*Berenice*, trans. Neil Bartlett. *Three Plays*. London: Oberon, 2010.

——*Complete Plays*, trans. Geoffrey Alan Argent. University Park, Pa.: Penn State University Press, 2010–.

——*Complete Plays*, trans. Samuel Solomon. 2 vols. New York: Random House, 1967.

——*Dramatic Works*, trans. R. B. Boswell. 2 vols. London: G. Bell, 1889–90.

Racine, Jean. *Five Plays*, trans. Kenneth Muir. London: MacGibbon & Kee, 1960.

—— *Iphigenia, Phaedra, Athaliah*, trans. John Cairncross. Penguin: Harmondsworth, 1963. Loughcrew: Gallery Press, 1996.

—— *Phaedra*, trans. Agnes Tobin. San Francisco: John Howell, 1958.

—— *Phaedra*, trans. Derek Mahon. Oldcastle: Gallery Press, 1996.

—— *Phaedra*, trans. Edwin Morgan. Manchester: Carcanet, 2000.

—— *Phaedra*, trans. Richard Wilbur. San Diego: Harcourt Brace Jovanovich, 1986.

—— *Phaedra: A Verse Translation*, trans. Robert Lowell. London: Faber and Faber, 1963.

—— *Phedra*, trans. Robert David MacDonald. In *Three Plays*. London: Oberon Books, 2010.

—— *Phèdre*. Dual Language Edition, trans. Margaret Rawlings. London: Penguin, 1961.

—— *Phèdre*. *Theatre 2*. Paris: Garnier-Flammarion, 1965.

—— *Phèdre/Phaedra*, trans. R. C. Knight. Edinburgh: Edinburgh University Press, 1971.

—— *Phèdre: A New English Translation in Rhymed Alexandrine Couplets*, trans. William Packard. New York: Samuel French, 1966.

—— *Phèdre: A New Translation*, trans. Ted Hughes. London: Faber and Faber, 1998.

—— *The Best Plays*, trans. Lacy Lockert. Princeton: Princeton University Press, 1936.

—— *Three Plays*, trans. George Dillon. Chicago: University of Chicago Press, 1961.

Raine, Craig. *'1953'*. London: Faber and Faber, 1990.

Ramsey, Paul. 'Free Verse: Some Steps Toward Definition'. *Studies in Philology* 65 (1968): 98–108.

Rands, William Brighty. *Lilliput Levee*. London: Alexander Strahan, 1867.

Reed, Beatrice Szczepek. *Analysing Conversation: An Introduction to Prosody*. Houndmills: Palgrave Macmillan, 2011.

'Rhythm in Twentieth-Century British Poetry'. Special Issue of *Études britanniques contemporaines* 39 (December 2010).

Ricks, Christopher. 'Racine's "Phèdre": Lowell's "Phaedra"'. *Arion* Third Series 1.2 (Spring 1991): 44–59.

—— *The Force of Poetry*. Oxford: Oxford University Press, 1984.

—— *Milton's Grand Style*. Oxford: Clarendon Press, 1963.

Ridley, M. R. *Keats's Craftsmanship: A Study in Poetic Development* (1933). London: Methuen, 1963.

Rimmon-Kenan, Shlomith. 'The Paradoxical Status of Repetition'. *Poetics Today* 1.4 (1980): 151–9.

Rostand, Edmond. *Cyrano de Bergerac*, trans. Christopher Fry. London: Oxford University Press, 1975.

Roth, Sister Mary Augustine. *Coventry Patmore's 'Essay on English Metrical Law': A Critical Edition with a Commentary*. Washington, DC: Catholic University of America Press, 1961.

Rothstein, Eric. *Restoration Tragedy: Form and the Process of Change.* Madison: University of Wisconsin Press, 1967.

Roubaud, Jacques. *La Vieillesse d'Alexandre: Essai sur quelques états récents du vers français.* 2nd edition. Paris: Ramsay, 1988.

Rudy, Jason. *Electric Meters: Victorian Physiological Poetics.* Athens, Oh.: Ohio University Press, 2009.

Russell, Trusten Wheeler. *Voltaire, Dryden, and Heroic Tragedy.* New York: Columbia University Press, 1946.

Russett, Margaret. *Fictions and Fakes: Forging Romantic Authenticity, 1760–1845.* Cambridge: Cambridge University Press, 2006.

Saintsbury, George. *A History of English Prosody from the 12th Century to the Present Day.* 3 vols. London: Macmillan, 1906–10.

Scott, Clive. *French Verse-Art: A Study.* Cambridge: Cambridge University Press, 1980.

——— *Riches of Rhyme: Studies in French Verse.* Oxford: Clarendon Press, 1989.

Scott, Sir Walter. *Selections from the Poems*, ed. Alexander Hamilton Thompson. Cambridge: Cambridge University Press, 1922.

Shakespeare, William. *Henry VI Part One*, ed. Andrew S. Cairncross. London: Methuen, 1962.

Shaw, Alan. 'Phaedra in Tact'. *Hudson Review* 40.2 (1987): 225–32.

Shaw, Mary Lewis. *The Cambridge Introduction to French Poetry.* Cambridge: Cambridge University Press, 2003.

Sinclair, J. McH. 'Taking a Poem to Pieces'. In Roger Fowler, ed., *Essays on Style and Language: Linguistic and Critical Approaches to Literary Style.* London: Routledge and Kegan Paul, 1966. 68–81.

Singh, Sarup. *The Theory of Drama in the Restoration Period.* Bombay: Orient Longmans, 1963.

Skandera, Paul, and Peter Burleigh. *A Manual of English Phonetics and Phonology.* Tübingen: Narr Verlag, 2011. 20–5.

Skelton, Robin, ed. *Poetry of the Thirties.* London: Penguin, 2000.

Smith, Barbara Herrnstein. *Poetic Closure: A Study of How Poems End.* Chicago: University of Chicago Press, 1968.

Solomon, Samuel. Review of Lowell, *Phaedra. London Magazine* (October 1966): 29–42.

Spenser, Edmund. *Shorter Poems*, ed. William A. Oram et al. New Haven: Yale University Press, 1989.

Stallworthy, Jon. 'Versification'. In Ferguson, Salter, and Stallworthy, eds., *The Norton Anthology of Poetry*, 2027–52.

Steele, Joshua. *Essay towards Establishing the Melody and Measure of Speech to be Expressed and Perpetuated by Peculiar Symbols.* London: J. Almon, 1775.

Steele, Timothy. *All the Fun's in How You Say a Thing: An Explanation of Meter and Versification.* Athens, Oh.: Ohio University Press, 1999.

——— *Missing Measures: Modern Poetry and the Revolt against Poetry.* Fayetteville, Ark.: University of Arkansas Press, 1990.

Stein, Gertrude. *Lectures in America.* New York: Random House, 1935.

Stein, Gertrude. *The Yale Gertrude Stein*, ed. Richard Kostelanetz. New Haven: Yale University Press, 1980.

Stetson, R. H. *Bases of Phonology*. Oberlin, Oh.: Oberlin College, 1945.

——*Motor Phonetics*. 2nd edition. Amsterdam: North-Holland Publishing Company, 1951.

Stewart, Garrett. 'Keats and Language'. In Susan J. Wolfson, ed., *The Cambridge Companion to Keats*. Cambridge: Cambridge University Press, 2001. 135–51.

Stewart, Susan. *Poetry and the Fate of the Senses*. Chicago: University of Chicago Press, 2002.

Stewart, W. McC. 'Racine's Untranslatability and the Art of the Alexandrine'. In T. E. Lawrenson, F. E. Sutcliffe, and G. F. A. Gadoffre, eds., *A Modern Miscellany Presented to Eugene Vinaver*. Manchester: Manchester University Press, 1969. 230–42.

Strand, Mark, and Eavan Boland, eds. *The Making of a Poem: A Norton Anthology of Poetic Forms*. New York: Norton, 2000.

Surrey, Henry Howard, Earl of. *Poems*, ed. Emrys Jones. Oxford: Clarendon Press, 1964.

Swinburne, Algernon Charles. *Selected Poems*, ed. L. M. Findlay. Manchester: Carcanet, 1982.

Swinden, Patrick. 'Translating Racine'. *Comparative Literature* 49 (1997): 209–26.

'Symposium'. *British Journal of Aesthetics* 50.1 (2010): 77–106.

Tambling, Jeremy. *Re: Verse: Turning Towards Poetry*. Harlow: Pearson Education, 2007.

Tarlinskaja, Marina. 'Metrical Typology: English, German, and Russian Dolnik Verse'. *Comparative Literature* 44 (1992): 1–21.

——*Strict Stress-Meter in English Poetry Compared with German and Russian*. Calgary: University of Calgary Press, 1993.

Taylor, Dennis. *Hardy's Metres and Victorian Prosody*. Oxford: Clarendon Press, 1988.

Tennyson, Alfred, Lord. *Poems*, ed. Christopher Ricks. London: Longmans, 1969.

Tennyson, Hallam. *Alfred, Lord Tennyson: A Memoir*. London: Macmillan, 1897.

Thomières, Daniel, ed. *Le Rythme dans les littératures de langue anglaise*. Reims: Presses Universitaires de Reims, 2005.

Thompson, John. *The Founding of English Metre*. New York: Columbia University Press, 1961.

Tonkin, Boyd. 'Translating a Trapped Tiger'. *Poetry Review* 99.3 (Autumn 2009): 81–6.

Turco, Lewis. *The New Book of Forms: A Handbook of Poetics*. Hanover, NH: University Press of New England, 1986.

Untermeyer, Louis, ed. *Modern British Poetry*. New York: Harcourt, Brace & Howe, 1920.

Vendler, Helen. *The Art of Shakespeare's Sonnets*. Cambridge, Mass.: Harvard University Press, 1997.

—— *Our Secret Discipline: Yeats and Lyric Form*. Oxford: Oxford University Press, 2007.

—— *Poems, Poets, Poetry: An Introduction and Anthology*. Boston: St Martin's Press, 1997.

Voss, Richard F., and John Clarke. '"1/f Noise" in Music: Music from 1/f Noise'. *Journal of the Acoustic Society of America* 63.1 (1978): 258–63.

Wainwright, Jeffrey. *Poetry: The Basics*. London: Routledge, 2004.

Weismiller, Edward. 'The "Dry" and "Rugged" Verse'. In Joseph H. Summers, ed., *The Lyric and Dramatic Milton*. Selected Papers from the English Institute. New York: Columbia University Press, 1965. 115–52.

—— 'Triple Threats to Duple Rhythm'. In Paul Kiparsky and Gilbert Youmans, eds., *Phonetics and Phonology*, I: *Rhythm and Meter*. San Diego: Academic Press, 1989. 261–90.

Wheatley, Katherine E. *Racine and English Classicism*. Austin, Tex.: University of Texas Press, 1956.

White, R. S. *Keats as a Reader of Shakespeare*. London: Athlone Press, 1987.

Wilkinson, John. 'Counterfactual Prynne: An Approach to "Not-You"'. In *The Lyric Touch*. London: Salt, 2007. 5–20.

Williams, Rhian. *The Poetry Toolkit: The Essential Guide to Studying Poetry*. London: Continuum, 2009.

Williams, William Carlos. *Pictures from Breughel and Other Poems: Collected Poems 1950–1962*. New York: New Directions, 1962.

Wimsatt, W. K. 'One Relation of Rhyme to Reason'. In *The Verbal Icon*. Lexington, Ky.: University of Kentucky Press, 1954. 152–66.

—— ed. *Versification: Major Language Types*. New York: Modern Language Association, 1972.

—— and Monroe C. Beardsley. 'The Concept of Meter: An Exercise in Abstraction', *PMLA* 74 (1959): 585–98; reprinted in Wimsatt, *Hateful Contraries: Studies in Literature and Criticism*. Lexington, Ky.: University of Kentucky Press, 1966. 108–45.

Wolfson, Susan J. *Formal Charges: The Shaping of Poetry in British Romanticism*. Stanford, Calif.: Stanford University Press, 1997.

—— and Marshall Brown, eds. 'Reading for Form'. Special issue of *Modern Language Quarterly* 61.1 (2000).

Wordsworth, William, and S. T. Coleridge. *Lyrical Ballads*, ed. R. L. Brett and A. R. Jones. London: Methuen, 1965.

Yeats, W. B. *The Poems. The Collected Works*, vol. I, ed. Richard J. Finneran. London: Macmillan, 1991.

Index

Printed and bound by CPI Group (UK) Ltd, Croydon, CR0 4YY